Words and Deeds

AMS STUDIES IN MODERN LITERATURE, NO. 8

ISSN 0270–2983

Other Titles in This Series
1. Richard E. Amacher and Margaret F. Rule. *Edward Albee at Home and Abroad: A Bibliography, 1958 to June 1968.* 1973.
2. Richard G. Morgan, ed. *Kenneth Patchen: A Collection of Essays.* 1977.
3. Philip Grover, ed. *Ezra Pound: The London Years, 1908–1920.* 1978.
4. Daniel J. Casey and Robert E. Rhodes, eds. *Irish-American Fiction: Essays in Criticism.* 1979.
5. Iska Alter. *The Good Man's Dilemma: Social Criticism in the Fiction of Bernard Malamud.* 1981.
6. Charles Lee Green. *Edward Albee: An Annotated Bibliography, 1968–1977.* 1980.
7. Richard H. Goldstone and Gary Anderson. *Thornton Wilder: An Annotated Bibliography of Works By and About Thornton Wilder.* 1982.
11. Clifford Davidson, *et al.*, eds. *Drama in the Twentieth Century: Comparative and Critical Essays.* 1984.
12. Siegfried Mews, ed. *"The Fisherman and His Wife" : Günter Grass's "The Flounder" in Critical Perspective.* 1983.
15. Partisan Review *Fifty-Year Cumulative Index.* 1984.

'Words and Deeds,

ESSAYS ON THE REALISTIC IMAGINATION

WITHDRAW

Taylor Stoehr

AMS PRESS, INC.
NEW YORK

Library of Congress Cataloging-in-Publication Data

Stoehr, Taylor, 1931—
 Words and Deeds.

 (AMS Studies in Modern Literature, ISSN 0270-2983; no. 8)
 Bibliography: p.
 1. Realism in Literature—Addresses, Essays, Lectures. 2.
Gothic Revival (Literature)—Addresses, Essays, Lectures. 3. Fic-
tion—19th Century—History and Criticism—Addresses, Essays,
Lectures. 4. Fiction—20th Century—History and Criti-
cism—Addresses, Essays, Lectures. I. Title. II. Series.
 PN3340.S84 1986 809.3'912 83-45286
 ISBN 404-61578-3

Published by

AMS PRESS, INC.
56 East 13th Street
New York, N.Y. 10003

To my teachers

W. EDWARD CLARK, who taught me to love literature

HENRY NASH SMITH, who taught me the importance of the wider culture

PAUL GOODMAN, who taught me how to read the deeper meanings

Contents

Preface

Realism has been the most popular of the literary manners, and therefore we know more about it than we do about naturalism, cubism, expressionism, and others yet unnamed. Nonetheless (and despite recent enthusiasm for theory among literary critics) we have not progressed very far since Ian Watt did the spadework almost thirty years ago in *The Rise of the Novel*. Our terminology is still poverty-stricken, much of it borrowed from other arts, and our concepts are vague and slippery. We have hardly touched the question of what a literary manner is, how it appropriates different genres, to what degree it determines or interacts with style, how it expresses cultural mood or an historical moment. So far as I am aware, for instance, no one has noticed that the gothic is a fully developed literary manner competitive with realism, not just a minor genre that flourished during the romantic movement. Obviously there is much to be done here. My own contribution is suggestive and exploratory rather than systematic, yet I do have a line of argument to present, which the reader may find it helpful to bear in mind.

I begin by describing the devices and conventions of realism, trying to firm up our vocabulary for discussing the ways in which a fiction may be true to life. At the outset I raise the question whether any single literary manner is likely to provide a better account of reality than others, but not until my final chapter do I attempt to answer it. The essays in between explore the assumptions and implications of such a question, with particular attention to the rival claims of the two chief contenders, realism and the gothic.

However important it is to be clear about formal conventions and their mimetic possibilities, literary manner is ultimately a function of an author's view of the world, his attitude toward reality and his faith in the imagination. To get at once to the problematic areas, my early chapters deal with two writers who were not realists at all but anti-realists, Hawthorne and Poe, tellers of gothic tales that hinge on the paradoxes and pitfalls of mimesis; only after considering their qualms do I turn to Henry James, who, though he too had misgivings about the "art of illusion," remains our great champion of realism, and then to D. H. Lawrence, the great purifier of the imagination.

My essays on Hawthorne and Poe are linked, each examining a different solution to the besetting anxiety of authors in the gothic manner—solipsism. Like their confrères the romantic poets, gothic writers were deeply skeptical about the world and uneasy about their access to it through the imagination. Hawthorne shuddered at the unpardonable sin because it sometimes seemed to be his own temptation, a despairing vision of the world as evil. Beware lest dream become reality!—as it did for Young Goodman Brown. Poe was still more desperately in the grip of doubt. For him reality existed as a feat of consciousness. Like the mesmerist narrator of "The Facts in the Case of M. Valdemar," he believed that the world would melt away the moment he relaxed his will. The same linguistic disappearing act is repeated over and over to prove it.

Thus do gothicists make the mirroring of reality in words either a fatal delusion or the only truth. The issue stands at the center of James's work as well, but quite differently conceived—in *The Princess Casamassima*, for example, as a contest between the claims of politics and those of art, pressing on his poor little hero who has sworn his artist's soul away for the sake of the revolution.

Especially during the middle period of his career James prided himself on his portraits of society, inviting comparison between the facts as history reconstructs them and the fictive rendering of what he called his *donnée*. Such comparisons are particularly telling for political novels, where one expects a critique of life, a laying bare of reality that aims at changing it. Here realism may be brought to the test. Along with other "terrorist" authors from Turgenev to Conrad, James is intrigued by the idea that words may have the force of deeds—intrigued, and profoundly disturbed, for he took little comfort in the activist doings of his fellowman. Like Hawthorne, whose sensibility he admired in spite of its gothicizing bent, James was suspicious of do-gooders, people who thought they had the answers. Commitment to a cause was virtuous only in the revulsion that might come on its heels, like Hyacinth Robinson's humanizing second thoughts about his vow. However bitter, the welling-up of consciousness was for James the only truth worth having. Realism thus ends where the gothic does, in the head.

At least as much as James, D. H. Lawrence wrote fiction that was a criticism of life, and he too worried about the uses and abuses of the imagination. But for Lawrence the locus was sexuality rather than society or politics, and his bugbear was fantasy instead of enthusiasm. Lawrence's sexually explicit scenes and diction are widely misunderstood: their intent was to expurgate sexual excitement from the novel by rubbing the reader's nose in it, so to speak, a crusade *against* titillation and what he called "mentalized sex." To his credit Lawrence saw the similarity between the passion for vicarious experience that gives realism its vast audience and the addiction to masturbatory fantasy that underwrites pornography. To his shame and confusion he himself fell into the trap of consciousness, and wrote books that have become classics of the very indulgence he abhorred. Like Brecht's *Threepenny Opera*, *Lady Chatterley's Lover* has been most popular in the enemy's camp.

The muddle in Lawrence comes from his acceptance of the taboo against masturbation that grew up side by side with the modern novel. Because masturbation has been regarded with horror and disgust for the last two hundred years, it has seemed necessary to maintain—by law as well as by criticism—a deep gulf between pornography and decent literature. Having broached this subject with Lawrence, I go on in my next essay to consider just where pornographic fiction does fit in the spectrum of literary experience. The matter has ramifications for the theory of mimesis, as was known to writers as sophisticated in the ways of the imagination as Rousseau and Proust. This is not simply an argument over censorship or public morals, though these are far from trivial concerns for critics or teachers of the young. What answer are we to make to Lawrence's accusation that the great preponderance of Victorian fiction, lubricious or not, is pornographic because it caters to the vice of consciousness? Supposing we could diminish or altogether eliminate the sexual content of pornographic fiction, how far would its naked forms and conventions mimic those of the traditional novel? And in what literary manner would its imaginative appeal have its most characteristic force?

In the chapters just sketched out I bestow much attention on audience and effects, how a reader experiences the commerce between art and reality. This is an ethical, not to say moralizing approach to the realistic imagination. I now go back to the more psychological approach of earlier chapters, asking once again how it is that an author's stance or world view determines his literary manner. My final example is the fiction of Paul Goodman, who was widely known as the philosopher of the New Left in the sixties, but who was also a prolific writer of short stories and literary criticism for three decades before his fame. Goodman was himself interested in theory, and used his own experiments to illustrate the kinds and degrees of alienation that shape literary manner. His career is especially apt for my argument because the self-conscious, "non-committal" cubism of his early years gradually developed into an engaged, realistic stance, and finally eventuated in the abandonment of fiction altogether, in favor of social criticism and political action. It might be tempting to say that Goodman had "written himself out" by 1960, but it is more suggestive to put it another way: he wrote himself *into* the world when he gave the title "Here Begins" to the final chapter of his last major fiction, and then sat down to write *Growing Up Absurd.*

In my concluding essay on "Realism and Ethics" I have written not a summary but a diatribe. There is no point in rehearsing it here, but perhaps it will be helpful to spell out a few of the ways in which I think this polemic addresses the issues raised earlier.

I should admit that my own taste is neither for realism nor for the gothic, though I have been drawn to each at different periods of my life. I prefer the hybrid strain of expressionism found in Hašek's *The Good Soldier Švejk,* Brecht's epic theatre, Chaplin's films, or more recently in Goodman's *The Empire City* and Peter Schumann's Bread and Puppet Theatre. Expressionism flirts with realism, sometimes impatiently, sometimes lovingly, but finally cannot take the prevailing social order seriously enough to grant it reality, to enter into its world mimetically. Indeed, the comic upsetting of our illusions about the way things are makes up a large part of expressionism's business. But I have noticed that this does not provoke laughter in most people. If my book barely mentions expressionism and is only incidentally concerned with other literary manners, even the gothic, the reason is that the enormous popular audience for fiction shares the vision of life on which realism is based, and in fact refuses to recognize any work as a "novel" unless it agrees to maintain the fictions of our culture. We must begin here.

Furthermore, in a healthy culture I believe that realism can serve its audience well. As Tolstoy, the greatest of all the realists, said, the chief end of literature is the education of the feelings. Another version of the same truth is Goodman's formulation, set down in his journal under the heading "Language":

> So-called "complex words," poems and orations, that develop into feeling and action—akin to the songful polysyllabic concretions of primitive speech, as Jespersen reconstructs it—are the premises in ethics. The positivists are in error; ethics does not consist of prescriptive commands and the sentences deduced from them; rather, it states the relations in the soul between how I am in the world and what I command myself to do. Poems and rhetoric give us these premises in a synthetic form; the implications must be drawn out by criticism. This justifies the vague and seemingly pompous carryings-on in the literary reviews. As Arnold said, Literature is the criticism of life, but it is not easy to know what it is saying. Similarly, belief is expressed in puzzling scriptures that require rabbinical exegesis. But there is no help for it. Simplicity or precision is not to be hoped for. If it is achieved, something is wrong, since ethics and faith are in present motion.

Whether we take feelings, sentiments, or the moral sense as the dimension of character on which literature works its tonic effect, I think it will be agreed that the mimetic modes—fiction, theatre, film—have been the important ones for our time, and among literary manners realism and the gothic particularly lend themselves to these modes because they encourage the total absorption that we call being "in" the fictive world, with obvious advantages for the kinds of soul-work Tolstoy and Goodman have in mind.

In some ways the gothic might seem the more likely method for establishing intercourse between the self and the world. Just as the goal of the pornographer is to provide an immediate physiological validation of mental life, so every gothicist is fascinated by the power of the will to control experience. This was what Poe was after with his hoaxes, shaggy-dog stories, and other self-reflexive narratives that end by "consuming" themselves. Of course not all gothic writing has the aim of binding reality to this desire for the perfect orgasm of consciousness. The impiety of such a project was the theme of Hawthorne's tales of mad scientists: it was what he meant when he cried, "Keep the imagination sane!" And when reminding ourselves of the great achievements in the gothic manner, we think not of Poe and his ilk but of Hawthorne, the Brontë sisters, or E. T. A.

Hoffmann. As a vision of life the gothic can be full of operatic power and epistemological subtlety, the good side of its stagey conventions and its obsession with consciousness. Nonetheless, it shrinks the world too much, albeit for the sake of an authentic passion of the human spirit.

In short, I come out for realism in my final essay; I defend it—especially against recent critics who treat the connection between spirit and world as arbitrary or merely formal, on the model of language, and who like the gothicists make art into a game of consciousness. Let me not anticipate my polemic, but simply say that whatever realism's drawbacks—and much of this book is devoted to them—it still seems worth defending. The lives of ordinary people are always interesting, often beautiful, when examined closely with an eye to their representativeness of the human condition. Realism is decidedly not grand opera, but it too can reach tragic heights and move us to tears.

ACKNOWLEDGMENTS

These essays were first published, some of them under different titles and in slightly different versions, in the following journals: chapter 1 in *Texas Studies in Literature and Language*, chapter 2 in *Nineteenth-Century Fiction*, chapter 3 in *South Atlantic Quarterly*, chapter 4 in *ELH*, chapter 5 in *Novel*, chapters 6, 7, and 8 in *Salmagundi*.

1

Realism and Verisimilitude

Fiction does not imitate life in the way that mirrors do, though we sometimes talk about its "mirroring of reality," nor does it pretend to be real in the way wax bananas do, or in the way that plastic simulates cowhide. Except for some odd cases in the early period of the novel, only a very few special sorts of frauds and spoofs pretend to be what they are not. Obviously a work acknowledged as fiction cannot also claim factuality, although it may assert its over-all lifelikeness, or even say "this is the way things *really* were in the thirties." Thus we distinguish fiction from history or reportage, even when our examples of the latter belong in the category of imaginative literature on other than mimetic grounds. Borderline cases, like the historical novels of Scott, or like the fictionalized biographies of Howard Fast, show the division to be a sharp and not a fuzzy one, for in reading such hybrids, we always first decide what sort of book it chiefly is, and then regularly shift gears for the "atmosphere," whether in the background or the foreground, which we know (often at some cost to our pleasure) is only history or only fiction and not the essential thing.

When it comes to the general question of *how* an artist makes the world he makes, it is hard to see that the problems of representing reality differ very much from fiction to nonfiction. The task of both is to formulate experience in words; both demand materials from which a selection and arrangement must be made. The primary differences seem to be in the applications of the two kinds of representation. The author lets us know whether to take his story as fiction or not, and accordingly we judge it by different criteria, and to different ends. Truth-to-life is not valued in the same way as truth. A reporter must get his facts straight, and a historian must have a regard for the complete, undistorted picture; while the novelist *cannot* make a factual mistake or hide crucial counterevidence. What do we care if the sperm whale is not really the largest of mammals? For the purposes of reading *Moby-Dick*, at most we wish it were.

Yet Melville's boner is certainly a lapse in some sense. If he had made a similar error with regard to men, and supposed some of them to be the size of Lilliputians or Brobdingnagians, we should have objected. On the other hand, Swift manages a sort of mimetic effect quite successfully, in spite of such outlandish departures from reality—in fact everyone agrees that his manipulation of these inconsistencies among kinds and degrees of verisimilitude is the secret of his ironic technique in the first two books of *Gulliver's Travels*. There seem to be different kinds of truth-to-life, different degrees of it, and different criteria for it. What are they? When must the novelist stick to the facts, and when may he invent them?

I believe it makes sense to begin, as we have here, with the distinction between fiction and nonfiction, taking the former as the field of mimetic art. This allows the point to be made early that the truth of truth-to-life is not the essential thing in mimesis, or at least not in the same way that truth is important for history or philosophy. What immediately arises then is the question of distinguishing the kinds of literature left over after we have eliminated those whose primary purpose is truth. For example, how are we to regard a work like *The Fall of the Great Republic*, a dull, anonymous precursor of *1984*, written as if history, without a detail of scene to suggest its world, even without a character to enliven its weary chronicle of power struggles that never took place, battles that never were fought, catastrophes that scarcely deserve the name "imaginary"? That it is fiction rather than lies is clear enough from its two title pages, one dated 1885 (genuine), the other 1895, with the imprimatur "By Permission of the Bureau of Censorship" (part of the fiction). But can such a work be called mimetic?

One wants to answer yes, and damn it on grounds thus established. It is an attempt to represent experience—albeit experience not possibly experienced by anyone and therefore liable to the usual disasters of utopian fiction. The inference, accordingly, is that mimetic literature need not be successfully so, just as a work of history may fail to live up to the demands of accuracy and consistency without losing title to its place among the DA's on the shelves of the Library of Congress.

Most of the theorizing on the subject of mimesis is concerned with a literary manner, realism, rather than with the representation of reality, mimesis—that is, with one means of effecting verisimilitude rather than with verisimilitude itself. The various literary manners—realism, symbolism, naturalism, and so on into those without names—are the different means writers have developed to present experience in words, and the theory of mimesis is the theory of the foundations of all such manners, their common problems, built into the relations of language and life.

Apparently it is hard to avoid slipping into diction that tends to confuse realism and verisimilitude. In some critical parlance verisimilitude becomes a mere tool of realism, a trick of the practiced ear or eye by which an author enhances his illusion of life, piecing in "authentic" bits of dialogue, clippings from the daily press, or other such flotsam and jetsam, as in the "ash can" and "pop" schools of painting. There are names for some of these devices, as we shall see, but "verisimilitude" is not properly or usefully one of them.

Another, more sophisticated mistake is to suppose that, although only a set of conventions, realism is in some ways better suited to the imitation of reality than other literary manners. If the physical world were reducible to objects, human character to speech habits, and human action to chronology, and if the representation of these in language consisted in denotation, dialogue, and the orderly specification of time and space, then truth-to-life might depend on reference—mentioning things like watches or bolts of Holland cloth; on grammatical and orthographic tricks—parataxis, pleonasm, or phonetic spelling; on plotting by map and calendar; and it would follow that the techniques of realism are the best means of achieving verisimilitude. Leaving aside the limitations of such a view of reality, there remains the question-begging catalogue of mimetic virtues; the inference that names, dialogue, and dates are the most direct linguistic means of representing objects, speech, and action really depends on treating names, dialogue, and dates as if they *were* objects, speech, and action, realism as if it *were* verisimilitude. The convention or manner is conflated with its purpose, for if one set of techniques were in some special, necessary touch with reality, then it would not be a set of techniques at all, but a guaranteed mirror of life, in which no realist could fail to reflect the truth he turned it on.

Let us consider some of the traditional topics of mimesis, attempting to separate these matters of technique from matters of truth-to-life.

FAMILIARITY

Both familiarity and particularity (the next heading below) are aspects of the relation between language and reality that allows us to use the one to speak of the other. Both grow out of the referential capabilities of language, a matter of shared experience not only of words but also of things.

The representation of reality, insofar as reality consists of the world of physical objects, must partly depend on the availability of words to "stand for" objects. However, it is not clear that "stand for," in the sense of "refer," is equivalent to "represent," a matter of mimesis. The difficulty here is in determining the meaning of "like" in the expression "lifelike," the meaning of "true to" in "true to life." Except in cases of onomatopoeia and quotation, the referential relation between word and thing is not iconic, but arbitrary and conventional. It is also doubtful whether any correspondence theory of the relation of sentences to situations—as in, say, the map-territory notions of the general semanticists, or in the "pictorial" view of the early Wittgenstein—can establish principles of structural correlation between propositions and states of affairs (let alone the vast range of nonpropositional utterance which makes up the bulk of speech and which has no truth value in the logician's sense) that we would be able to accept as an explanation of mimetic effects. Yet if mimetic representation is not a matter of structural correspondences at the referential or propositional levels of language, it nevertheless must depend on them at least to the degree that truth-to-life must be truth-about-life; whatever interpretation we give to "true to" or "like," it seems certain that "about" comes first, that reference must be logically prior to any aspect or quality of presentation such as resemblance or accuracy or authenticity. If we cannot allude to something, it would seem to follow that we cannot get it into language in any way.

Abandoning hope for an account of reference that has rules for verisimilitude built into it, perhaps we can find instead some guidelines in our sense that the lifelikeness of a work often goes back to its mentioning of familiar things, as for example in Defoe. His example is a useful one to begin with, for in him we can see quite readily the distinction to be maintained between particularity and familiarity: the inventory of his imagination, although it endlessly enumerates the familiar, is rarely enlivened by particularizing details, unless we are willing to count the mere naming of a thing as particularization. Depending as he does on this mere naming of the commonplace to produce his mimetic effects, Defoe is closer in many ways to late-nineteenth-century naturalism than to the realism of his immediate successors, Richardson and Jane Austen—and this circumstance will help us make another interesting observation concerning the historical relativity of mimetic effects, an important facet of the topic of familiarity.

No doubt some parts of a culture, including some parts of its language, fade faster than others, and of its physical objects and the names for them, those which are commonest and thus most often in people's mouths are the most lasting. Supposing the extreme case, that, through the passage of time, a word should lose its familiarity by losing all its reference, become an "x" which the reader must solve for—or supposing the more ordinary possibility, that a large number of the things mentioned in a novel should slowly lose their original functions, so that the words for them (which would also have been changing, covering more or less ground) no longer denote what they once did: simplicity, and especially the simplicity of Defoe and his nineteenth-century counterparts, the naturalists, with their characteristic subject matter, might seem more likely to preserve, if not verisimilitude, then at least a tinge of familiarity for the modern reader. Compare Scott's phrase in *The Heart of Midlothian*, "the useful and patient animals on whose produce his living depended," with its denotative equivalent, "his cows." Throughout *The Heart of Midlothian* (excepting the handling of the Scots dialect) the expansive style blurs even pictures we know to be grounded in historical fact. It is hard to resist repeating: what is true is not necessarily true to life, and actual referents are no better than fictional ones as a means to verisimilitude, especially when there is so much language between them and us.

If we are looking for the qualities of language that do facilitate verisimilitude, a direct and unadorned style is not likely to prove much more availing than Scott's periphrasis. Or at least not as a function of simplicity alone. Granting that there is a point beyond which "his cows" are scarcely recognizable, still, even in regard to familiarity and whatever realistic coloring it may lend a fiction, the writer who somewhat elaborates his prose has an advantage over the reporter of bare facts—and not merely an advantage of flavor or complexity. This is another distinction between realism and naturalism, one which depends on clarifying the relation of denotation to other kinds of linguistic meaning. Examine Defoe's account

of Robinson Crusoe loading a makeshift raft with goods from his castaway
ship:

> . . . I brought away several Things very useful to me; as first, in the
> Carpenter's Stores I found two or three Bags full of Nails and Spikes, a
> great Skrew-Jack, a Dozen or two of Hatchets, and above all, that
> most useful Thing call'd a Grindstone; all these I secur'd together,
> with several Things belonging to the Gunner, particularly two or three
> Iron Crows, and two Barrels of Musquet Bullets, seven Musquets, and
> another fowling Piece, with some small Quantity of Powder more; a
> large Bag full of small Shot, and a great Roll of Sheet Lead: But this
> last was so heavy I could not hoise it up to get it over the Ship's Side.
>   Besides these Things, I took all the Mens Cloaths that I could find,
> and a spare Fore-top-sail, a Hammock, and some Bedding; and with
> this I loaded my second Raft, and brought them all safe on Shore to my
> very great Comfort.

Compare this with another well-known looting of an abandoned ship by a
pair on a raft, Huck Finn and Nigger Jim:

> We got an old tin lantern, and a butcher knife without any handle,
> and a bran-new Barlow knife worth two bits in any store, and a lot of
> tallow candles, and a tin candlestick, and a gourd, and a tin cup, and a
> ratty old bed-quilt off the bed, and a reticule with needles and pins and
> beeswax and buttons and thread and all such truck in it, and a hatchet
> and some nails, and a fish-line as thick as my little finger, with some
> monstrous hooks on it, and a roll of buckskin, and a leather dog-collar,
> and a horse-shoe, and some vials of medicine that didn't have no label
> on them; and just as we was leaving I found a tolerable good curry-
> comb, and Jim he found a ratty old fiddle-bow, and a wooden leg. The
> straps was broke off it, but barring that, it was a good enough leg,
> though it was too long for me and not long enough for Jim, and we
> couldn't find the other one, though we hunted all around.

Of the two hauls, the items on Crusoe's raft, being older and also
somewhat more specialized, have lost more of their familiarity ("Sheet
Lead" for example), but as a simple matter of reference, Huck's "Barlow
knife," "buckskin," and "curry-comb" may be on the way to a similar
junkyard for words and things. Nevertheless, Huck's rummage will last
without footnotes longer than Crusoe's, regardless of the nature of the
objects or their names, because of the characterizing additions with which
Twain allows himself, sparingly, to fill out the human meaning of his list.
Compare Defoe's "that most useful thing" with Twain's wonderfully

comic insinuations covering a whole range of degrees of uselessness—the main organizing motif of the passage. The wooden leg is carefully led up to. "Butcher knife without any handle" tells us more than that knives usually have handles; we are reminded of the uses of knives, what can and cannot be done with them, how their function as a specialized extension of the hand may be lost. In Twain's catalogue, and in realism generally as opposed to naturalism, denotation—the pointing to the thing—is less important than connotation—not, strictly speaking, a matter of associations but of the whole range of quality, use, and circulation of the thing in the human world, which entitles the thing to its name, and which, linguistically considered, is not a matter of reference but of sense. Although still crude by philosophical standards, this distinction will serve to indicate the dividing line between words that, by naming, fix the attention on things being talked about, and words that themselves constitute the talking-about. Huck's phrase "ratty old" is not a name, not even of a quality or attribute, but rather an instance of qualifying or attributing, of making sense about something. Just as names change their appropriateness according to usage, so too, and probably to a greater degree, expressions of sense depend on application, which continually reinforces or undermines their meanings. The repetition of "ratty old" in the paragraph from Twain is a typical instance of the way sense develops: our initial understanding of the phrase is conditioned by the "bed-quilt" it qualifies (as "threadbare," "dirty," "stained," perhaps literally infested with or chewed by rats), but the sense is both extended and diluted by the second use, applied to "fiddle-bow," which cannot be "threadbare" although its horsehair may be thin, and is probably not "dirty" or "stained" so much as "scratched" or "peeling"; "ratty old" means "worn-out," "junky," "useless" in this passage, and this sense of the expression grows out of its use, not only in particular applications, but also in the full context, which tells us to attend to the varieties and degrees of obsolescence in everything mentioned.

It ought to follow from what has been said, not only that the language of realism should preserve its own familiarity better than that of naturalism, insofar as the latter leans on reference for its main relation to reality while the former more frequently qualifies its reference with guides to the sense in which its expressions are to be taken, but also, since this second sort of meaning is extremely fluid and adaptable to the needs of any situation in life, that the realistic manner should reflect the changing human notions and uses of things in reality more responsively than a "purely referential" style with its strictly kept inventory of nameable objects. But this leads us into our next topic. So far as we are concerned with the familiarity of the things talked about and the ways of talking about them in a novel, verisimilitude would seem to be a matter not of absolute faithfulness to some eternal facts of life, but of fidelity to ways of taking life, to views of life that alter with time. As regards the more stable truths, the coincidence of tastes and perceptions of author and reader (the strongest sort of familiarity) would seem not to create verisimilitude so much as to facilitate it, allowing a reader to judge more easily whether or not a novel is true to life, by virtue of the author's concentrating on subjects the reader knows something about, and to the extent that they talk the same language—all of which seems to be one possible function of realism.

PARTICULARITY

An author may try to make his fiction seem like life by choosing to fill it with references to particulars, using a high proportion of names of physical objects and spending time characterizing these objects, not because he expects them to be more familiar to the reader, but because he finds such things more real than others. Along the same lines, he may suppose particularizing details, whether of objects, characters, or events, to possess a reality in themselves, or give special access to reality, that an equivalent attention to the general or abstract nature of things and people and occurrences, concentrating on what is common to classes of men, what is typical of groups or kinds, cannot afford.

Details are the irreducibles of someone's experience, particulars noticed or responded to. Generalizations are patterns attributed to experience, groupings, similarities, relationships which someone apprehends or believes in. Only in extreme cases of language disorder—aphasia—does one see either particularization or generalization usurping the entire linguistic field (patients unable to name things presented to them, although they may recognize the things and even use their names in spontaneous sentences; others who can name things but cannot make sentences with the words they use). Both varieties of awareness are essential to writing and thinking, and the ratio of one to the other is an important index of an author's style. Certain rough proportions may be seen playing a role in distinguishing the kinds of literary manners, realism being a blend that emphasizes the *characteristic* detail (that is, the detail immediately generalized), and naturalism one that moves from lengthy enumeration of apparently *given* details to generalization by induction, imitating popular conceptions of science in the nineteenth century. For example, the realist's good ear for dialogue enables him to render the words of others with convincing fidelity to their habits of speech, local idiom, and so forth. This ability, although apparently a matter of detailing only, is hindered in naturalism by the inhibition of the generalizing faculty: if the writer is unwilling immediately to grasp the peculiarities of another person's speech *as characteristic*, that is, as habits or localism or clichés, then although he may be able to remember and report verbatim particular instances of dialogue, and even to classify them after collecting enough data, he will not be able to invent extensions of them, in utterances which he has not actually heard. *His* good ear in such a case turns out to be not much better than the microphone of a tape-recorder, an automatic stimulus-response facility and not really a literary talent at all.

Details and generalizations are not limited to the language of objects and classes of objects, any more than the whole realm of experience is grasped only through names and designations. Details are the bits and aspects of experience considered as unique, individuated to the point where nothing else is quite like *this*. The primary act of detailing is pointing one's finger at something, rendered linguistically by the demonstrative pronouns. Details are thus associated very closely with *what is*, the present actuality of the writer, although one invents details in a novel, out of one's experience with factual reality. Generalizations, on the other hand, grow up out of a regard for what is like something else rather than what is distinctive. While in one sense it is true that no two things are alike, in another it is true that nothing is unique. The generalizing faculty sorts and orders experience; the whole range of sameness and difference, choices, suitable alternatives, appropriateness, hierarchy, and the like, is contemplated and understood by its agency. The primary act of generalization is the act of recognition, of seeing that something is the same sort as another of the sort—akin to naming ("it is an apple"). This, of course, is quite different from the singling out which detail perception involves, for the generalizing act does not focus on the context of a thing so much as on its concept, its family, other members of which may or may not be present. Generalizing is therefore more like remembering or imagining than reporting, and generalizations are associated with *what was* or *what may be* rather than *what is*, with opinion and wish, hypothesis and faith, rather than with immediate impressions of actual fact located in time and space.

Of course, realism is not a literary manner we think of as especially having to do with subjunctives or imperatives. The systematic investigation of the moral and the ideal, though more central to the purposes of Jane Austen or George Eliot than to those of the naturalists, is nevertheless so solidly grounded in the minute details of character and action that the realists have sometimes been supposed to shy away from abstraction and devote themselves entirely to particularity. Although such suppositions are misleading, especially if taken as exclusively identifying the push of the realist's interests, it is nonetheless true that other writers, in other literary manners, furnish our favorite models for the contrary emphasis, on generalization. Fielding, for example, is always telling us that men of such-and-such a sort will do thus-and-so, and characters like Tom Jones appeal to the imagination because they are put forth as representatives of possible kinds of men, and even of the desirable qualities found in human nature. Fielding's manner, although neither realism nor naturalism, is also a means to mimesis; but it is one to which critics of our own time have agreed to allow more truth than life, though no one accuses him of not being lively. Yet qualities like good nature, prudence, generosity, and the rest are found in life as often as dry-goods and furniture; indeed, if asked to state the important truths about anyone or anything in ordinary life, we are more likely today as always to offer general remarks than individualizing details.

Fielding's manner makes use of details as well as generalizations, and indeed the balance of the two is very like that sought by the realists, though the seeking and its uses seem at first to be reversed. Whereas the realist hunts the revealing detail, that will lay bare the underlying characteristic, Fielding invents the exemplary detail, that will perfectly illustrate an already formulated, almost classic truth. Both the manner of Fielding and that of the realist present a world that is stable and familiar enough to name, attractive enough to describe in detail, orderly enough to provide standards of relevance and systems of implication. Much in such a world may be taken for granted, both as regards the value and permanence of things and as regards what is essential to say about them. In this basically confident picture of reality, the focus is on critical areas where, in spite of the general acceptance of things as they are, the realist (and Fielding) finds something to complain of and improve. Hence the ironic stance of such writers, founded on a shared sense of what is plausible and proper in an ordered and reasonable world, often with comic results, author and reader secure on their own ground, laughing at the follies and misunderstandings of characters whose views are limited or whose behavior is out of touch with the facts of life. These manners differ from naturalism, which finds the world less reasonable and trustworthy. Since the naturalist can take nothing for granted, everything must be catalogued, and he is at further pains to steer clear of qualifying or evaluating details that might undermine the authenticity of the data. Frequently—and even involuntarily, especially in cases of unselfconscious naturalism, as Defoe's—tremors of irony vibrate across the prosy, flat surface of the narrative, for the withholding of judgment and the refusal to discriminate among particulars seems automatically to tempt interpretations at a more abstract level: every meaning appears at once dubious and possible, and life seems full of hidden malevolence or cosmic absurdity. Thus in the etiology of literary manners, while that of Fielding seems a more confident ancestor of the realist's, realism in turn tends to settle into naturalism, and naturalism moves toward symbolism. The criteria of verisimilitude accordingly shift, as the meaning of life and the sense of what is real vary from relatively clear and integrated to increasingly confused, disguised, beyond ordinary perception or control and available only to private sensibility. It remains a challenge to literary historians to plot such shifts, and to show their correlations with other aspects of cultural history, to bring mimetic theory into a livelier relation with the most immediate concerns of our tradition and of our own times.

PLAUSIBILITY AND PROBABILITY

Whether or not a certain person, thing, or event could occur in life is surely a relevant question in judging the verisimilitude of such an occurrence in a novel. Whatever is not possible in life cannot be true to life in a fiction. This dictum seems clear enough, but even here there are difficulties, and difficulties significant for the distinction between verisimilitude and realism. Men differ over what they believe possible in real life; even more over what they want to believe possible; and still more over what they are willing to believe, so long as it is put to the test only in fiction. Realism and other literary manners cope differently with plausibility and play variously with the slack between what men do and want to credit. To begin with a nonrealistic example: when, at the end of Lewis's *The Monk*, Lucifer appears to carry Ambrosio off to his death, are we to say positively that this is an impossibility and therefore a lapse in verisimilitude? Or is there perhaps some question about what an impossibility consists of, in this case? Coleridge thought (John Berryman points to it in his introduction to *The Monk* as a curious remark, though he sees it as curious in still another way) that Lewis violated the rules of naturalness when he allowed Ambrosio, fresh from his first encounter with the devil—which Coleridge imagines ought to have shaken him to his roots—to hasten straightaway to an attempt on Antonia's chastity, that is, so little affected by his supernatural experience that he can immediately be moved "by so fleeting an appetite as that of lust."[1] No doubt this is not a modern view of the power of lust (therefore Berryman calls the remark curious), but still less is it a modern view of the kinds of experience people are likely to have. In the very midst of a complaint about the verisimilitude—"contrary to nature," he calls it—of Ambrosio's feelings and actions, Coleridge seems not a bit bothered that the natural response he finds wanting is precisely a response to something *super*natural. Of course, this does not mean that Coleridge thought devils common as cabbages, any more than moderns do. It is only that he distinguishes different kinds of implausibility. The supernatural has its place alongside the natural, so long as it is clearly labeled "supernatural" and does not threaten to become merely unnatural. The criterion, it is worth noticing, is one of verisimilitude—a matter of what can happen in nature (what cannot, yet does, is either miraculous or supernatural, and allowable in literary manners other than realism); contrariwise, the criterion for Coleridge's complaint about Ambrosio's lust is realistic, and thus, one would suppose, relatively inappropriate to the Gothic manner.

Some such formulation will hold for works like *The Monk*, but one cannot imagine anything supernatural occurring in *Joseph Andrews* or *Persuasion* without offending the decorum of plausibility. One can imagine supernatural events in *Bleak House* (although, strictly speaking, there are none), for the same reason that one can accept them in *The Monk* or *The Marble Faun*, that is, because the contextual requirements for the convention—the Gothic atmosphere, the subject matter of family curses and unnatural crime, the dreamlike logic of the plot—are met in this literary manner. In other words, the conventions of some literary manners (but, for the most part, not realism) allow for and neutralize violations of strict plausibility.

Moreover, from the point of view of verisimilitude, there seem to be degrees of plausibility, so that while some actions in a novel may seem impossible in life, and therefore violations of verisimilitude, others may be just barely possible, or hardly likely, or extraordinary, or common enough. The criterion of plausibility shades off into the criterion of familiarity where they come together in the area of the ordinary and the commonplace. Readers may disagree about the plausibility of Ambrosio's lust in certain marvelous circumstances, but no one would claim that it is unnatural (always barring the fact that she is his sister) once he has gained entrance to the lady's chamber: it is not so much to be described then as a "possible" thing as it is a "familiar" one. All this is evidence to show that plausibility, so far as it is a criterion of verisimilitude, is primarily a negative matter, marking the boundaries beyond which the author's fancy must not take us (though the lines are drawn with difficulty) but not of much use to him in establishing the techniques of any literary manner, even realism. Indeed, the most plausible story need not seem very lifelike; that which is trivial or mundane will hardly be trusted as faithful to experience, for reality cannot be so drab as all that. This is the notorious weakness of certain varieties of naturalism, as for example in Sinclair Lewis. Another sort of naturalism appears to favor the sensational rather than the commonplace, but the sensation aroused by a Zola or a Dreiser comes from their willingness to mention the all-too-common that others wish to regard as aberration. Such sensationalism can be tedious in its own way too, witness Charles Reade and Hubert Selby, Jr.

When we move from what could happen to what might happen in ordinary life, we move from the natural to the social sciences, from laws, out of man's control, which are descriptive and delimiting, to regularities and norms, which, less unalterable, are the more likely to be taken as prescriptive. If the laws of plausibility are largely negative, the statistics of probability are for many writers positively enjoining. Here too there are degrees; however, probability shades not into familiarity (the absence of the unusual) but into consistency—upon which Melville remarks in *The Confidence Man*: "True it may be urged that there is nothing a writer of fiction should more carefully see to . . . [yet t]hat fiction, where every character can, by reason of its consistency, be comprehended at a glance, either exhibits but sections of character, making them appear for wholes, or else is very untrue to reality. . . ." Although it ultimately has something to do with the way life is, probability is first of all something an author "sees to," a matter of the formal integrity of a work of art, the nice adjustment of the parts to each other and to the whole so that there are no loose ends, no inconsistencies, no gaps or excessive strains in the structure of relationships. Formal excellence is, of course, a virtue comprehended in any literary manner. Its place on the scale of fictional values, however, is less high for Melville or Dreiser than for James, whose working notes and prefaces are our fullest sourcebook for the methodology of probability. The realist, and especially the realist in a transition period (to naturalism), is most attentive to the order and proportion of his materials: he still relies on traditional views of life, still believes in the reality of received forms, taste, ethics, rules of conduct; he sees and resents those others unable to trust any but raw materials, undigested subject matter, whether the rumination of a phenomenologist gazing out to sea or the tropism of a behaviorist drudging at his piecework. The latter types are, in other words, not so willing to admit relations between plausibility and probability; expectations have been deceived, and the solution has been to expect no longer, but instead either to play a waiting game (Dreiser) or to wait a playing game (Melville). To the realist like James, such solutions must appear frivolous or cynical, since plausibility and probability *are* related, if one only takes the trouble in life or in art to study them out. What can happen will happen, and just as much of it as possible, in the usual orderly fashion. A *donnée* has its implications and tendencies, not so much to be trusted as to be embraced.

In any case, the facade of realism is maintained in a novel primarily by the coherence and stability of this superstructure of probability, and once a support gives way, chinks appear everywhere. One recalls, for example, the unfortunate conclusion of *Huckleberry Finn*, where all the probabilities and necessities of plot, character, and theme established earlier in the novel are abandoned at once, with consequent spoiling of the realism and the verisimilitude. Note the different but related effects in this case of the simultaneous violation of plausibility and probability. It is inconceivable that any actual persons, in such circumstances, should act in the way most of the characters do at the end of the novel; it is artistically improbable, given the obvious theme and intentions of the book, the development of the characters, the direction of the plot, and so on, that its outcome should be so inconsistent, should have so paltry a meaning, so petty an unwinding. Either the implausibility or the improbability would be enough to sabotage the ending, but of course they go together. In serious realism they always go together: the givens of incident, character, and theme are selected because they are the interesting and important materials of life; their elaboration and working out is the attempt of the artist to make sense of life as he conceives it, to imagine it in its proper relations, which seem true to life because they satisfy not merely our notions of plausibility but also our desire to see how things are ordered, to have some account of the world— which is, after all, what we often mean by "truth."

Other manners maintain different relations between what is possible and what is likely in the formal circumstances. High naturalism, so attached to the actual, seems almost to court the improbability of anticlimax, for instance, as if it were a guarantee of authenticity. Later variations, moving toward symbolism, display impatience with the plausible. Consider the following account of a late naturalist's movement into symbolism: ". . . I boldly adopted the device of introducing angels and other miraculous incidents to open out again the dead-ends of worthlessness into which the characters' 1940 dispositions had betrayed them. The angels speak unintelligible syllables; the incidents are causally improbable, though not necessarily artistically improbable."[2] For still further examples, one would go to Kafka and Genet, which ought to tell us something about the history of literary manner and of verisimilitude in our century.

SIMULATION AND ILLUSION

Devices like the autobiographical mode, the epistolary narrative, the quotation of invented (or genuine) documents, newspaper articles, manuscripts, letters, poems, and so forth, are among the means which some authors use to convince readers of the truth-to-life of their novels, by simulating (not the same as imitating or representing) things familiar in everyone's experience. The range of possibilities here is mainly limited to verbal artifacts (Wordsworth's inscriptions on rocks are a curiously inverted exception), and even these are not fully available to simulation. To take the strongest case, the use of the autobiographical point of view, although it is true that in most ways the conditions of reading a simulated (not pretended, still another possibility) autobiography do not differ from those of reading a genuine one, the difference of knowing that the one is simulated and the other authentic is everything; our attention is differently directed, our concern otherwise oriented, our sense of the relation of the book to life thoroughly altered. Similarly with letters and other documents. I remember a striking illustration of this difference of context, when, reading a novel in manuscript, I discovered at the beginning of one chapter a newspaper clipping taped neatly to the page, to serve as epigraph. The clipping had already lost much of its "authentic" context—or rather had acquired a new one—and was on its way to another. It could no longer be just a bit in the newspaper; that part of its meaning was not to be simulated in any novel, though it might be represented there. The device of copying actual documents into a fiction belongs to naturalism more than to realism, and its characteristic effect is that of the still life or snapshot: it incorporates the passing scene in approximately the same way that a photograph, in its pattern of variously tiny points of light, is able to capture reality, reflecting nothing more than the similar pattern of light which obtained in the space and moment when the mechanical eye of the shutter clicked. The meaning of the photograph is not the same as the meaning of the moment photographed except in this rather artificial (if essential) regard.

The most famous use of simulation is in *Pamela*. Readers who complain of Richardson's awkward attempts to account for Pamela's having enough paper and pens, energy and occasion, to keep up her journal letters, do not understand the nature of the many references to her writing. It is not that Richardson is embarrassed by the epistolary device he has chosen; there is so much to-do about the letters because they are the central fact of the novel, and attention must be drawn to them. They are, for example, the means of the peripety, for it is Mr. B——'s perusal of them that results in his change of heart (and they are later trusted to work a similar effect on his sister). That Pamela should sew some of them in her skirts is thus symbolically perfect. All this is marvelously suited to Richardson's whole scheme, for as critics have observed, his great achievement was to give the reader a fantastically detailed rendering of a human consciousness at work, and the device of the letters is first his means of doing this, and then also (a value not available to the "interior monologue" writer) his means of laying that sweet consciousness before Mr. B—— so that he, like the reader, may be captivated. Thus are plot, character, point of view, theme, and effect all bound up together in that curious book. This integrity of elements has something to do with the feeling one has that the novel is true to life in spite of its tiresomeness. Simulation joins with probability to foster a lifelikeness we might not otherwise be able to respond to.

Literary historians often point to the influence of Bunyan as crucial for the development of mimetic virtues in fiction, and in particular they draw attention to his use of dialogue, which, as Ben Franklin observed, is "very engaging to the reader, who in the most interesting parts finds himself, as it were, brought into the company and present at the discourse." Franklin also makes the connection to Defoe and Richardson, the classic genealogy, but what most concerns us is his early recognition of the relation between dialogue, the most common device of simulation in fiction, and what is known as the "illusion of reality." Obviously, on the face of it, the utterances of men are more susceptible to quite literal imitation in a linguistic medium than any other aspects of life or behavior—and, as we have just seen, written utterances are the most susceptible of all, since there is no problem of transcription to contend with. But dialogue has far outlasted epistle as a mimetic technique, and for reasons which will help us understand the relations between simulation and illusion, two topics that are often, wrongly, supposed one.

By the term "illusion" (which is probably not apt, though traditional), I believe we usually mean nothing more than being caught up in the story. Expressions like "the illusion of life" are thus especially treacherous, since they tend to conflate our sense of the verisimilitude of a work with our attentiveness to it. When Franklin says that the reader "finds himself, *as it were*, brought into the company and present at the discourse," he is careful to qualify because he knows, as we all do, that no one really imagines himself "actually there" when reading dialogue. If a reader has any thoughts beyond those which the author has written out for him, the spell (the "as it were" effect) is immediately broken, by precisely those interrupting thoughts. And if those thoughts are something like, "How true! How lifelike!" then we are thinking about the spell, not under it. Caught up in the world of the novel, one loses touch with other surroundings, much as in a daydream, and any comparison of the fictive world with the real world is sure to bring one back to his senses; indeed, only then can one notice how rapt he has been.

There is one sense in which we may say that the reader, as he becomes engrossed in the dialogue of a fiction, is actually there, where the characters are. Like all the utterances of the novelist, when they fully command our attention, the expressed thoughts of a character are our own thoughts; reading them is thinking them, though not thinking them up. So that the reader, although he is not really there, of course, shares a good deal with the characters who are—primarily their thoughts, but also the thoughts they are responding to (an advantage of dialogue over other devices of simulation), and, to a certain degree, varying with the centrality of the character, the sense of the significance of the thoughts in the context of the whole novel, its world and its action. Something like this is behind the notion of "identification," another corollary to "illusion." Again, it does not mean that we suppose we *are* Huck Finn or Isabel Archer, but only that we "have" their thoughts, insofar as they find utterance in the fiction. Often we "identify" in this sense with the novelist himself, since *all* the words are his—and especially with realists, interestingly enough, Jane Austen, George Eliot, Mark Twain, and so on. Still more frequently (and here is another reason for the persistence of dialogue as a technique of fiction) our identification is with the dramatic play of character and event. Dialogue is dramatic, or tends to be, because something is likely to be at stake there, in a way that it is not in narrative, since the dialogue gives the impression of being out of the author's control (and, as anyone who has written dialogue knows, it *is* less docile than narrative). There is also the obvious fact on which the dramatic power of dialogue rests, namely the dialectic inherent in two voices addressing one another. Paul Goodman, the novelist quoted above, testified elsewhere that he could never bring himself to put in the mouth of any character, no matter what his role in a fiction, any sentiment he could not imagine himself saying with conviction. Not all authors would go so far perhaps, but one insight of modern criticism has been the interpretive value of taking everything said by a novelist, no matter whose the fictional responsibility, as somehow meant, a partial revelation of the author's total world of sayables. To affirm, then, that our identification is with the dramatic play of character and event, with the excitement of what may grow at any moment out of the dialectic of the author's different fictive voices, is to say once again that identification, like illusion, is not merely a matter of realism, although it may be a matter of verisimilitude. We can point to highly abstract, unrealistic, nonfictional works as being just as engrossing as stories, with the same consequent loss of awareness of one's immediate surroundings, and similarly, we know we can become absorbed in the dramatic play of thought confronting thought in any speculative work. Illusion and identification are only special terms, used in talking about fiction, for more comprehensive notions like interest, attention, entrancement, absorption, conviction, assent, conversion.

Just how much illusion and identification have to do with verisimilitude it is difficult to say at this point. Something, to be sure, but the subject opens up a view of large gaps in our knowledge of the relations between the nature of address and the nature of reality. How much our categories have to do exclusively with realism is an easier question. Probably it is a confusion to rank them so high in importance for realistic technique as they usually are (they are scarcely techniques at all, rather effects of numerous evanescent variables), and critics who have the words often in their mouths are not to be trusted, including James, who, one fears, knew too well the advantages of professional hocus-pocus.

If the "illusion of reality" is thus to be discounted as a criterion for realism, nonetheless we must yet deal with one further general problem of mimesis often considered under such a rubric. In the preceding pages formulations like "the impression of life" or "convincing representation" have played some part in the phrasing of the successful mimetic effect. This diction too is misleading, though hard to avoid. It is a difficulty rooted in most of our terminology of mimesis, even in such expressions as "lifelike," which also leaves room for the possibility of a fiction attempting only to seem true to life without actually being so. The implication is misleading because, as we saw at the outset, representations of reality are rarely intended to fool the reader in the manner of *trompe l'oeil*. They are intended to convince him that life is precisely as they say it is, an altogether different aim.

It is important to reaffirm this point, because there is a tendency to suppose that, although other literary manners may tell truths about life honestly and accurately enough, they are nevertheless not mimetic, in any strict use of the term, while realism alone both "tells" and "shows" the truth about life, through special aptitudes and devices which somehow mimic reality so well as to exert an almost hallucinatory effect on the reader. It has been a large part of my purpose here to deny this special aptitude of realism, and to substitute a formulation which allows each literary manner its own mimetic subject matter, equally part of reality and equally capable of being rendered with the most thoroughgoing verisimilitude. Our views of mimesis, however, have been so historically conditioned by the rise of realism (and naturalism) that the topics under which we consider the problem of imitation are to a great extent the topics of realism rather than of verisimilitude itself; although there are things to say, for instance, about probability or plausibility as relations between literature and life, our ordinary uses of the terms lead us away from such questions, or narrow them to technical concerns with plotting and coherence. To be sure, realistic criteria can be applied to non-realistic writers, at least as intelligently as in James's study of Hawthorne, but the methodology is not really suited to them, and cannot take account of mimetic virtues which these writers—exclusively—command. Indeed, we are left without even names for the literary manners of books like *Tom Jones* or *The Scarlet Letter, Wieland* or *Bleak House.* Symbolism covers some cases, yet is stretched too far, and, to the confusion of the theory of literary manners generally, is rarely seen as mimetic at all, but as an alternative or even contrary set of techniques.

Even topics as broad as we have been examining here exclude too much, predetermine too much, at the initial stages of the analysis of verisimilitude. Questions about the influence of familiarity are premature until we know more about the different ways that saying something about something may be a function of the relations between speaker and hearer; problems of tone and voice, the general categories of such relations, are especially important to mimetic theory, not only here, but also in the discussion of illusion and identification, insofar as they link such areas with a range of associated inquiries into the nature of assent, belief, and faith. The discussion of reference, pursued here under the headings of familiarity and particularity, needs the larger context of a general theory of semiotics, including some treatment of the function of extended tropes in the reference systems of whole cultures, or in scientific models like the Newtonian universe. Would it be helpful, for example, to think of fiction as always providing its own reference system, a world view based on some scheme of tropes acting as a sort of lens for reality? Along similar lines, plausibility and probability, insofar as they are matters of formal limitations and coherence, might usefully be considered as founded on the interplay between culturally derived metaphors for reality and the writer's own system of tropes—realism perhaps being the case where the two are in most complete adjustment. Simulation, as treated here, has seemed a relatively minor concern, but in a fuller view of mimesis it would be worth going deeper into the practice of introducing fragments of "actual" reality into literature; what is the relevance of the drama, where mimesis is a kind of enactment with everything simulated? Might fiction also be considered a performing art, with improvisation, impersonation, and acting-out, as in Dickens and Twain? Or, like music, a notation system (stage directions) which the reader follows in a privately imagined performance?

2

Hawthorne's Faith in Words

I

The tellers of tales—in America, writers like Poe, Hawthorne, Melville, and later Mark Twain—construct their fictions around some single and striking figure of speech, at once abstract and concrete, an idea embodied in an action, object, circumstance, or the like, so that it becomes, as it were, a trope of life. The tale's main "effect"—to use Poe's term for it—reduces again and again to some bizarre image: a house collapsing with the death of its owner, a woman dying with the removal of her birthmark, a stutterer whose speech is act, a package of limburger cheese mistaken for the putrescence of a corpse, a chandelier of human torches, a "Pygmalion" figurehead for a ship, a "writer" who would "prefer not," a burglar-alarm system with a will of its own. This is in contrast with authors like James, who write a different genre, the short story, and who are concerned with character, situation, life or a slice of it. The teller of the tale carefully leads up to or surrounds his central conception with a series of events which may sometimes look like a realistic plot, but which differ in that they comprise something like a closed system, the elements inter-connected and interdefined (like a perfectly logical language), and all organized by the dominant image. If there is often a good deal of ornament along the way, it is neither naturalistic nor gratuitous. Detail is not offered for its own sake, nor in the interests of verisimilitude, but is part and parcel of the "effect." Generally in Poe and Twain the end of the tale is the final clicking into place of the essential cog, for the sake of which everything else exists—the revelation of the secret, the discovery of the truth, the

23

magic word, the punch line, the gimmick or nub or snapper. In Hawthorne and Melville it is the reader's job to discover the key; then, as in the analysis of dreams, the fantastic filigree of secondary elaboration collapses to a single symbolic image, the dream-thought or hidden content.

Clearly this is not realism, nor is the purpose of these writers to hold the mirror up to nature. And yet it would not be fair to say that their tales have nothing to do with life or reality or truth. What sort of an imagination is it, and what sort of a vision of the world does it imply, when an author is continually blowing up fictional balloons only to pop them or to invite the reader to reduce them to a neat little bang?

The comparison to dreams may be helpful at this point, for these writers used the analogy themselves. Poe addressed himself "to the dreamers and those who put their faith in dreams as in the only realities." Hawthorne said he chose Brook Farm as the scene of *The Blithedale Romance* because, "being certainly the most romantic episode of his own life,—essentially a day-dream and yet a fact," it thus offered "an available foothold between fiction and reality," and Melville approvingly described his reading of *Mosses from an Old Manse* as being spun "round about in a web of dreams." Twain too finally came to rest on similar insubstantial ground, for example in *The Mysterious Stranger*, where Satan pronounces the final truth toward which everything in that gloomy story (and much in Twain's development as an author) has been heading: "*Life itself is only a vision, a dream. . . . Nothing exists save empty space—and you! . . . And you are not you—you have no body, no blood, no bones, you are but a thought. I myself have no existence; I am but a dream—your dream, creature of your imagination.*" We are reminded of Ishmael on the mast-head, White-Jacket in the water, or Pierre, who did not see "that all the great books in the world are but the mutilated shadowings-forth of invisible and eternally unembodied images in the soul; so that they are but the mirrors, distortedly reflecting to us our own things."

Already we will be noting differences in the views of our authors, but we may begin in general by saying of them that the solipsistic bent is in none of them a genuinely philosophical attitude. It is instead a particular artistic stance, in its most extreme version a promotion of fiction to a rank of reality above life, and a conception of experience as predominantly verbal, or at least gaining its significance from expression in language rather than from acting-out in life. It is not so much that these writers can believe in nothing but the reality of their own fantasies—though Poe often pretends to such a view and Twain bitterly toys with it at the end of his career—but rather that the sense that they are able to make of the world automatically frames itself in fantasy, and that this is by virtue of some very specialized uses of language to render experience. It should be emphasized that "dreams, visions, fiction," a triad of equivalencies found in *The Mysterious Stranger*, are terms closely related, if not synonymous, in all four writers; accordingly the correspondences of dream and reality are to a great extent problems of verbal imagination, referential language, and literary mimesis. "To dream" is to use language about life and the world in special ways.

In brief, these special uses of language may be stated as follows: for Poe, a kind of word-magic built chiefly on metonymies, in which words are treated as if they were naturally or supernaturally rather than conventionally and arbitrarily attached to their referents; for Hawthorne, a heavily metaphorical style, in which whatever is described seems always on the verge of turning into its metaphorical description, and in which one often cannot tell the difference between the imaginary and the real; for Melville, a similar ambiguity, based on irony rather than metaphor, words turned against themselves, until reference disappears at the other end of Poe's blind alley; for Twain, a hyperbolic use of language, in which most expressions turn out to be heightened and distorted inventions, exaggerations, even lies, about the ordinary world.

The center or kernel of Poe's tales is frequently a visual pun taken literally and in deadly earnest—as Hop-frog puts the torch to the human chandelier, or Dupin finds "The Purloined Letter" in plain sight on the thief's letter rack. In Hawthorne some metaphor, such as "Life figures itself to me as a festal or funeral procession" ("The Procession of Life"), is allowed to flower into or to cap with one all-encompassing emblem a series of similar images. Melville focuses on bits of human speech—or the lack of it, in "Billy Budd"—and reiterates until all meanings have been canvassed, and *none* are left. Twain in his turn tells the tall tale, built on a succession of whoppers, and reserving some monstrously inflated absurdity to ring down the curtain.

Poe and Twain typically end their tales with a sort of explosion—it is the dreaded revelation in Poe, when, as in "Morella," the name calls the thing named into being, and the narrator's consciousness goes blank in horror (this blankness or blotting out is the familiar abyss or maelstrom in Poe, "the end"); in Twain, it is the deflation of the hyperbolic balloon, when the last great puff of hot air from the narrator, who has gone *too* far this time, leaves the audience collapsing with laughter. In both cases, the end of the fictional structure is likely to come with a sudden neatness; the last words fall into place and, with a shock, we are back in our own reality again, where we become aware that we are holding our breath, or our sides.

Some of Hawthorne's tales go this way also, emphasizing the literal boundaries of fiction, the beginning and the end. More often, however, and especially in his best pieces, Hawthorne (like Melville) puts the confrontation between the imaginary and the real directly into his plots, as the focus of interest rather than as the means to an effect. One might even say—and this will be a large part of our concern in what follows—that a tale like "Young Goodman Brown" is *about* the relations of fiction and reality, a study of the true-to-life, a sketch for a theory of mimesis.

The structure of events in Hawthorne's tales is not linearly, that is to say temporally, conceived as in Poe's, where disaster awaits at the end, but rather cyclically or spatially, as befits thematic rather than anecdotal organization—and of course the built-in predispositions of emblematic art lend themselves to such a method. Hawthorne's tales sometimes have plots, but when they do they are mere pretexts for the configurations which he wants to present. Most of his tales exist for the sake of a single scene or image, and the reverberations he can make it echo with. One thinks of "The Minister's Black Veil," "The Bosom Serpent," "The Wedding Knell," "The Birthmark," and so on. In some cases, as for example the processional "My Kinsman, Major Molineux," the crucial image is reserved for the climax, but more usually it is present from the beginning, an emblem which Hawthorne can constantly refer to as a source of moral comment and fanciful speculation. The emblematic moment recurs again and again in different guises and contexts. Very often it builds to some physical confrontation of the characters, standing in different moral planes, for example the deathbed scene in "The Minister's Black Veil" or the final coming-true of the prediction of "The Prophetic Pictures." This is the methodology of Hawthorne's novels as well, which are rather like collections of tales strung together as series of tableaux showing the characters in a variety of physical and moral postures *vis à vis* one another. One almost wants to say that nothing else happens *in* the novels; all the action takes place behind the scenes and in the wings.

The central images on which Hawthorne bases his tales are easy to isolate and study; many of them are precisely formulated in the *American Notebooks*, for example:

> A man to swallow a small snake—and it to be a symbol of cherished sin. ["The Bosom Serpent"]
>
> The semblance of a human face to be found on the side of a mountain, or in the fracture of a small stone, by a *lusus naturae*. The face is an object of curiosity for years or centuries, and by and by a boy is born, whose features gradually assume the aspect of that portrait. At some critical juncture, the resemblance is found to be perfect. A prophecy may be connected. ["The Great Stone Face"]
>
> To make one's own reflection in a mirror the subject of a story. ["Monsieur du Miroir"]
>
> . . . An essay on the misery of being always under a mask. A veil may be needful, but never a mask. ["The Minister's Black Veil"][1]

Here as in Poe we see a fondness for the bizarre or grotesque image, but unlike Poe, Hawthorne usually conceives his emblem as having a moral, as embodying some truth, and in the actual working out of the tale he invariably directs it to some meaning for ordinary life. One need only compare the morals pointed at the ends of "Drowne's Wooden Image" or "The Prophetic Pictures" or "Edward Randolph's Portrait" with the more simply fantastic treatment of the same sort of idea in Poe's "The Oval Portrait" to see the difference in intention—all the more strongly highlighted in this case by a similarity in both design and effect. Pursuing the comparison a bit further, it is surprising to discover the number of entries in Hawthorne's *American Notebooks* which suggest or actually parallel tales developed by Poe. Had he had access to them, there are several entries that would have made Poe hesitate, in his review of *Twice-told Tales*, before accusing Hawthorne of transcendentalist symbol-hunting and (what is more ironic) unconscious plagiarism. Here are some examples which show how far toward the purely fantastic Hawthorne might have gone, had he not been committed to the "metaphor run-mad," as Poe called his rival's technique:

> To make literal pictures of figurative expressions;—for instance, he burst into tears—a man suddenly turned into a shower of briny drops. An explosion of laughter—a man blowing up, and his fragments fly-

ing about on all sides. He cast his eyes upon the ground—a man standing eyeless, with his eyes on the ground, staring up at him in wonder-
ment &c &c &c. [Cf. Poe's "A Predicament"]

Questions as to unsettled points of History, and Mysteries of Nature,
to be asked of a mesmerized person. [Cf. Poe's "Mesmeric Revelation"]

The strange incident in the court of Charles IX (*sic*, for VI) of France:
he and five other maskers being attired in coats of linen covered with
pitch and bestuck with flax to represent hairy savages. They entered
the hall dancing, the five being fastened together, and the king in
front. By accident the five were set on fire with a torch. Two were
burned to death on the spot, two afterwards died, one fled to the
buttery, and jumped into a vessel of water. It might be represented as
the fate of a squad of dissolute men. [Cf. Poe's "Hop-Frog"; Hawthorne had this idea from Froissart's *Chronicles* in 1838 and Poe
probably from a secondary source when he later developed the
anecdote.][2]

There are dozens more of these grotesque ideas recorded in the
American Notebooks, the majority of which never found their way into
Hawthorne's tales. Of those that finally did grow to full treatment, most of
them have a moral already pointed in the first conception, and if they do
not originally have moral significance, are given it in their fictional elabo-
rations. This, of course, was what Poe found offensive and "transcendental" in Hawthorne. Probably he would have been all the more vexed to find
that the image or emblem ordinarily occurred first to Hawthorne, and was
then pressed for some symbolic meaning or significance. Often one sees
him groping unsuccessfully for a meaning in the notebooks—"A person to
catch fireflies, and try to kindle his household fire with them. It would be
symbolical of something"[3]—and it was precisely this difficulty of finding
a meaning adequate to his symbols that, in his last years, proved
Hawthorne's stumbling block (see Davidson's editions of *Dr.
Grimshawe's Secret* and the other unfinished manuscripts). The central
struggle of his art is to maintain a tension between the terms of his
symbols, to enliven dead metaphors, to force his daydreams into a certain
relation with everyday life without giving up their essential strangeness.
Hawthorne's typical stance may further be distinguished from Poe's in
that the narrative point of view of a moral tale is outside the tale itself,
whereas in the tale of pure fantasy the teller is not only part of the tale, but,
in Poe at any rate, peculiarly identical with it. The usual Poe narra-

tors—men like the morbid husband of Ligeia—become the characters in Hawthorne—like Ethan Brand or Young Goodman Brown or Rev. Hooper. (Rappaccini and Hawthorne's other evil scientists are like Poe's Dupin, or like Poe the poet-critic of "The Philosophy of Composition"; and it is interesting that the ratiocinative figure in Poe is rarely the narrator unless Poe is speaking in his own voice—the women are generally the abstruse and metaphysical ones.) Hawthorne maintains a certain essayistic distance from his characters and their stories. He presents his tales as purported translations, parts of an unpublished book, stories told him by others, imagined historical events, and so forth, and his prose is full of little reminders of the narrator's essential uninvolvement: "It only remains to say . . . ," "the historian of the sect affirms . . . ," "at that moment, if report be trustworthy . . ."

Hawthorne's narrative stance is different from Poe's because Hawthorne wants to bridge the gap between imagination and reality while Poe prefers to fall in. The former's emblems are *of* something, have bearing on life, while the latter's are grotesque climaxes marking the boundary-line of fantasy and its sharp division from the ordinary world, which, so far as his tales are concerned, might as well not exist. In Poe there is no distinction between the expressions of language and what those expressions express. All reality but that of language is denied, and Poe is like his character in "The Power of Words" who speaks the stars into existence. Whereas Hawthorne does not deny extra-linguistic reality, he does assign it a peculiar status in his view of things. He does not believe "in dreams as the only realities," as Poe does, but he says—or allows his narrator in *Blithedale* to say—that their "airiest fragments, impalpable as they may be, will possess a value that lurks not in the most ponderous realities of any practicable scheme." [4] The contrast between dream and reality is what interests Hawthorne. The world, he writes in "The Old Manse," is "tormented by visions that seem real to it now, but would assume their true aspect and character were all things once set right by an interval of sound repose." His advice to the world, to "take an agelong nap," is fancy carried to Hawthorne's most annoying extreme of whimsy, but serious analyses of the relations between dream and reality occur in tale after tale. In these, Hawthorne sometimes trusts the dream, sometimes the reality, sometimes cannot decide between them. Perhaps he is more often found on the side of the dreamer than that of the realist—Clifford rather than Judge Pyncheon, Owen Warland rather than Robert Danforth,

Violet and Peony rather than their father—and moreover, the whole evidence of his choice of subject matter and method, the preponderance of tales over essays, fables over sketches, attests his nearness to Poe's stance as a pure fantast. But while Poe wants to blot out reality and allow fantasy to fill the consciousness, Hawthorne is more interested in exploring the relations between the two.

II

Probably the most interesting of Hawthorne's tales, seen in this light, is "Young Goodman Brown." The core of the plot is a pun—not taken with perverse literalness as it would be in Poe, but preserved as a pun and pressed to its full ambiguity in the course of the tale. Young Goodman Brown, an ordinary young and good man, has a sweet and doting wife whose name is Faith. By the end of the narrative, Brown has grown old, is no longer good in any ordinary way, and has lost his Faith, that is, his religious faith, his faith in his fellowman, his faith in his wife. The story opens with Brown taking leave of his wife for an overnight trip. She begs him to remain, says she fears that bad dreams will visit her in his absence, but he tells her to say her prayers and no harm will come to her. He himself, as it turns out, is off to a Witches' Sabbath, a gathering of the devil's own in the forest, where tonight several converts are to be admitted to the communion. On his way he meets the devil, who looks very like Brown's own father. Disconcerted by his companion and his "serpent" staff, Brown hesitates, finally refuses to go on to the meeting, even though he has meanwhile discovered that he is to be in the company of all the most valued of his religious guides and counselors—Goody Cloyse, Deacon Gookin, and even the village pastor himself. Apparently everyone he respects is a hypocrite, actually a partaker of the devil's sacrament. Still reluctant, he is next astonished to hear what seems to be the voice of his own wife as she prepares to join with Satan's revellers in the distant clearing, and, as a token of her apparent defection, a pink ribbon which she wore "fluttered lightly down through the air."

> "My Faith is gone!" cried he, after one stupified moment. "There is no good on earth; and sin is but a name. Come, devil! for to thee is this world given."

Brown now proceeds to the clearing where the whole town appears to be gathered, including his wife. Even yet there seems to be one more chance for Brown and his Faith. They approach Satan's altar where they are to pledge themselves to him. Satan welcomes them:

> "Depending upon one another's hearts, ye had still hoped, that virtue were not all a dream. Now are ye undeceived! Evil is the nature of mankind. Evil must be your only happiness. Welcome, again, my children, to the communion of your race!"

At the last moment Brown calls out to his Faith: "Look up to Heaven, and resist the Wicked One!" Immediately his surroundings change, take on their ordinary appearance, and he is alone. Apparently he is saved. He does not know whether his wife has saved herself too or not. Indeed, it seems equally possible that he has merely "fallen asleep in the forest, and only dreamed a wild dream of a witch-meeting." Yet, dream or no, the experience produces a profound change in Brown. Although his wife greets him with unsuspecting joy the next morning, his faith is gone. He now mistrusts all men, his life becomes a succession of suspicions and secret judgments, and "his dying hour was gloom."

Even this bare outline of the tale presents us with some interesting puzzles. If, as seems apparent, Brown does look up to heaven at the last moment, with the consequence that the whole evil scene disappears and he is left alone in the woods, is not this circumstance an indication that he has preserved his faith after all, by refusing the devil's communion? How then are we to explain his later behavior? Alternatively perhaps we are to take the whole episode as a dream. Hawthorne has a plan in the *American Notebooks* for a tale to be composed like a dream:

> To write a dream, which shall resemble the real course of a dream, with all its inconsistency, its strange transformations, which are all taken as a matter of course, its eccentricities and aimlessness—with nevertheless a leading idea running through the whole. Up to this old age of the world, no such thing ever has been written.[5]

But if "Young Goodman Brown" is an outgrowth of this idea, it has surely changed considerably. Among other things we are missing the "eccentricities and aimlessness," although we have the "matter of course." Further, "Young Goodman Brown," if it has a dream in it, must also have a reality, and there are no very clear boundaries marking the one off from the other. Where does it begin? And what does it mean?

If we do take Brown's experience as a dream, we must then regard his loss of his faith, both wife and virtue, as a kind of wish—at least we may say that *he* imagines the loss, and thus far chooses it. He similarly imagines the worst of all mankind, and by so imagining these horrors, he wakes into the condition of believing them. If the reader has trouble distinguishing the boundary between dream and reality here, all the more is Brown unable to discern it, for his dream becomes his waking life—what he imagines comes true for him.

The ambiguity of Brown's experience, both chosen and forced upon him, imaginary and real, is worth dwelling on, for it is at the center of the problem of faith as Hawthorne conceives it. So far as we know, Brown himself never questions the reality of his adventure in the woods. And, if we suppose with him that it all really happened, I think we have to admit that Brown has good reason for his loss of faith—at least in his fellowman—since everyone except himself seems to be in the devil's service. Supposing, however, that it was only a dream, then we must judge Brown harshly, as having chosen his loss, just as Ethan Brand seems to choose his fate in that tale. But Hawthorne seems to leave the question in the air; he will not say for sure, nor give us any certain evidence, that Brown's experience was either dream or reality. Nor is it something between the two (whatever that could mean); in a way it is both. To make this clear, we must return again to the text.

The language of Hawthorne's tales is particularly abundant with expressions of *apparent circumstance*: "as if," "as though," "it appeared that," "it seemed that," "it might have been," "it must have been," "doubtless," "perhaps," "were such a thing possible," "he fancied that," "as it were," "some affirm that," and so forth. There are at least thirty such expressions in this tale, not counting subtler versions. Going hand in hand with these is the vocabulary of surfaces—faces, facades, visages, countenances, aspects, images, tokens, types, symbols, and the like—all quite appropriate to the presentation of fantasy and dream-vision. In most writers we expect such expressions to signal statements and descriptions which we are not to take literally but rather metaphorically. Moreover, in a case like Hawthorne's, where the tales are so thoroughly permeated with "as if" and "as though" constructions, we are tempted to take the whole as allegorical, a highly organized saying of one thing to mean another. In Hawthorne, however, this is not quite the effect. His emblematic technique is less allegorical than "hypothetical," less a matter of systematically reading other meanings into the literal statement than a matter of withholding judgment on all apparent meanings, which are nonetheless offered as possibilities.

In proposing the term "hypothetical" to characterize Hawthorne's method, I wish to emphasize that it must be taken here in the loosest sense. Hawthorne does not present a hypothesis which he expects in any way to be verified or verifiable, as, for example, a writer of utopian fiction like Bellamy or a Chicago realist like Henry Blake Fuller might. In most of Hawthorne's tales—certainly in "Young Goodman Brown"—the statements put forth are not to be regarded as either true or false, or even possibly so, except in the broadest meaning of "truth-to-life." We are not to imagine that what happened to Goodman Brown really happened to someone, or will, although much of the account Hawthorne gives could stand just as it is, had there been such a person with such a history. Nor are we asked to "suspend our disbelief" in reading the tale—not at least in any strict sense of that expression. In reading Hawthorne, as a matter of fact, we are constantly to bear in mind that it is only a fiction we are engrossed in. We take the story as neither true nor false, not by agreeing to leave such questions in abeyance, but by recognizing (and in Hawthorne, even concentrating on) the fact that such questions do not apply in the ordinary way. As with certain other kinds of imaginative accounts—for instance daydreams or jokes—we are required to put an "as if" construction on everything, to begin the experience with a silent "Supposing that . . ." which determines our attitude toward what we read. Again as in daydreams, jokes, and so forth, it is obvious that our attitude of "supposing" is quite different from an attitude of "believing" or even "pretending to believe." Imagine believing or pretending to believe in "Young Goodman Brown"! This does not mean that we do not take such fiction seriously, for certainly we do, but only that our serious reaction to it is different from what it would be in the case of non-fiction. One does not write letters to the *Times* protesting the outrages committed in a tale (unless one happens to be a literary critic); one does not pass the hat for the relief of fictional orphans. Like as not, one takes thought rather than action.

Obviously there is much more to say about the logical implications and psychological effects of fiction as opposed to non-fiction. We have gone far enough, however, to see that "Young Goodman Brown," with its insistence on its own "as-ifness," is a rather special sort of tale, peculiarly about itself, about the nature of belief in imagined realities, and about the status of such realities. What happened to Young Goodman Brown in the woods is, first and foremost, a part of a fiction invented by Hawthorne. Brown of course cannot know this; that would be a twist for a modern novelist or playwright. Brown *can* know that his experience is in direct contradiction to his everyday sense of things, and that one or the other of them must be false—if they are to be regarded as matters of truth and falsity at all. This is just his difficulty. Logically, either Satan is right when he says, "ye had still hoped, that virtue were not all a dream. Now are ye undeceived! Evil is the nature of mankind," or else Brown *had* "fallen asleep in the forest, and only dreamed a wild dream of a witch-meeting." But how is Brown to decide which of the two accounts to trust? Remembering always that this is a *logical* question only if the accounts *are* true or false, let us go on to see what criteria or means of deciding are open to him. Perhaps he has some subtle moral sense, some faculty of intuition that could tell him. Hawthorne sometimes seemed to believe in such a faculty, as in this passage from the *American Notebooks*:

> A person, while awake and in the business of life, to think highly of another, and place perfect confidence in him, but to be troubled with dreams in which this seeming friend appears to act the part of a most deadly enemy. Finally it is discovered that the dream-character is the true one. The explanation would be—the soul's instinctive perception.[6]

Such an "explanation" might fit "Young Goodman Brown." Assuming for the moment that it does, we should observe that it is not necessarily the apparent dream that is to be distrusted; distrust itself, to put it another way, is likely to lead to mistakes about reality:

> Distrust to be thus exemplified [another entry in the Notebooks reads]:—Various good and desirable things to be presented to a young man, and offered to his acceptance,—as a friend, a wife, a fortune; but he to refuse them all, suspecting that it is merely a delusion. Yet all to be real, and he to be told so, when too late.[7]

Back again with a character who needs "to be told" which is dream, which reality, we see Hawthorne here identifying the lack or loss of faith with a sort of suspicious pessimism—rather like that which Young Goodman Brown is said to arrive at as a consequence of his loss of faith. Perhaps instead it *constitutes* that loss.

Let us look at one more striking example of the sort of dilemma posed in these entries and in "Young Goodman Brown"—a situation in "Rappaccini's Daughter" that is so instructive an illustration of the problem that I must quote from it at some length. The hero, Giovanni, has fallen in love with the beautiful but deadly Beatrice. He has discovered that Beatrice is so imbued with the poisons of her father's garden that her very breath is fatal. At first unbelieving, he exclaims, "It is a dream . . . surely it is a dream," but

> he could not quite forget the bouquet that withered in her grasp, and the insect that perished amid the sunny air, by no ostensible agency, save the fragrance of her breath. These incidents, however, dissolving in the pure light of her character, had no longer the efficacy of facts, but were acknowledged as mistaken fantasies, by whatever testimony of the senses they might appear to be substantiated. There is something truer and more real, than what we can see with the eyes, and touch with the finger: On such better evidence, had Giovanni founded his confidence in Beatrice, though rather by the necessary force of her high attributes, than by any deep and generous faith, on his part. But, now, his spirit was incapable of sustaining itself at the height to which the early enthusiasm of passion had exalted it; he fell down, grovelling among earthly doubts, and defiled therewith the pure whiteness of Beatrice's image.

As it turns out, so far as the reader can tell, Giovanni was quite right to be suspicious of Beatrice. Although he is certainly cruel to her, and although his attempt to achieve earthly happiness with her by administering powerful antidotes to the poison in her system is unquestionably fatal to her, yet surely he made no mistake about her potent infirmity. Yet Hawthorne says, "had Giovanni known how to estimate" Beatrice's virtues properly, they "would have assured him that all this ugly mystery was but an earthly illusion." If we ask what difference that could have made, considering the realistic circumstances, the only answer that presents itself—and it is surely a curious one—is that Hawthorne could have invented some sort of loophole for his hero, if only his hero had had the "high faith" worthy of such a miracle. This may sound like the literary critic grasping at straws, but I believe that it is somehow Hawthorne's point—that after all, it is only a story, that the characters might have acted differently, the outcome might have been whatever they wanted, had they only realized it.

Both here and in "Young Goodman Brown," Hawthorne seems to throw the blame on his characters, while at the same time he gives them no means of saving themselves. He undermines his condemnation of them by telling their dreams as realistically as he does their actual experiences, so that even the reader can see little difference between the two. Were the author not on hand to put us right, by dropping an "as if" here and there, or, in "Rappaccini's Daughter," by explicitly telling us what to think, would we know that Brown and Giovanni are to be condemned for their tragic losses—any more than Brown and Giovanni know it themselves? Hawthorne's technique puts us in nearly the same position as his characters, except that we are given some additional hints as to how we should come to terms with *our* dream, the tale we are reading.

For us it is a case of "supposing," which we are to take seriously but not literally. We are to learn from it, as another of Hawthorne's notebook characters who never made it into fiction:

> A person to look back on a long life ill-spent, and to picture forth a beautiful life which he would live, if he could be permitted to begin his life over again. Finally to discover that he had only been dreaming of old age,—that he was really young, and could live such a life as he had pictured.[8]

For this character, as for his readers, the typical Hawthorne illusion turns out well enough, but the Young Goodman Browns have no kindly author looking out for their interests, allowing them to "discover" that all is a dream. One feels that Hawthorne would have preferred to have all his tales come out so luckily for their characters. He worried over the unrelieved gloominess of *The Scarlet Letter* and wanted to include a few lighter pieces with it. Persuaded to separate publication by Fields, he followed it with an attempt at a book with more sunshine in it, *The House of the Seven Gables*, and if one reads through the complete works, the surprising thing is how many dreary cheerful things he did write—often for children. But at his best he invariably sees things at their worst. For a man who is always complaining about his characters' lack of faith, Hawthorne himself is singularly dubious about the possibilities of life and human nature. To quote the *Notebooks* once again, he frequently seems to be in the following situation:

> A person to be writing a tale, and to find that it shapes itself against his

intentions; that the characters act otherwise than he thought; that unforeseen events occur; and a catastrophe comes which he strives in vain to avert. It might shadow forth his own fate, —he having made himself one of the personages.[9]

One suspects that Hawthorne had his own experience in mind here. In any case, it is certainly related to the experience of Young Goodman Brown, whose dream turns into his reality merely by virtue of his belief in it. If Brown "strives" at all, it is certainly "in vain" to avert *his* catastrophe; ditto his creator.

Hawthorne's tales are attempts to find meanings adequate to the emblems of life with which he fills his notebooks. In this respect he may be said to be rather like his Concord neighbor Thoreau, taking the measure of worldly facts, reading them as signs, and worrying a transcendental meaning out of them. But even in *The Seven Gables* Hawthorne's beans come up with scarlet blossoms, and his pond is a Maule's well. Thoreau uses language to create a world in which his spirit can breathe, which is neither entirely factual, past, and dead, nor entirely fanciful and unattainable. To borrow the rather Thoreauvian pun with which Hawthorne concludes one of his tales, he tries to "look beyond the shadowy scope of Time, and living once for all in Eternity, . . . find the perfect Future in the present." But Hawthorne, like the protagonist of "The Birthmark" so enjoined, cannot live up to such advice, or, as almost seems to come to the same thing for him, his characters cannot live up to it. Looking into the hearts of his Giovannis and Young Goodman Browns, Hawthorne finds no warrant for the faith he seeks. His "supposings" for them regularly issue in disaster.

Hawthorne's tales do tell us that things need not be what they seem, that there is always another, better world possible to faith. But contrariwise, the means to this faith is itself through fiction and related activities of the imagination, dreams and visions. As he also says in "The Birthmark," *à propos* of Aylmer's dream: "Truth often finds its way to the mind close-muffled in robes of sleep, and then speaks with uncompromising directness of matters in regard to which we practise an unconscious self-deception, during our waking moments." This, especially in the context of Aylmer's experiment, is a gloomy version of something Emerson says in *Nature*, "that a dream may let us deeper into the secret of nature than a hundred concerted experiments."[10] Hawthorne's position is in some wise an Emersonian or Thoreauvian optimism, but without the grace to find his faith supported by the dreams which he and his characters are assailed by. Not that their dreams don't come true, but that they turn out nightmares, like Aylmer's or Young Goodman Brown's.

While exploring the problem of faith through his characters, Hawthorne does not hesitate to probe the question of his own disappointment in them. He seems to recognize that if the fault is somehow in his characters, it is no less in himself, in his very decision to explore and experiment with their moral natures. Here we come at last to the perennial crux in Hawthorne, what in one way or another keeps him from being a transcendentalist—the unpardonable sin. Among the speeches of Satan to Brown and his wife as they are welcomed to the communion is the following:

> "This night it shall be granted you to know their secret deeds. . . . By the sympathy of your human hearts for sin, ye shall scent out all the places—whether in church, bed-chamber, street, field, or forest—where crime has been committed, and shall exult to behold the whole earth one stain of guilt, one mighty blood-spot. Far more than this! It shall be yours to penetrate, in every bosom, the deep mystery of sin, the fountain of all wicked arts, and which inexhaustibly supplies more evil impulses than human power—than my power at its utmost!—can make manifest in deeds."

Despite his refusal to join the devil's communion, Brown comes out of his experience—be it dream or reality—with precisely the power here promised him. The knowledge of good and evil (mainly evil) which he thereby gains is a curse. In it consists his loss of faith —in all senses of the word—for he now *sees* the sin in his wife and in his fellowman, and he believes that the world is the devil's. The exercise of this power of secret knowledge is what, in the *Notebooks* and later in "Ethan Brand," Hawthorne calls the "Unpardonable Sin"—"a want of love and reverence for the Human Soul; in consequence of which, the investigator pried into its dark depths, not with a hope or purpose of making it better, but from a cold philosophical curiosity."[11]

Although Hawthorne uses the phrase "cold *philosophical* curiosity," it should be noted that the unpardonable sin, breaking the "magnetic chain of humanity," is not the exclusive propensity of the calculating scientists in Hawthorne; the artists too are liable to pry too deeply into the "mystery of sin" in others, with the result that they are as much responsible for that sin as the sinners themselves. So the painter of "The Prophetic Pictures" asks himself, "Was not his own the form in which that destiny had embodied itself, and he a chief agent of the coming evil which he had foreshadowed?" And yet, how can the painter help seeing what he sees, foretelling what his power of vision reveals?

The difference between Hawthorne's artists and his scientists is that while the former, men like the painter of "The Prophetic Pictures" or Holgrave in *The House of the Seven Gables*, have the ability to transcend the here and now through a kind of artistic clairvoyance, the latter, like Aylmer, Rappaccini, and Chillingworth, are meddlers with time and space, Dupin-like reasoners who, since they can never get beyond the alchemical confines of their methodology, end up destroying the subjects of their experiments. As Aylmer discovers in "The Birthmark," ". . . our great creative Mother, while she amuses us with apparently working in the broadest sunshine, is yet severely careful to keep her own secrets, and, in spite of her pretended openness, shows us nothing but results. She permits us, indeed, to mar, but seldom to mend, and, like a jealous patentee, on no account to make." The artists are also tempted to *act* on their special knowledge of "the mystery of sin," the "dark depths" of the human soul, but the best of them characteristically refuse to go so far, or, if they do allow themselves *even* the painter's mimetic act, they are by so much the less possessors of the "high faith" that is the ultimate value in Hawthorne.

What disturbs Hawthorne most, and in fact gives rise to his conception of the unpardonable sin, is that his artists, like his scientists, may after all be guilty of attempting to "make" reality, and consequently, by virtue of their insight into the recesses of the human heart and their power to portray what they see with Pygmalion-like verisimilitude, they may actually call into being what would otherwise lie dormant, may sacrilegiously "commit" the sins they "imagine" in others. Obviously this fear has special import for Hawthorne's own situation. As Melville said in his review of *Mosses from an Old Manse*, one cannot finish reading "Young Goodman Brown" ". . . without addressing the author in his own words—'It shall be yours to penetrate, in every bosom, the deep mystery of sin.'" But this is a question for a more psychoanalytic reading of him than I am now attempting.

One might extract from Emerson a fuller view of language to help explain how Hawthorne gets out of his mimetic dilemma, in so far as he does get out:

> Words [Emerson says] are signs of natural facts. The use of natural
> history is to give us aid in supernatural history. The use of the outer
> creation is to give us language for the beings and changes of the inward
> creation.
>
> It is not words only that are emblematic; it is things which are emble-
> matic. Every natural fact is a symbol of some spiritual fact.
>
> The world is emblematic. Parts of speech are metaphors because the
> whole of nature is a metaphor of the human mind. The laws of moral
> nature answer to those of matter as face to face in a glass.
>
> In like manner, the memorable words of history, and the proverbs of
> nations, consist usually of a natural fact, selected as a picture or
> parable of a moral truth. [12]

By this account, truth-to-life is a necessary result of the proper use of
language. The emblematic writer like Hawthorne cannot help but be in
touch with reality. This is not a matter of mere factual or literal description; on the contrary, Emerson tells us we must "rise above the ground line
of familiar facts," to figurative language, images, and metaphors. [13]

As the *American Notebooks* amply testify, Hawthorne believed with
Emerson that "Every natural fact is a symbol of some spiritual fact," and
that "The laws of moral nature answer to those of matter as face to face in a
glass." It is only a little step further to a thorough reversal of the realist's
theory of mimesis; holding the mirror up to nature becomes, in gothicists
like Hawthorne, not a means of seeing nature, but a means of seeing,
reflexively, back into the seer himself, which is the point of the passage
from *Pierre* cited at the beginning of this study. To quote Emerson again,

> These are not the dreams of a few poets, here and there, but man is an
> analogist, and studies relations in all objects. He is placed in the centre
> of beings, and a ray of relation passes from every other being to him.
> And neither can man be understood without these objects, nor these
> objects without man. [14]

The ordinary realist, a writer of short stories, wants to "reproduce" reality,
or some aspect of it, in language. Words are thus conceived and valued as
indicators of things, referring to the various "facts" of life and nature, and
the writer is advised, for example by Henry James (though it was not exactly his practice), to take notes on his experience, the better to render it

later in fiction. Ordinary realism is premised on the view, whether tenable or not, that the writer can "match up" the things in his fiction to the things of life, through the agency of words, which act as neutral conductors, like the "half-tone dots" of a newspaper photograph. By contrast, in Hawthorne's mimesis with its dependence on emblematic language, what is "imitated" is not nature at all, but the supernatural—"moral law," "spiritual fact," "the beings and changes of the inward creation"—and these by means of natural emblems. In Emerson, this is one way of defining faith itself, "man's power to connect his thought with its proper symbol, and so to utter it." "[P]icturesque language," he says, "is at once a commanding certificate that he who employs it, is a man in alliance with truth and God."[15] For him it is the essence of faith to find the natural world only a metaphor for the spiritual: he can act in this world enlivened by imagination; there is a universe for him. Belief, desire, and act are amalgamated, and one creates reality as one goes along: I make things happen, and thus *prove* my existence *and* the existence of what happens.

But for Hawthorne these "creative imitations" of the spirit are always accompanied by the admonition *not* to take them as reality, not to act upon them as upon evidence or fact. The products of the imagination, though they may comprise the highest truths of all, are only "supposed" truths, "as ifs" which crumble at the touch or disappear in the daylight, as Hawthorne coyly warned the reader of *Twice-Told Tales*. This is not regarded as a disadvantage so much as a safeguard, nor is he so sure of its invariable efficacy. As we have seen, his emblems carry a somber meaning, one which produces in him a nagging sense of guilt, as if he were to blame (and who else?) for the truths he divines. He keeps reminding us of the danger of taking the symbolic burden of an emblem literally, like Ahab in *Moby-Dick*, and thus destroying oneself in pursuit of an illusion—which for Melville too is tantamount to calling it magically into life. Less concerned with faith than with its loss, Hawthorne offers the following analysis: once we treat a spiritual truth as a natural truth, as something to act on, it immediately becomes a chimera breathing real fire; *active* belief is fatal to desire, and we are left with only half of faith, if not doubt then horror. His refuge was a theory of mimesis, or the rudiments of one: fictions, and their truths, are not matters of truth or falsity at all. For him, faith depends on remaining *out* of doubt, on maintaining the aesthetic distance.

3

"Unspeakable Horror" in Poe

In many of Poe's tales the voice of the narrator seems to be the only thing a reader can count on; the tale proper, in its setting, characters, and events, may be a mere projection of the teller's diseased imagination. More than one critic, for example, has attempted to explain the supernatural events of "Ligeia" as hallucinations produced in the teller by opium. Poe himself, even if he intends us to entertain such possibilities, never admits that his narrators are only "seeing things," so the best we can say is that these peculiar tales seem both realistic and hallucinatory. With these queer self-involved narrators, there is no tension, no difference, between the realistic and the hallucinatory—that is Poe's trademark, the "effect" he aimed at in his most characteristic tales. Thus in the beginning of "The Fall of the House of Usher" it does not matter whether, as the narrator says, the gloom of the scene depressed his spirits, or, as seems equally possible in the context, his gloomy imagination endowed the scene with its bleakness. Already we begin to accept the simultaneity of inner and outer, the congruence of subject and object. There are no relevant criteria for deciding between these possibilities.

As everyone knows, Poe's interest in such effects shows itself in numerous ways. His fascination with "intermediate states of consciousness," as in mesmeric trances, hallucination, visions, suspended animation, the passage from dreams to waking, and so on, almost amounts to an obsession with the borders of awareness. This of course places him squarely in the gothic tradition, especially the more self-conscious school of second generation gothicists like Maturin and Hoffmann, whose commerce with the outposts of psychic experience exceeded even Poe's.

Nor does one have to explore very far to find analogues in the work of most of Poe's major contemporaries in the United States—Hawthorne and Melville, Emerson and Thoreau, each in his own way fixated on the problems of self and other, world, faith, and transcendence.

More than either his gothic models or his contemporaries, Poe spent his energies on the lunatic fringe of such realms. I mean this quite literally as well as metaphorically. Unlike Hawthorne's Young Goodman Brown or Melville's Tommo, for example, a Poe hero tends to loiter on the verge of the woods or at the entrance to the fatal valley, be it paradise or devil's playground. Once they tumble over the precipice, Poe's characters have little to do, and like Pym it seems they cannot wait to scramble back for another try, as if there were some possibility of falling into another world altogether if one could only get the formula right. It is this aspect of Poe's fiction that I want to examine, especially as it shows itself in his attitude toward language—not so much his style, the words on the page, but his belief in language as a means to transcendence, a way out of mundane reality and a way in . . . to what mystic country of the mind?

Poe's narrators are highly articulate and his narratives are rich in their vocabulary, subtle in syntax, profusely rhetorical. Yet all the armory of stylistic devices produces a prose which is often as vague as it is pellucid. Leaving aside problems of pomposity and stilted elegance, we may locate this curious imprecision in Poe's subject matter itself, in the sort of thing he wished to communicate. Here, for example, are some relevant passages from two of the tales:

> Ah, word of no meaning! behind whose vast latitude of mere sound we intrench our ignorance of so much of the spiritual.   ["Ligeia"]

> Words are impotent to convey any just idea of the fierceness of resistance with which she wrestled with the Shadow.   ["Ligeia"]

> Through a species of unutterable horror and awe, for which the language of mortality has no sufficiently energetic expression . . .   ["Ligeia"]

> . . . was conveyed in terms too shadowy here to be restated . . .   ["The Fall of the House of Usher"]

> Yet I should fail in any attempt to convey an idea of the exact character of the studies. . . .   ["The Fall of the House of Usher"]

> I would in vain endeavor to educe more than a small portion which

should lie within the compass of merely written words.
["The Fall of the House of Usher"]
I lack words to express the full extent. . . .
["The Fall of the House of Usher"][1]

This list might be greatly expanded, of course, to include "inarticulate breathings," "indefinite shadows," "unutterable woe," "unspeakable horrors," and so on. Its significance lies in Poe's evident fascination with the inexpressible. "Unspeakable horror" is so often Poe's subject, his return to it again and again in the tales raises some paradoxical questions. How can language express the inexpressible? If there are no words for what he finally wants to say, how can he say it at all? At first one suspects Poe of a calculated coyness, or at best a clever use of indefiniteness to heighten suspense; for in the end the inexpressible always does seem somehow to get expressed. Yet this explanation does not go far enough.

"Ligeia" is one of the two quarries for the list above. Like its earlier and much shorter model "Morella," this is a story of resurrection, the passage from life to death and back again, a passage accomplished through the power of the will and the mystical use of words. The narrator describes his beloved Ligeia, recounts something of their life together, her death and his unhappy remarriage to Rowena, the sickness and death of his second wife, and finally the revivification of Rowena's body, which Ligeia's spirit enters and transforms into her own likeness. Certain passages stand out in the tale as peculiar. The narrator is strangely forgetful. Not only does he have the continual difficulty with language which the passages already quoted display; he is also unable to recall—if that is the word for his curious lapses—a number of things about Ligeia:

I cannot, for my soul, remember how, when, or even precisely where, I first became acquainted with the lady Ligeia.

And now, while I write, a recollection flashes upon me that I have *never known* the paternal name of her who was my friend and my betrothed. . . .

There is no point, among the many incomprehensible anomalies of the science of mind, more thrillingly exciting than the fact—never, I believe, noticed in the schools—that, in our endeavors to recall to memory something long forgotten, we often find ourselves *upon the very verge* of remembrance, without being able, in the end, to remember. And thus how frequently, in my intense scrutiny of Ligeia's eyes, have I felt approaching the full knowledge of their ex-

pression—felt it approaching—yet not quite be mine—and so at
length entirely depart!

In spite of his protests that memory and language fail him at the brink of
discovery, the narrator does finally communicate what it is that the expression of Ligeia's eyes tells him:

> Of all the women whom I have ever known, she, the outwardly calm,
> the ever-placid Ligeia, was the most violently a prey to the tumultuous
> vultures of stern passion. And of such passion I could form no
> estimate, save by the miraculous expansion of those eyes which at
> once so delighted and appalled me—by the almost magical melody,
> modulation, distinctness, and placidity of her very low voice—and by
> the fierce energy (rendered doubly effective by contrast with her
> manner of utterance) of the wild words which she habitually uttered.

The "passion" which she expresses in both her eyes and her "wild words"
is pure will, a force which in this tale overcomes death itself. The "wild
words" seem to be connected with Ligeia's recondite studies in areas of
"forbidden" knowledge (mentioned, for example, in the paragraph immediately following that just quoted), so that the reader is led to suppose
that Ligeia's speech has something of the character of black magic, an
incantation, a mysterious formula by which she finally imposes her will on
physical nature. "Man doth not yield him to the angels, *nor unto death
utterly*, save only through the weakness of his feeble will," she exclaims
on her death bed, quoting the mystical pronouncement (which Poe
scholars have been unable to trace) that stands as epigraph to the tale itself.
   Actually, Ligeia's words are not the means of her resurrection at the end
of the tale; the emphasis on her speech here merely foreshadows a more
potent incantation. The narrator, in spite of his strange aphasia regarding
Ligeia's family name, is more than able to remember her given name, and
after her death he can summon up her image by repeating it to himself:

> Ligeia! Ligeia! Buried in studies of a nature more than all else adapted
> to deaden impressions of the outward world, it is by that sweet word
> alone—by Ligeia—that I bring before mine eyes in fancy the image of
> her who is no more.

The narrator tells us how he

. . . would call aloud upon her name, during the silence of the night, or among the sheltered recesses of the glens by day, as if, through the wild eagerness, the solemn passion, the consuming ardor of my longing for the departed, I could restore her to the pathway she had abandoned—ah, *could* it be forever?—upon the earth.

Finally, on the night of Ligeia's resurrection, the narrator sits alone by the corpse of Rowena his second wife, still brooding on the loss of his first, his "one and only and supremely beloved" Ligeia. Since he is now completely given over "to passionate waking visions of Ligeia," perhaps he is again pronouncing her name. After several mysterious preludes Rowena's body begins to show signs of life—to the narrator's "unutterable horror"—until finally she arises and stands before him. The cerements fall from her face, revealing "the full, and the black, and the wild eyes—of my lost love—of the Lady—of the Lady Ligeia!" As the culminating reference to her "wild eyes" suggests, it is partly through the effort of Ligeia's own will (of which the eye is a common symbol, as well as a specific one in the context) that she accomplishes her rebirth—but the narrator plays his part in the "hideous drama of revivification" too. By chanting her name, he has succeeded in reviving not merely her image, but her very body.

The passages that describe the first strange effects of pronouncing Ligeia's name lay particular stress on the necessity that it be pronounced aloud, and this circumstance, together with the fact that the narrator reports his own exact words in quotation marks only once in the tale, at the very end when he stammers out her name, suggests that the unutterable expression which he has throughout been struggling after may be none other than this very name, which of course he has known all along, unaware of its ultimate potency until the climax. "Ligeia" is thus a tale of the *logos*, names mystically producing their referents as consequences. The "wild words" and abstruse learning of Ligeia, once she is dead, are symbolically rediscovered by the narrator, whose weird aphasia about Ligeia represents the imminence of his "recalling" her to life.

Obviously, a full reading of the tale would have to take into account other features—the gothic themes of mysterious lineage, sexual mastery, exotic setting, and so on—and it can be shown that all of these cohere in something like the conventional gothic pattern. But the essence of the tale lies in the speaking of the "unspeakable," as a comparison with some others of Poe's tales, and even his criticism, will make clear. To take the easiest example, "Morella" is an even more explicit case in which the name of the heroine, pronounced by the narrator, brings her back to life. In that tale the heroine has given birth to a daughter (somehow the same as giving place to a second wife) at the moment of her own death. Years later the fatal denouement takes place:

> Thus passed away two lustra of her life, and, as yet, my daughter remained nameless upon the earth. "My child" and "my love" were the designations usually prompted by a father's affection, and the rigid seclusion of her days precluded all other intercourse. Morella's name died with her at her death. . . . But at length the ceremony of baptism presented [itself] to my mind. . . . And at the baptismal font I hesitated for a name. . . . What prompted me, then, to disturb the memory of the buried dead? What demon urged me to breathe that sound, which, in its very recollection was wont to make ebb the purple blood in torrents from the temples to the heart? What fiend spoke from the recesses of my soul, when, amid those dim aisles, and in the silence of the night, I whispered within the ears of the holy man the syllables—Morella? What more than fiend convulsed the features of my child, and overspread them with hues of death, as, starting at that scarcely audible sound, she turned her glassy eyes from the earth to heaven, and, falling prostrate on the black slabs of our ancestral vault, responded—"I am here!"

Other tales do not treat the utterance of the unutterable quite so boldly (with an exception to be examined in a moment), but analogous plots abound in Poe's fiction. In the "MS. Found in a Bottle" the narrator finds himself "thoughtlessly" daubing a folded sail with a tar brush, so that when unfurled it spells out the word "Discovery." In "A Tale of the Ragged Mountains" Bedloe is "Oldeb conversed," once again fate folded in a name. The *Narrative of Arthur Gordon Pym* climaxes with the scream "Tekeli-li!" and its looming embodiment in the vast white figure arising out of the "chasm" of the antipodes. It would be easy to list other examples, but a passage in the "Marginalia" is more useful at this point, since it begins to make a connection for us between the denotative "power of words" and Poe's monomaniacal fascination with the edge of ordinary time and space, death and resurrection, consciousness and oblivion, catalepsy and trance.

> How very commonly we hear it remarked, that such and such thoughts are beyond the compass of words! I do not believe that any

thought, properly so called, is out of the reach of language. I fancy, rather, that where difficulty in expression is experienced, there is, in the intellect which experiences it, a want either of deliberateness or of method. For my own part, I have never had a thought which I could not set down in words, with even more distinctness than that with which I conceived it:—as I have before observed, the thought is logicalized by the effort at (written) expression.

There is, however, a class of fancies, of exquisite delicacy, which are *not* thoughts, and to which, *as yet*, I have found it absolutely impossible to adapt language. I use the word *fancies* at random, and merely because I must use *some* word; but the idea commonly attached to the term is not even remotely applicable to the shadows of shadows in question. They seem to me rather psychal than intellectual. They arise in the soul (alas, how rarely!) only at its epochs of most intense tranquility—when the bodily and mental health are in perfection—and at those mere points of time where the confines of the waking world blend with those of the world of dreams. . . .

Now, so entire is my faith in the *power of words*, that, at times, I have believed it possible to embody even the evanescence of fancies such as I have attempted to describe. In experiments with this end in view, I have proceeded so far as, first, to control (when the bodily and mental health are good) the existence of the condition:—that is to say, I can now (unless when ill) be sure that the condition will supervene, if I so wish it, at the point of time already described. . . .

I have proceeded so far, secondly, as to prevent the lapse from *the point* of which I speak—the point of blending between wakefulness and sleep—as to prevent at will, I say, the lapse from this border-ground into the dominion of sleep. Not that I can *continue* the condition—not that I can render the point more than a point—but that I can startle myself from the point into wakefulness—and *thus transfer the point itself into the realm of Memory*—convey its impressions, or more properly their recollections, to a situation where (although still for a very brief period) I can survey them with the eye of analysis.

For these reasons—that is to say, because I have been enabled to accomplish thus much—I do not altogether despair of embodying in words at least enough of the fancies in question to convey, to certain classes of intellect, a shadowy conception of their character.[2]

Although these remarks are directed most obviously to the borderline between dream and waking states, they also apply to all the varieties of Poe's concern with the "world" that "exists" in the midst of paradox, the realm he posits in the intersection of mutually exclusive conditions of existence. His "faith in the power of words" to describe this realm is, more than anything else, a justification of his art, since so many of his tales exist for this purpose alone. Here as elsewhere much emphasis is put on the elusiveness of the objects of Poe's efforts, but there is something fishy about his argument. It begins to appear that Poe's linguistic aim is not really descriptive at all, but creative—an attempt to find the talismanic words that will, as he says, "embody" the supernatural event, or at least bridge the unbridgeable gap between opposite mental states. Part of the formula consists of disclaimers, to the effect that the magic words are unpronounceable, but this hesitation is merely an incantatory buildup to the final ecstatic abracadabra. The essential task of Poe's art is to prepare the way, by various interlocking linguistic expectations and probabilities, for a culminating sentence that will somehow both say and be the desired apotheosis.

Poe and his narrators are practitioners of word-magic. They believe that there is a natural (or supernatural) connection between the word and what it names—not merely a conventional semantic relationship. Of course not all of Poe's tales reduce to a single magical word, but most of them are built around a single magical act of perception ("mere points of time") in which some image or symbol—a portrait, a letter hanging on a letter-tape, a group of men dangling from a chandelier, a mirror image—turns out, horrifyingly, to *be* what it only seemed to stand for or reflect or represent—so that the "oval portrait's" lifelikeness results in the death of its subject, the hiding place of the "purloined letter" turns out to be a letter-tape, the King and his councillors in "Hop Frog" are lit like candles as they hang from the chandelier, William Wilson and his mirror-double are a single suicide-murderer. These cases are all varieties of metonymic perception, a kind of primitive word-magic carried to its utmost extreme. To a large extent, Poe's literary method is summed up in this paradigm of the talismanic word which calls into existence what it names.

A full and characteristic example is "The Fall of the House of Usher." The structural principle of this tale is hinted in its title, namely the metonymic pun ("'House of Usher'—an appellation which seemed to include, in the minds of the peasantry who used it, both the family and the family mansion") which we discover we must take literally: in typical gothic fashion, the physical house collapses at the same time that the lineage of the hereditary house is cut off. The physical constitution—or, more precisely, configuration—of the house is represented in the opening pages as a puzzle much like the inexpressible mystery of Ligeia's wild eyes or the evanescent "border-ground" between sleep and waking. The narrator asks himself "What was it—I paused to think—what was it that so unnerved me in the contemplation of the House of Usher? It was a mystery all insoluble; nor could I grapple with the shadowy fancies that crowded upon me as I pondered. I was forced to fall back upon the unsatisfactory conclusion, that while, beyond doubt, there *are* combinations of very simple natural objects which have the power of thus affecting us, still the analysis of this power lies among considerations beyond our depth."

He describes the building: "No portion of the masonry had fallen; and there appeared to be a wild inconsistency between its still perfect adaptation of parts, and the crumbling condition of the individual stones." As we later find, Roderick, the last of the Ushers, believes that "some peculiarities in the mere form and substance of his family mansion, had, by dint of long sufferance, . . . obtained [an influence] over his spirit—an effect which the *physique* of the gray walls and turrets, and of the dim tarn into which they all looked down, had, at length, brought about upon the *morale* of his existence." Part of this strange reciprocity consisted in the sentience of the house, the conditions of which Usher believed were "fulfilled in the method of collocation of these stones—in the order of their arrangement. . . ." That is, there is something organic, even syntactical, about the house. Finally, we are also told that Usher is peculiarly sensitive, and in particular he seems to be able to hear movement in any part of the house. Since the house itself is sentient, we may assume that Usher is aware of movements throughout the house as one might be aware of his own body. The house and the scion are one, and each exists by virtue of the other.

As in "Morella" and "Ligeia" so in this tale, the climax is a resurrection scene. Roderick Usher's twin sister Madeline—with whom he has "sympathies of a scarcely intelligible nature"—has been prematurely buried in a vault deep beneath the house. Again, magical words are the means by which she is recalled to life, but in this case it is not the pronunciation of her name that revivifies her, but a more elaborate incantation. The narrator is reading to Usher when the final catastrophe takes place. The "antique volume" recounts "an entrance by force" which, as the narrator pronounces the words, is echoed in the house of Usher itself. Passage by passage, "the voice of the dry and hollow-sounding wood," "the dragon's unnatural shriek," the "terrible ringing sound" of the shield, are heard coming closer and closer. Roderick finally exclaims:

"Not hear it?—yes, I hear it, and *have* heard it. Long— long—long—many minutes, many hours, many days, have I heard it—yet I dared not—oh, pity me, miserable wretch that I am!—I dared not—I *dared* not speak! *We have put her living in the tomb!* Said I not that my senses were acute? I *now* tell you that I heard her first feeble movements in the hollow coffin. I heard them—many, many days ago—yet I dared not—I *dared not speak!* And now—to-night—Ethelred—ha! ha!—the breaking of the hermit's door, and the death-cry of the dragon, and the clangor of the shield!—say, rather, the rending of her coffin, and the grating of the iron hinges of her prison, and her struggles within the coppered archway of the vault! Oh whither shall I fly? Will she not be here anon? Is she not hurrying to upbraid me for my haste? Have I not heard her footstep on the stair? Do I not distinguish that heavy and horrible beating of her heart? Madman!—here he sprang furiously to his feet, and shrieked out his syllables, as if in the effort he were giving up his soul—*Madman! I tell you that she now stands without the door!"*

As if in the superhuman energy of his utterance there had been found the potency of a spell, the huge antique pannels to which the speaker pointed, threw slowly back, upon the instant, their ponderous and ebony jaws. It was the work of the rushing gust—but then without those doors there *did* stand the lofty and enshrouded figure of the lady Madeline of Usher.

All the mysterious affinities—of Roderick, his house, his sister, and the "antique volume"—are ingeniously orchestrated here in a single metonymic pun. For days Roderick has known of his sister's life in the tomb, but "dared not speak" the "unspeakable horror." After Madeline's interment but before the reading of "The Mad Trist," "a tremulous quaver, as if of extreme terror, [had] habitually characterized his utterance." Roderick then appeared as if he were trying "to divulge" some "oppressive secret." Once the tale of Ethelred, with its strange reverberations, had begun, Roderick's "lips trembled as if he were murmuring inaudibly." Now, as the house physically echoes each phrase of "The Mad Trist," Roderick's voice begins to vibrate in unison with it. Up until the last moment, however, the house does Roderick's talking for him: the sounds of Madeline's revivification travel through a "long archway . . . sheathed with copper"—not unlike a throat—and finally burst through "ponderous and ebony jaws" in a "rushing gust" of breath. At this point Roderick joins with the house to scream out his last words, and, as if "in the superhuman energy of his utterance there had been found the potency of a spell,"

Madeline is, so to speak, enunciated.

The "hideous import" of Roderick's final speech consists in its power to create, to embody, whatever it says, just as in "Morella" and "Ligeia." As Poe explains more metaphysically (how seriously it is hard to tell) in his curious little fantasy "The Power of Words," all creation is the result of "impulses upon the ether"—"the *physical power of words*." Thus one of the speakers in that dialogue "in a few passionate sentences" creates a star. This power depends somehow on the physical nature of the words themselves. They must be sounded or written, and their particular sound or look is intimately related to the characteristics of the things they name. In the *Narrative of Arthur Gordon Pym*, for instance, the hieroglyphics are landscape as well as message, both name and thing named. Or again, Poe's interest in "autography" betrays a similar tendency to identify name and person named. His "Chapter on Autography," compared, for example, with Hawthorne's "A Book of Autographs," shows him not so much a psychologist of expressive forms, as Hawthorne was, but a mystical chirographer, interpreting signatures more than handwriting, and trusting to private intuition rather than to any theory available in the psychology of the day, or to common sense. "The Fall of the House of Usher" merely takes such word-magic one step further, in positing similar supernatural ties between configurations or collocations—in architecture or in syntax—and the combinations in "reality" to which they presumably correspond: Usher and his house, "The Mad Trist" and its symbolic reverberations, and so on.

Poe's practice thus melts into his principles of artistic creation. His notion of the "power of words" is both formulated and demonstrated in his most characteristic tales, and these seem almost "written to order" from the conception of art that he propounded in his more theoretical works. In *Eureka*, for example, one finds an analogy between fiction and reality that is merely the denouement of "The Fall of the House of Usher" philosophized:

> In the construction of *plot*, for example, in fictitious literature, we should aim at so arranging the incidents that we shall not be able to determine, of any one of them, whether it depends from any one other or upholds it. In this sense, of course, *perfection* of *plot* is really, or practically, unattainable—but only because it is a finite intelligence that constructs. The plots of God are perfect. The Universe is a plot of God.[3]

Instead of the "physical" emphasis on names—the "reverse onomatopoeia" of "The Power of Words" or "The Philosophy of Composition"—Poe
here concentrates on the "perfect" collocation, the syntax of Creation. In
order to create—whether a tale or a universe—it is necessary to build an
interrelated linguistic world, entirely self-contained and self-referring,
like mathematical language. "In the whole composition" of a tale, Poe
insisted in his 1842 review of Hawthorne, "there should be no word
written, of which the tendency, direct or indirect, is not to the one pre-
established design." Only then would art have its proper
"effect"—namely, to become reality for the reader's time-being.

For the *time-being*, because Poe's theory of creation encompasses its
end as well as its beginning: in the initial action is contained the reaction;
in the "perfect plot" of *Eureka* the denouement springs "out of the bosom
of the thesis—out of the heart of the ruling idea . . . arising as a result of
the primary proposition—as inseparable and inevitable part and parcel of
the fundamental conception of the book." The "end of all things [is]
metaphysically involved in the thought of a beginning; seeks and finds in
this origin of all things the *rudiment* of this end; and perceives the impiety
of supposing this end likely to be brought about less simply—less directly—less obviously—less artistically—than through *the rëaction of the
originating Act*."[4]

In "The Fall of the House of Usher" this "creative" principle of action
and reaction is maintained in Madeline's immediate dissolution after her
resurrection, and also reflected in Roderick's own death, the subsequent
collapse of the house, and the expiration of the tale itself. All these
creations are mere words, which have their existence only in the moment
that they come into being. Poe (or his narrator) holds the fictitious world
together only for that moment, "upon the very verge" of destruction—at
the lip of the maelstrom, the edge of the abyss, the brink of the
tarn—symbols of the oblivion that even the creating *logos* cannot dispel
for more than an instant. The final words of the incantation are pronounced; afterwards there is nothing: "there was a long tumultuous shouting sound like the voice of a thousand waters—and the deep and dank tarn
at my feet closed sullenly and silently over the fragments of the '*House of
Usher*.'"

This structure—the chanting of a charm of words to call life into being,
and the collapse of the creation into nothingness once the terrible vivifica-
tion has occurred—is the primary movement of Poe's tales. Not only do

many of the plots exhibit such a pattern, but the genre itself, as Poe conceived it, invoked this paradigm. In his tales Poe creates a fantasy world by means of a highly stylized use of language, with many of the characteristics of ritual incantation; this world takes precedence over the ordinary world so long as the tale continues, so long as the hypnotic voice of the narrator wills it into being. No other world is believed in; the dream is the only reality: "During the hour of perusal the soul of the reader is at the writer's control," he said in the review of Hawthorne. But the vision can be maintained only until the charm is finished, and then the fantasy collapses back into nothingness again; as the final words are written the fictional world dissipates, and the reader is back in reality—while the narrator himself (a part of Poe) ceases to exist, falls indeed into oblivion and nothingness.

From a certain point of view, this is a description of all fictive art, all literary experience that depends on a linguistic texture to focus and concentrate the attention on an imagined reality. Yet Poe's conception of artistic language is really very peculiar—at the extreme of gothic idealism. On the one hand, as we have seen, there is a sense in which he believes that language is the only reality, that nothing exists save the tales his narrators tell. Yet on the other hand, he does not really believe in language *qua* language, for he wishes to use it not as a conventional system of conventional meanings but as a magical system of forces. He insinuates that language is bound to reality, not by convention or usage, but by mystic affinities and supernatural necessities. Perfect diction, perfect syntax, perfect rhetoric, perfect plot will result, he seems to say, in the instantiation of the reality named or recounted. But of course there is no such language or art, and Poe's tales are therefore completely out of phase with everyday life. They do achieve—for some readers, especially at certain ages—a remarkably powerful impression, almost hallucinatory in its grip on consciousness, and not unlike the "effect" Poe aimed at. And yet for other readers the tales are all surface and show, a veneer of style behind which hides a talented hack. Whether you fall into one camp or the other depends on how successful you are in giving your mind over totally to the voice of the narrator. It is fatal to reserve even the slightest recess of consciousness; a single glance of comparison toward ordinary existence and the vision instantly fades. This is why Poe was so insistent that the tale be short enough to read "in a sitting," for any interruption would break the spell.

A curious corollary to these fundamentals of the genre is that, despite the assumed magical connection between words and reality *within* a fiction, Poe's tales have scarcely any intent vis à vis a reality external to them. They aspire to total self-containment and interdependence, each part having its significance only in terms of the other parts, without reference to the non-fictive world. Thus they are all façade, emblem, appearance, fantasy—without any underlying, concomitant sense to be made or seen. Of course I do not mean that we cannot talk about the tales in terms of their relations to other phenomena—but they themselves do not suggest such relations. Their settings are purely conventional scenes, gothic labyrinths that never ask for comparison with the real world. The characters are stock types, agonizingly sensitive narrators, studious and willful heroines, and so on; many are mere corpses, character as prop. Events are saturated with probability, and Poe's favorite model of plotting is *Caleb Williams*, which Godwin wrote "backwards," starting with his denouement. In short, everything is as self-reflexive as possible. It is not surprising then to find Poe denying Truth and Morality as ends of literature in "The Poetic Principle." Beauty—the formal relation of parts, freed from any necessity of application to the ordinary world of facts or of good and evil—is the highest aim of poetry, whereas Passion and Terror are recognized (in the review of Hawthorne) as the goals of the prose tale. Here again is the ground of Poe's theory of words and reality: everything is calculated for effect rather than significance. The only Truth that can be allowed is the merely formal Truth of his tales of ratiocination, self-enclosed puzzles with no bearing on anything outside the confines of the page. Only thus can the mystic identity of language and its reference be guaranteed, when it points to what it in fact helps to make, a linguistic construct. Not surprisingly, Poe's hobbies are music and mathematics.

Although Poe is continually hinting that there is some hidden meaning lurking behind every appearance, about to be dreadfully revealed, in fact the "unspeakable horror" is precisely that there is nothing there: the magic words are pronounced, the doors burst wide, the dead open their eyes, and—everything collapses, the characters fall into the abyss, the story ends. The whole process is summed up in M. Valdemar's seven month's suspended animation, achieved through mysterious mesmeric "passes," a means of "composing" the patient which keeps him at the point of death so long as they are continued, but once reversed allows of no "re-composure," so that the body instantly decomposes, the tongue being the last to go, shouting "dead! dead!" as it crumbles and liquifies. A gruesome fantasy, but in fact very accurate as a description of Poe's literary method. Whatever is "willed" into existence also must pass out of existence once the will is relaxed. Reality is a pulse of the *logos*. From this point of view, the "unspeakable horror" is both the void and all reality, a horror only so long as it *is* unspeakable, and nothing at all once spoken. Roderick Usher is correct when he predicts, "I must abandon life and reason together, in some struggle with the grim phantasm, FEAR." To put it another way, what terrifies Poe and his narrators is just this abandonment of life and reason, the life and reason that exist for them only by virtue of language.

In Poe's second, 1847 review of Hawthorne, he complained of his "metaphor run-mad," a habit of allegorizing that Poe blamed on the transcendentalists—"cut Mr. Alcott, hang (if possible) the editor of 'The Dial,'" he advised. He hated the "mysticism" of "Young Goodman Brown" because there Hawthorne had asserted that language is arbitrary and conventional, that metaphor is the essence of man's linguistic freedom from things, and that the life of the imagination is precarious, always teetering between faith and despair, the equal possibilities of *acting* on one's fantasies. This attitude toward reality and consciousness Hawthorne did partly "imbibe" from Emerson and the transcendentalists, though the ambivalent twist he gave it was all his own. And Poe's view of the relations of language and life is exactly the opposite of Emerson's, in *Nature*, that all language rests on material things, and that the principle of its use is metaphor. Poe despises metaphor as mere ornament. He attempts a language that is absolutely literal. In his solipsistic world all reality will ultimately rest on words. Poe's work then is not, as Emerson's so clearly is, a coping with reality, or as Hawthorne's, a cautionary fable; Poe is in full flight to hallucination, fantasy, nightmare. His value is that he brings us into contact with a kind of perception which we all have at one time or another, the horror of a world where everything is surface. But he is too much a case study, too little an artist. What starts as a denial of the everyday realm of things ends trapped in nothing but linguistic arti-facts—"word-things" in a world that has no bearings in any other reality. It is like the endless string of manuscripts in *Melmoth the Wanderer*, each one plunging the reader deeper into an infinite regress of art from which the only escape is exhaustion and disgust. Some of Poe's contemporaries, especially Melville in *Pierre*, went much further in assessing the gothic relations of art and life, and later writers, notably Wilde and Kafka, became virtuosi of the paradoxes of self and the infinite regress. Poe is not the last or best of the gothicists, but he thoroughly explored at least one of these dead-end alleys—so far as to lose himself in its depths.

4

Propaganda by the Deed in James

I

"If one was to undertake to tell tales and to report with truth on the human scene," wrote Henry James in the preface to *The Princess Casamassima*, "it could be but because 'notes' had been from the cradle the ineluctable consequence of one's greatest energy: to take them was as natural as to look, to think, to feel, to recognise, to remember, as to perform any act of understanding."[1] If we want to know just what James meant by "notes," or precisely what relation he thought there was between them and the story or its truth to the human scene, we shall have to raise the question in a much broader context than the preface to the New York Edition of the novel supplies; the grammatical bridge here, "it could be but because," is hardly adequate to the heavy and peculiar traffic between James's "notes" and his novels, the span between the life observed and the life rendered which he thought of as the points of departure and arrival of his art.

Still, this is a good place to begin inquiry into a problem that much interested James, namely, the problem of realism in the novel. Is it, for example, a necessary, perhaps even a sufficient condition of truthful reports on the human scene that they should begin with notes of direct observation? The question is raised with good reason in the case of *The Princess Casamassima*, for not only did James declare that "this fiction proceeded quite directly . . . from the habit and the interest of walking the streets" of London, and from "the urgent appeal, on the part of every-thing, to be interpreted and, so far as may be, reproduced,"[2] but further, critics have hastened to corroborate or to contradict James's own testi-mony (which certainly has something defensive about it), by comparing

59

his finished portrait with its original, or what remains to us of that, thus to provide a sort of "truth-test" for the novel and some account of the realistic manner itself. And, as regards certain London streets and certain dingy rooms and halls, like the Rose Street Club in Soho, the Berners Street Club and the *Morgenröthe* in the East End, it is further a question whether to praise or to blame James for meddling in a subject he himself admits he knew next to nothing about—the revolutionary movement of the early eighties—any answer largely depending on how satisfied one can be with James's own justification, "that the value I wished most to render and the effect I wished most to produce were precisely those of our not knowing, of society's not knowing, but only guessing and suspecting and trying to ignore, what 'goes on' irreconcilably, subversively, beneath the vast smug surface."[3]

Thanks to critics and historians, we can know much of what "went on" as well as what "went into" *The Princess Casamassima*, and this ought to be an advantage to any study of the realistic manner, for the "report with truth on the human scene" should imply somewhere a human scene to be faithful to, and comparison would seem the first step in verification. On the other hand, the "verities" (a Jamesian phrase), are not always or merely a function of "veracity" (another), nor is it so easy to say these words without the taste of irony on the tongue. For instance, just what is the best guarantee of verisimilitude—honesty, accuracy, factuality, plausibility, authenticity? The shades of truth in "truth-to-life" are subtle enough for even a James.

One might hope for a further advantage in beginning with *The Princess Casamassima*, in that, as a political novel, it ought perhaps to engage, even to interfere, with reality rather than merely represent or comment on it. Certain writers, like Camus (whose title, *Actuelles*, conveys his position), have identified such engagement as the great prerequisite of realism: "create dangerously" is their motto. But none of James's three "novels of social criticism," as *The Bostonians* (1886), *The Princess Casamassima* (1886), and *The Tragic Muse* (1890) have been called, points its treatment of society with so sharp a polemic aim; not, at least, in comparison with contemporary examples like *The Bread-winners* (1883), *Caesar's Column* (1891), or *The Anarchists* (1891), which made no bones about being calls to action.

James is in another tradition of political novelists, whose works include *Sentimental Education* (1869), *The Possessed* (1872), *Virgin Soil* (1877), and *Under Western Eyes* (1911),[4] to name some especially relevant examples—a conservative tradition that tests the claims of political life against those of the artistic, and that seems to counsel withdrawal (to the aesthetic distance) as the wisest political gesture. From a point of view like that of social realism, these novels would appear scarcely political at all, and thus realistic only in a meaningless, bourgeois sense of the term; nonetheless, in their fully argued refusal to participate in propagandistic exercises (unless one counts their renunciation of politics as propaganda), they furnish a revealing commentary on the relations between language and reality that must lie behind any theory of realism. One might go so far as to say that the novels of this tradition are about little else but theories of realism, and that their divided and suicidal heroes—frustrated novelists like Frédéric Moreau, lame poets turned stumbling revolutionaries like Alexai Nejdanov, scholars turned men of action by default like Kirylo Razumov—are all victims of the difference between language and reality, and that the fatal division of thought and action in each of them is the result of one or another mistaken view of the nature of art, of the relations of life and literature, in short, some false notion of mimesis.

"How can one tell the truth from lies?" Razumov asks the prosy narrator of *Under Western Eyes*. "The colour of the ink and the shapes of the letters are the same." The latter suggests some possibilities—"The character of the publication, the general verisimilitude of the news, the consideration of the motive, and so on" (158-159)—but he too is suspicious of language, by profession: "Words, as is well known, are the great foes of reality. I have been for many years a teacher of languages. It is an occupation which at length becomes fatal to whatever share of imagination, observation, and insight an ordinary person may be heir to. To a teacher of languages there comes a time when the world is but a place of many words and man appears a mere talking animal not much more wonderful than a parrot" (1).

Conrad's narrator is safe from the dangers of imagination and insight, through over-exposure to words; such is our guarantee that the story he tells us is truth—this, and his claim to have done little more than piece the facts together from the diary of Razumov himself, "documentary evidence" the credibility of which, perhaps inconsistently, the narrator never doubts. Although Razumov too is a man "who had read, thought, lived, pen in hand" (301), he is as well supplied with imagination as the narrator is devoid of it. His linguistic inventiveness amounts to a fatal passion, for despite his cynical view "that speech has been given to us for the purpose of concealing our thoughts" (220), he is ultimately horrified to find himself so resourceful in deceit that, so to speak, he has lied himself out of existence. Only his diary, which apparently renders a true account of his experience, preserves his sanity, and only his confession, which his diary finally becomes (301), allows "his escape from the prison of lies" (305).

If words have led Razumov to suicidal isolation, they have also saved him from it in the end. His elaborately fabricated identity—concocting it "was like a game of make-believe" (265)—is replaced by the true "story" or "tale" (Conrad uses each word twice at the crucial juncture, 298) of his part in the betrayal of Haldin. The one a lie, the other true, both are mere structures of words, and among other things, Conrad wants us to see that neither is entirely free from illusion, since neither is reality itself. If language is not necessarily always the "foe of reality," in the sense that we can never tell the difference between truth and lies, it is nonetheless evident that truth and reality are not the same thing, and that the truth-to-reality of any particular utterance is largely a matter of chance—sometimes depending on the knowledge, skill, and honesty of the speaker, but more often on the mere accident that the statement *is* true. What is important, apparently, is that the speaker mean to tell the truth.

For a novelist to present such a view is a little disturbing perhaps, but not so surprising. What cannot the skilled concocter of "circumstantial falsehoods" make us believe? No doubt it is partly a professional hazard, like that Conrad's narrator runs, a suspicion of words and their mimetic power.

Turning from the latest to the earliest example of these conservative political novels, we find the treatment of language and reality less explicitly put forth, but perhaps more than anywhere else fully embodied in the structure of the story. In *Sentimental Education* we are told almost immediately that Flaubert's hero "nursed an ambition to become the Sir Walter Scott of France" (26), and, to him, Madame Arnoux "looked like the women in romantic novels. He would not have wanted to add anything to her appearance, or to take anything away. She was the point of light on which all things converged; and lulled by the movement of the carriage, his eyelids half closed, his gaze directed at the clouds, he gave himself up to an infinite, dreamy joy" (22). Through most of the book, however, we hear little of Frédéric's utterly romantic literary dabblings. Instead we watch as the novelist manqué stumbles through political and love affairs, casting himself as hero, villain, victim, in a series of fantasies ironically blended and juxtaposed with reality. Once or twice Frédéric approaches a kind of awareness of his "literary" way of life, as in the revealing passage where he is tempted to "act" decisively to clear his path to Madame Arnoux:

> Arnoux was sleeping with his arms outstretched; and as his musket was resting at a slight angle, with its butt on the floor, the muzzle was under his armpit. Frédéric noticed it and took fright.
> "But no! I'm a fool. There's nothing to be afraid of. All the same, if he happened to die. . . ."
> And straight away an endless succession of pictures passed through his mind. He saw himself in a postchaise with her at night; then beside a river on a summer evening; and in the lamplight at home, in their own house. He even dwelt on domestic details and household arrangements, seeing and savouring his happiness already, and all that was needed to bring it about was the cocking of the musket's hammer. He could push it with the tip of his big toe; the gun would go off; it would be an accident, nothing more.
> Frédéric brooded over this idea, like a dramatist writing a play. Suddenly he felt that it was going to be put into action, that he was going to play his part in it, that he wanted to; and then panic seized him. In the midst of his anguish he felt a certain pleasure, into which he sank deeper and deeper, with a horrified awareness that his scruples were vanishing; in his wild reverie the rest of the world grew dim; and he was no longer conscious of himself except through an unbearable tightness in his chest. (314)

There would be much to say about this passage—about the ambiguity involved in the metaphor of the play, and whether it is Flaubert's metaphor or Frédéric's, about the juxtaposition of murderous thoughts and Frédéric's big toe, about the dimming of the real world as the fantasy grows strong—but for our present purposes it is enough to recognize how typically Frédéric loses his chance to "act" by spending too much time imagining himself in the role. Indeed, he always prefers the role of actor to that of agent. Arnoux wakes up and the fantasy dissipates into the coarse reality of Arnoux's "Shall we have a drop of white wine?" Living as Frédéric does for such moments of excited reverie, the real thing is always a let-down for him, and if he learns anything at all in the course of the novel, perhaps it is that he cannot have his role on stage and off. His refusal of Marie's favors at the end of the book might suggest this—if he *chose* to keep her on the pedestal—but probably he has not even discovered this lesson, for more likely the let-down has already come, when she takes off her hat to reveal her white hair, which strikes him "like a blow full in the chest" (414). Frédéric ought to have been a novelist; it might have saved him from his illusions (as Flaubert perhaps supposed it *had* saved *him*). But instead, as novelist manqué, he believes everything he tells himself—just as the various villains and fools of '48 believe their own private accounts of reality and try to force them on others.

Peter Verkhovensky of *The Possessed* is another concocter of plausible fictions. "His articulation was amazingly clear; his words fell from his lips like large, smooth grains, always carefully chosen and always at your service. At first you could not help liking it, but later on you hated it, and just because of his too clear enunciation, of this string of ever-ready words. You somehow could not help feeling that he must have a sort of peculiarly shaped tongue in his head, a sort of unusually long and thin one, very red and with an exceedingly sharp and incessantly and uncontrollably active tip" (188). More like Razumov than Frédéric, he is perfectly aware of his power and the art behind it, if not always in control of its effects. Peter's father, Stepan Trofimovich Verkhovensky, is closer to Flaubert's ridiculous hero, a frustrated writer always imagining things, dabbling in politics and love without really getting his feet wet, yet thinking he is in up to his neck.

At times Peter seems to have only contempt for language and speech, as for his father: "in my view all these books, Fourier, Cabet, all this talk about the 'right to work,' all this Shigalyov business—all are like novels, of which you can write a hundred thousand. An aesthetic pastime. I realize that in this provincial hole of a town you are bored, and so you rush to pick up any piece of paper that has something written on it" (407). And again, "let me ask you which you prefer: the slow way consisting of the composition of social novels and the dry, unimaginative planning of the destinies of mankind a thousand years hence, while despotism swallows the morsels of roast meat which would fly into your mouths of themselves, but which you fail to catch; or are you in favor of a quick solution, whatever it may be, which will at last unite your hands and which will give humanity ample scope for ordering its own social affairs in a practical way and not on paper?" (408). But the next minute, having condemned his audience's foolish reliance on the written word, on "chatter" instead of "immediate action," he uses the very device of "paper prescriptions" he has been ridiculing: "I'm afraid I'm not very good at talking. I came here with certain communications . . . ," and then, having tantalized and awed his hearers with these (nonexistent) communications, "Ladies and gentlemen, I see that almost all of you have decided to act in the spirit of the leaflets. . . ." When his grandiose plot is revealed, not at this meeting of fools but shortly thereafter, to Stavrogin, on whom it depends, we see that Peter is really the paradigm of all the mad authors of *The Possessed*: his idea is to "spread a legend" that Stavrogin is Ivan the Crown-prince, pretender to the throne. As a political plot Peter's scheme is too absurd to interest Dostoyevsky, but as the plot of a kind of fiction it is central to the themes of the novel. As Peter himself says, "The main thing is the legend!" (423). When his hero Stavrogin coolly refuses to act his role in the plot, Peter loses his nerve and discloses just how like a fiction his plan really is: "I can't give you up now. There's no one like you in the whole world! I invented you abroad; I invented it all while looking at you" (424). Stavrogin explains Peter's strange "literary" madness very clearly when he first introduces him in the novel: "He always, as it were, scribbles away when telling you something"—adding, ironically as it turns out—"please, remember that being a realist he cannot tell a lie and that he puts the truth far above his own interests" (203).Precisely the opposite description of Peter would be more accurate—he values his lies and fantasies above all, even above his own interests. He is a victim of the same delusions that afflict Frédéric and Razumov.

What Flaubert, Dostoyevsky, and Conrad seem to be saying, in obviously different ways and with varying insight and emphasis, is that numerous modes of discourse—inward or outward, conversational, epistolary, oratorical, historical—have the liability which, according to the realist, is the *sine qua non* of mimetic fiction: the "illusion of reference"—the power to delude and mislead men as to the nature of reality, by suggesting that something exists which may not, that the stories one tells oneself or others are true to something in experience.

Like the other novelists of this tradition, Turgenev concerned himself with problems of language and reality, but his treatment is somewhat more significant for our present purposes. He focused and simplified the subject by choosing to cast his hero as quite explicitly a literary man, whose difficulty is the struggle between his art and his politics. By virtue of this choice, Turgenev was able to develop a plot that gathers up elements and motifs running through other political novels and orders them in an almost paradigmatic sequence. No doubt it was this firm hold on his subject that first interested James in Turgenev's *Virgin Soil*, and that most influenced him when he came to write *The Princess Casamassima*. He discussed *Virgin Soil* with Turgenev before it was finished, reviewed it in *The Nation* upon its first appearance in English, and reread it in 1884, not long before he began work on his own political novel.[5] Although he thought Turgenev's book "the weakest of his long stories (quite)"[6] and accorded it only "a minor perfection"[7] when he passed his final judgment in 1897, James nevertheless borrowed liberally from it for *The Princess Casamassima*. The many parallels between the two novels have been discussed by Daniel Lerner,[8] so that it is not necessary to go through them here. More interesting is the way that Turgenev crystallized for James a certain sequential view of the problems we have seen raised by other political novelists in regard to the relations of language and reality.

The hero of *Virgin Soil*, Alexai Nejdanov, is the illegitimate son of a nobleman, and his flawed lineage rankles as much as Hyacinth Robinson's in *The Princess Casamassima* or Razumov's in *Under Western Eyes*. Like these later heroes, Nejdanov shows his breeding through his manners, and especially his speech—"Everything about him betokened his origin. . . . [H]is very voice was pleasant, although it was slightly guttural" (27). Throughout the novel, Nejdanov's speech habits are used as an index of his state of mind, as he wavers between two styles of life, political and artistic. "He was fastidiously accurate and horribly squeamish, tried to be cynical and coarse in his speech. . . . He was furious with his father for having made him take up 'aesthetics,' openly interested himself in politics and social questions, professed the most extreme views (which meant more to him than mere words), but secretly took a delight in art, poetry, beauty in all its manifestations, and in his inspired moments wrote verses" (27–28).

Nejdanov is already committed to the revolutionary cause at the opening of the novel, and when he is suddenly hired as a tutor by the suave landowner Sipiagin, whose "words flow[ed] from him as a stream" (20), a conflict begins to appear in his powers of speech. At table with Sipiagin and his aristocrat friends, Nejdanov "blushed, bent over his plate, and mumbled something; he did not feel shy, but was simply unaccustomed to conversing with such brilliant personages" (50). In other company, however, among his radical friends, Nejdanov finds his tongue with fatal ease. He falls into "wild fits" of eloquence that remind one of Hyacinth's speech at the "Sun and Moon" club in *The Princess Casamassima*. Also like Hyacinth, Nejdanov wants the "real thing," and says that "the time had come for 'action'" (151).

Nejdanov's eloquence comes and goes in a kind of seizure, and leaves him with something like a hangover. Returning from his all-night harangue at Markelov's, "He did not feel well. He had hardly slept, and then all that talk, all that useless discussion. . . . "[9] Later he asks himself, "Why this fatigue, this disinclination to speak as soon as he was no longer shouting and furious? What internal voice did he try to drown by that same furious zeal?" The next time he falls into this "intoxication" Turgenev takes pains to insist upon the metaphor:

> Soon there began what is called in the language of drunkards the build-ing of the Tower of Babel. A mighty noise and confusion arose. As the first snow-flakes twist and turn in rapid dance in the yet warm autumn sky, so in the heatened atmosphere of Golushkin's dining room words of every sort whirled, crossed, and encountered each other; progress, government, literature, taxation; the church question, the woman's rights question, the law question; classicism, realism, Nihilism, communism; international, clerical, liberal, capital; administration, organization, association, and even crystallization!

Finally, when he decides to prove his commitment to the cause by going directly "to the people," Nejdanov finds once again enforced upon him the ironic connections between language, politics, and drunkenness; the peas-ants make him drink vodka with them, and his powers of speech desert him completely:

> He seemed to be surrounded by purple noses, dusty heads of hair, tanned necks covered with nets of wrinkles. Rough hands seized him. "Go on!" they bawled out in angry voices, "talk away! The day before yesterday another stranger [Markelov] talked like that. Go on. . . ." The earth seemed reeling under Nejdanov's feet, his voice sounded strange to his own ears as though coming from a long way off. . . . Was it death or what?   (259)

Here at last Nejdanov confronts the full truth that has been slowly dawning upon him throughout the novel. Political expression—propaganda—is merely a sort of drunken rant, strange even to his own ears, and incom-prehensible to those whom he addresses. On the one hand, it is a "speaking with tongues" in its peculiar ecstatic origin; on the other, it is a "confusion of tongues" in its failure to communicate with any hearers, who, like the builders of Babel, speak another language. And, as the final sentence of the passage hints, the literal as well as the symbolic result of such linguistic isolation is death.

The alternative life open to Nejdanov is also primarily a matter of language, for he is a poet and secretly longs to give up politics for his art. Were he not illegitimate, with claims upon him from his mother's world—the dispossessed and cast-off world of the masses—he might find his own voice in literature, but as it is he oscillates hopelessly between politics and poetry, accomplishing little in either realm. His political "fits" are matched by literary paroxysms in which he composes sentimental verse. His sole outlet for genuine self-expression is the journal-letter he writes his friend Vladimir Silin, to whom he confesses all his doubts and failures. In these calmer moments of introspection and self-revelation, he approaches a solution to his difficulties, but again only in verbal terms. Finally he arrives at a statement of his dilemma:

> Well, what can one do? Start a secret printing press? There are pamphlets enough as it is, some that say, "Cross yourself and take up the hatchet," and others that say simply, "Take up the hatchet" without the crossing. Or should one write novels of peasant life with plenty of padding? They wouldn't get published, you know. Perhaps it might be better to take up the hatchet after all? But against whom, with whom, and what for? So that our state soldier may shoot us down with the state rifle? It would only be a complicated form of suicide! It would be better to make an end of yourself—you would at any rate know when and how, and choose the spot to aim at.   (241–242)

By the time of his drunken adventure with the peasantry, it is too late for Nejdanov to choose between politics and art. He announces his disillusionment with the cause, but his life is too entangled with it for him to withdraw anything less than his very existence.

Before the inevitable suicide, Nejdanov is brought to an even more explicit renunciation of politics than his letter to Silin. First, as in *The Princess Casamassima*, there is a call to action from the "Central Committee," in this case secret orders from the mysterious Vassily Nikolaevitch. Like Hyacinth's friends in *The Princess Casamassima* Mashurina is reluctant to pass on the letter, since such communications are always regarded in these novels as warrant of death. But even though Mashurina yields to sentiment and swallows the letter, its symbolic force registers as surely as Schinkel's loyal delivery of Hoffendahl's orders. The episode has no direct effect on Nejdanov's actions, since he never learns of the letter at all. Turgenev includes it to remind us of the linguistic nature of Nejdanov's involvement with politics, and to prepare the reader for the final statements of this theme, enunciated by a pair of scenes in which both Markelov and Nejd-anov contemplate the failure of their revolutionary efforts. Markelov, through the novel one step ahead of Nejdanov in exploits and one step behind him in sensitivity, has been betrayed by the same peasants who later get Nejdanov drunk. Now in the hands of the police he begins to doubt:

> Had he been mistaken about the thing he was striving for? Was Kisli-akov a liar? And were Vassily Nikolaevitch's orders all stupid? And all the articles, books, works of socialists and thinkers, every letter of which had seemed to him invincible truth, were they all nonsense too? Was it really so? And the beautiful simile of the abcess awaiting the prick of the lancet—was that, too, nothing more than a phrase? "No! no!" he whispered to himself. . . . "All these things are true, true . . . only I am to blame." (286)

The implication for the reader, of course, is that every item in this catalogue of verbal deceit may justly be laid at the door of the propagan-dists. But Markelov has a sure instinct of self-preservation, which prevents him from believing any of these charges and thus protects his illusory world from collapse. Nejdanov, on the other hand, more sensitive to verbal effects and slower to defend himself from catastrophe, admits to Mariana that he has lost all his political illusions:

> "I always thought . . . that I believed in the cause itself, but had no faith in myself, in my own strength, my own capacities. I used to think that my abilities did not come up to my convictions. . . . But you can't separate these things. And what's the use of deceiving oneself? No—I don't believe in the *cause itself*." (296)

The "use of deceiving oneself," it turns out, is that only by so doing can the political activist justify his existence. Once the heady world of rhetoric, the "furious zeal" Nejdanov wondered at in himself, has evaporated, noth-ing remains to live for. Very like Conrad's Decoud in *Nostromo*, Nejdanov kills himself in order to end an existence that is, for all ordinary purposes, already ended.

I have suggested that the lesson Nejdanov finally learns in *Virgin Soil* comes too late to do him any good. That is one way of putting it, and the way I believe Turgenev himself thought of Nejdanov's fate; but in the light of the other political novels in the tradition, it might be more accurate to say that such a discovery—of the untrustworthiness of language—must always come too late to do any good, since it undercuts the premises of almost all social life. Indeed, if words are not to be trusted, then the very account of that discovery must be suspect—one reason why these books end immediately after the discovery, with suicide or some other self-defeating act. It is as if the novelist himself had begun to mistrust the tendency of language to compel belief in the existence of whatever it mentions.

II

Supposing the function of discourse is to give man verbal access to his world, a further means of experiencing life beyond his senses and feelings, then a theory of language as primarily referential—a matter of names and propositions appropriate, accurate, and verifiable—is likely to result. As Frege put it classically in his essay "On Sense and Reference" (1892):

> A logically perfect language should satisfy the conditions, that every expression grammatically well constructed as a proper name out of signs already introduced shall in fact designate an object, and that no new sign shall be introduced as a proper name without being secured a reference. The logic books contain warnings against logical mistakes arising from the ambiguity of expressions. I regard as no less pertinent a warning against apparent proper names having no reference. . . . "The will of the people" can serve as an example; for it is easy to establish that there is at any rate no generally accepted reference for this expression.[10]

For Frege, "If words are used in the ordinary way, what one intends to speak of is their reference"[11] (although he also allows for another kind of meaning, "sense," and is quite clear about the difference between "logically perfect" and natural language). Further, sentences too, if they are propositions, have reference, consisting of their truth value. Thus, "Every declarative sentence concerned with the reference of its words is . . . to be regarded as a proper name, and its reference, if it has one, is either the True or the False."[12] Declarative sentences that are neither true nor false, as for example those in fictions, would therefore have no reference.

Such a view of language as primarily referential is behind most discussions of literary mimesis. Since, it is supposed, the ordinary uses of language are a sort of pointing to things or, in the case of sentences, to facts, it accordingly ought to follow that in fiction, so long as we are not forcibly reminded that the words have no referents in the usual way, readers are likely to fall (willingly enough) under the spell of a kind of "illusion of life," to quote James.[13] And the more apparently "referential" the language of a novel, the more likely we are to take it as true-to-life, if not as actually true. Ian Watt, in a chapter called "Formal Realism and the Novel," says that "the function of language is more largely referential [in novels like *Moll Flanders* or *Pamela*] than in other literary forms,"[14] and by this he means, of course, not *actually* more referential (words have reference or they don't, and in novels for the most part, they don't, being largely about non-existent people, places, things, events, and so on), but *functioning more like* referential discourse. According to this view of mimesis, realism depends, so far as the use of language is concerned, on words being used *as if* they referred to or specified things, and sentences *as if* they were statements of fact, which could be either true or false.

All very well for realistic novels, perhaps, say the writers of them that we have been concerned with, but very dangerous for the rest of life, especially political life. Fiction is one thing, "lies like truth" another. Theirs is a new despairing version of Socrates' banishment of the poets from the Republic. It is not merely a matter of the good or bad intentions of speakers and writers (although this is certainly part of it), but also a question of whether language, after all, is in any way reliable as a means of representing reality *truly*. What *is* truth to the human scene?—to come back to James's claim for his novel.

It will be remembered that James imagined *The Princess Casamassima* as a consequence of his observations and notes on the London streets. There is, however, nothing to suggest that these "notes" took the form of transcription or description. Although the working-notes for *The Princess Casamassima* have not survived, the equivalent documents for the early stages of much of James's fiction may be examined in *The Notebooks of Henry James*, which he seems to have used to sort and test out story ideas, but not to preserve material for the sake of its authenticity or verisimilitude.[15] Moreover, *The Princess Casamassima* is quite bare of the details of observation and specification that James leads us to expect. His "London streets" may be fairly represented by Madeira Crescent, to which the Princess retires in her slumming phase:

> The long light of the grey summer evening was still in the air and Madeira Crescent wore a soiled, dusty expression. A hand-organ droned in front of a neighbouring house and the cart of the local washerwoman, to which a donkey was harnessed, was drawn up opposite. The local children as well were dancing on the pavement to the music of the organ, and the scene was surveyed from one of the windows by a gentleman in a dirty dressing-gown, smoking a pipe, who made Hyacinth think of Mr. Micawber.   (353)

Well might Hyacinth's mind wander to Dickens, for the scene has the pastoral air of literary recollection rather than naturalistic reportage. Compare a contemporary account of another London street, observed in the year that *The Princess Casamassima* was published, by a man who was himself an anarchist:

> The yards that were separated from each other by crumbling walls reaching to a man's breast, and whose narrowness hardly permitted one to stretch out his arms, were filled with muddy pools of slimy filth; heaps of rubbish were piled up in the corners; wherever one looked, he saw broken things and furniture lying about; here and there a rag of gray linen was hanging motionless in the chilly air. The stone steps leading to the doors were worn out; the blinds of the windows, mostly broken, were swinging loosely on their hinges; the window-panes were cracked, hardly one was whole; the holes pasted over with paper; where the windows were open, bare walls were seen.
> . . . Slowly the friends tore themselves away from the wretched sight, and silently walked down the middle street. Sometimes a window was half opened, a bushy head thrust out, and shy, curious eyes followed half in fear, half in hate, the wholly unusual sight of the strangers. A man was hammering at a broken cart which obstructed the whole width of the street. He did not respond to the greeting of the passers-by; stupified, he stared at them as at an apparition from another world; a woman who had been cowering in a door corner, motionless, rose terrified, pressed her child with both hands against her breast hardly covered with rags, and propped herself, as if to offer resistance, against the wall, not once taking her eye off the two men; only a crowd of children playing in the mud of the street did not look up,—they

might have been taken for idiots, so noiselessly did they pursue their joyless games.[16]

This passage too is reminiscent of Dickens (*A Tale of Two Cities*), but it is not an imitation so much as it is a later, cruder instance of the same perception. In spite of clichés, rhetorical ineptitude, and imperfect translation (Mackay wrote in German), there is an authentic ring to these sentences, especially those which report sights that James also mentioned: "Mr. Micawber" becomes "a bushy head thrust out," "the cart of the local washerwoman" becomes "a broken cart which obstructed the whole width of the street," and "dancing on the pavement to the music of the organ" becomes "so noiselessly did they pursue their joyless games."

Of course Mackay is writing propaganda, not fiction, though his form is novelistic. James would have thought it a narrow purpose, and one likely to distort reality to its political ends. "Truth to the human scene" was not for James a matter of camera-like accuracy. He knew that there were more squalid scenes than he chose to notice on the London streets, and he refrained more out of a sense of what he owed his art than any personal squeamishness. Much as he believed that "The only reason for the existence of a novel is that it does attempt to represent life," he mistrusted the realistic theory of representation, even while he helped to formulate it. Like other novelists in the conservative political tradition, he struggled to free the realistic novel from its own conditions and theory, as they were tightening on the genre in the last half of the nineteenth century. James's major statement on these questions up to the writing of *The Princess Casamassima* was his essay on "The Art of Fiction," composed in 1884. "Write from experience and experience only," he says there, but carefully qualifies: "experience consists of impressions," and "A novel is in its broadest definition a personal, a direct impression of life: that, to begin with, constitutes its value, which is greater or less according to the intensity of the impression."[17] We are moved very quickly from the representing of "life" to the reporting of "experience" to the recording of "impressions." Accuracy seems less important than intensity. In these terms, and with these values, we can understand how his notebooks *were* records of experience, "the ineluctable consequence of one's greatest energy." The words and sentences that constitute his notes and his novels have no "truth value" in Frege's sense; they do not refer to anything in the ordinary way that names and propositions in the newspaper do, or are sup-

posed to. Rather they are responses and reflections, of more or less intensity and energy, called forth by the scenes writers like Mackay attempted
to "reproduce."

III

Before it is possible to assess James's response to the political and linguistic questions that he inherited from Turgenev and others in the tradition,
we must first take time to understand the way those questions presented
themselves in the 1880s. Some critics have attempted to defend James's
verisimilitude by appeal to a picture of revolutionary anarchism that is
rather misleading, and whether his response was a matter of recording
observations or rendering impressions, it would seem important to be clear
about the "human scene" before judging his "truth" to it. Lionel Trilling,
for example, has praised "the solid accuracy of James's political detail at
every point," instancing particular aims and attributes of the anarchists
that he finds mirrored in *The Princess Casamassima*.[18] He mentions the
anarchists' supposed desire for complete destruction of society, including
its art; their reliance on methods of conspiracy and terrorism; their authoritarian organization; their political naiveté and incompetence, especially
among the rank and file; their artisan backgrounds; and he ends with a
suggestion that James's Hoffendahl might have been modeled on Johann
Most, a particularly visible and violent propagandist for the deed. Another
critic, W. H. Tilley, has documented many of these and other popular
ideas about the anarchists and their position from contemporary sources,
especially *The Times*.[19]

There is little doubt that James believed most of what he read about the
anarchists in the newspapers, and that his broad conception of them in *The
Princess Casamassima* reflects his reading. But such knowledge of the
anarchists as could be gleaned from *The Times* scarcely goes beyond
catchwords, and hardly qualifies as authentic for purposes of verisimilitude, even if true. Moreover, James had the good sense and taste to avoid
the crudities other novelists borrowed from the press; such as the following:

> And on the swaying deck of the great liner, near the orphaned
> heiress, in patient, plotting self-counsel, the falcon eyes of Carl Stein
> were reading the stars as he dreamed of the victory of the "Cause
> without a Name,"—the awful propaganda whose flag is a crimson

stain! His heart was tied by all the madness of a perverted nature on the unspoken code whose sequence is the doom of modern society. "Revolution—Destruction—Annihilation"[20]

James could not think in such clichés, nor was he really interested in "petroleum's hidden work" or "Nobel's awful portable volcano," the trusty weapons of Savage's counter-revolutionary arsenal. The "imagination of disaster" that Trilling praises in James[21] was not founded on the rhetoric of violence which served both sides in the propaganda war. His conception of the anarchist peril was more refined, if no less inaccurate, than that of the popular imagination. Compare Savage and James on the subject of anarchist organization:

> [Savage—] There has lately been observed an organized movement of anarchists, and their abettors, aided with at least considerable funds, and we have developed the fact of increased correspondence and European direction in these incipient schemes. It looks as if an energetic apostle of Bakunin and Marx was stirring up the black flood to its depths. Manufacturing properties, especially mining plants and railway interests are subject to sudden losses from riot, fire, dynamite, or skilfully united mob action. . . . There seems to be a mental inertia about the better classes not at all creditable to them.[22]

> [James—] Nothing of it appears above the surface; but there's an immense underworld peopled with a thousand forms of revolutionary passion and devotion. The manner in which it's organised is what astonished me. I knew that, or thought I knew it, in a general way, but the reality was a revelation. And on top of it all society lives. People go and come, and buy and sell, and drink and dance, and make money and make love, and seem to know nothing and suspect nothing and think of nothing; and iniquities flourish, and the misery of half the world is prated about as a "necessary evil." . . . All that's one half of it; the other half is that everything's doomed! In silence, in darkness, but under the feet of each one of us, the revolution lives and works.
> (276)

Both Savage and James (a decade apart of course) seem to believe in an international plot, part of the drama of which resides in society's ignorance of it. But where Savage reacts to this situation with uncomplicated outrage (feigned or not), James's response is more ambiguous. He seems to savor the irony of "society's not knowing," and indeed returned to that as the explanation of his purpose in writing the novel when he offered his second thoughts in the preface to the New York Edition. Further, and perhaps even more relevant to James's "imagination of disaster," there seems to be a hint at least of welcome for the impending doom. It is quite in character for Hyacinth, at this point in the novel, to take some pleasure in these prophecies. What about James? What was his investment in Hyacinth's catastrophic vision?

We may discover that the vast conspiracy and its immediate threat to civilization was largely an invention of propagandists. An organization such as Savage and James seem to credit was perhaps the dream of some anarchists, among them Bakunin, but to imagine that London was the fermenting center of such plans is to give in to just the sort of hysteria that the militant anarchists of sensational fiction (and, to a lesser degree, fact) counted on. The London International Congress of 1881, the chief gathering of "nihilist fiends" in the period, never got much beyond the stage of advocating that revolutionaries bone up on chemistry. In the autumn of 1882, at the end of eleven boring months in London, Europe's sanctuary for political refugees, the leading anarchist of the day Peter Kropotkin and his wife "said to each other, 'Better a French prison than this grave,'" and crossed the channel, where they soon found themselves implicated in the Lyons bombing, and ended up in Clairvaux prison.[23] During the next few years the anarchist *Attentat* made the news more and more frequently, in Russia, on the continent, in America, but the English movement remained relatively unorganized and nonviolent. One only has to read Kropotkin's account of his return to England in 1886, when James was finishing *The Princess Casamassima*, to see that although more was stirring now to interest Kropotkin, there was little conspiracy or terrorism afoot. Lecturing "all over the country" in the autumn and winter of 1886, Kropotkin "stayed one night in a rich man's mansion, and the next in the narrow quarters of a working family."[24] He remarks on the missed chance of the movement in England, the Establishment's shrewdness in giving light sentences to agitators, middle-class charity in the East End, palliative measures generally. Granted that Kropotkin was not one of the violent faction in the movement (although he defended them when necessary, and went to jail with them more than once), still his account corresponds quite closely with others, for example, Mackay's version of the same period in London:

. . . in none is their swarm so mixed as in London. Nowhere does it draw so closely together; nowhere does it go so far apart. Nowhere are its own dissensions more bitter, and nowhere does it fight the common enemy with greater bitterness. Nowhere does it speak in so many languages, and nowhere does it give expression to a greater variety of opinions in a greater variety of accents.

It embodies all types; and it shows them all in their most perfect and interesting as well as in their most demoralized and commonplace forms. . . .

It seems at times as if the refugees had forgotten their distant enemy, so bitterly they fight among themselves. Individual groups secede from the sections of the parent society, and refuse to retain even the old name. A few individuals, filled with restlessness and ambition, try to avail themselves of the dissension for the purpose of gathering up the severed threads and keeping them—in their own hands. The controversies for and against them are carried on for weeks and for months to the degree of exhaustion, when they cease and leave no other traces than estrangement, a pile of papers full of insinuations and suspicions, and a useless pamphlet.[25]

There were dynamitings in London during the 1880s, but these were the work of the Irish Nationalists, whose methods attracted certain English novelists to do for them what Savage did for the anarchists. If America was so threatened by foreign perversion that Savage's hero could exclaim, "The destruction of the Atlantic passenger ferry would be a blessing to America!"[26] an Englishman might with equal justice complain of speeches in Faneuil Hall and Tremont Temple where Irish orators asked "the people of Boston to give all the aid they could. . . . He did not like dynamite, and the English did not [Laughter]; but he had no objection that the Irishmen in London or in Ireland should use all the dynamite they could get. [Applause.]"[27] In 1884 Sir Lepel Henry Griffith published a warning to Englishmen, *The Great Republic*, which dwelt long on the Irish menace in America, and the following year an anonymous novelist followed Griffith's lead with *The Fall of the Great Republic*, a fanciful history of how the Irish and the German anarchists combined to take over the United States—only to be quickly subdued by Allied troops from England, France, and Germany.[28]

James himself read Griffith's book and had the idea for "The Modern Warning"[29] from it, but the Irish question in that story is toned down to some vague talk about ancient racial hatred. In his letters too, James's

revulsion from the dynamite outrages of the earlier 1880s was generalized
to a sense of *"malheurs*—reverses, dangers, embarrassments, the 'decline,' in a word, of old England," as he wrote to Grace Norton two days
after "Westminster Hall and the Tower were half blown up . . . by Irish
Dynamiters." In 1881, when the news of Alexander's assassination
reached James in Milan, he inserted this reaction in the midst of a light and
gossipy letter to Fanny Kemble: "You must have felt *spattered*, like all the
world, with the blood of the poor Russian Czar! Aren't you glad you are
not an Empress? But you are. God save your Majesty!" In general James
took both Irish and anarchist propaganda by the deed rather coolly. He
concluded his political reflections to Grace Norton by suggesting, à
propos of England's "decline," that "the drama will be well worth watching from a good, near standpoint as I have here. But I didn't mean to be so
beastly political!"[30]—not exactly a cataclysmic vision when set against
contemporary fiction like Savage's *The Anarchist* or John Hay's *The
Bread-winners*, not to mention Ignatius Donnelly's *Caesar's Column*.

What then was James's interest in the anarchists and propaganda by the
deed? Some critics have pointed, as James himself did in reviewing *Virgin
Soil*, to his interest in "the moral and psychological side"[31] of his subject,
but this—accurate enough an observation—is too easy an answer; one
would hardly accept a similar one for *The Wings of the Dove*. However
much James thought politics a "drama" one might attend to or not ("I shld.
like to see a country in a state of revolution," he wrote to T. S. Perry in
1886),[32] there was more at stake for him in Hyacinth's story than curiosity,
or the desire to cash in on the popularity that his friends Henry Adams's
and John Hay's political novels enjoyed. From the evidence offered by
Mackay and Kropotkin, it is clear enough that James's "imagination of
disaster" was a fantasy, obviously fed by the press and even by the
anarchists themselves, but not based in the sort of fact that was (or could
be) reported in newspapers. And yet like most fantasy, James's had its
sources in reality, in a perception of reality, an "impression" to be judged
by its "intensity." Where was this reality?

IV

To any reader of both novels, it is apparent that James borrowed more
from *Virgin Soil* than he did from *The Times* for the details and the overall
plot of *The Princess Casamassima*. Paradigmatically viewed, *Virgin Soil*

reduces to the following sequence: a divided man confronts society; his inheritance from his father favors traditional and conventional modes of perception and expression—poetry—while from his nameless mother he receives the impulse to rebel against authority and tradition—revolutionary propaganda. Once committed to political life (the more traditional alternative is not open to him, being illegitimate), he is unluckily introduced to a society where the values of easy and poetic language are tantalizingly omnipresent—no less tempting because they are obviously premised on the ruthless suppression of any genuine political thought or life. Two modes of discourse are progressively elaborated as the poles of this tension—political language is chiefly "drunken" exhortation; poetic language is mawkish self-pity. Neither has any authentic relation to reality, nor can either successfully communicate with an audience. A third mode, the personal "journal-letter," half diary, half confession, provides the only viable language, but its avowals are useless in the immediate circumstances except as a means of undermining the false rhetoric of politics and poetry. Once the "confession" becomes "self-recognition," the hero sees that his only audience is himself. The despairing solipsist then acts out this knowledge, in suicide.

The action of *The Princess Casamassima* may be reduced to a similar sequence, also focused on the nature of the relationship between language and reality.

Hyacinth's father is an English nobleman, a "Duke," and his mother is of the lower classes, a "French impropriety" who murdered her lover in a jealous quarrel and died in prison for it. This heritage serves as the rather Dickensian premise for the rest of the book. Here is "the state of the account between society and himself" (43): Hyacinth is not legitimate; he is, as Paul Muniment puts it, "a duke in disguise" (379). But the Jamesian working-out of the situation is not a matter of revelations, long-lost wills, hidden affinities and resemblances, as in Dickens. James's heroes, as he himself said of Turgenev's, "are never heroes in the literal sense of the word, rather quite the reverse; their function is to be conspicuous as failures, interesting but impotent persons who are losers at the game of life. . . . Their interest, in his hands, comes in a great measure from the fact that they are exquisitely conscious of their shortcomings, thanks to the fine and subtle intelligence, that 'subjective' tendency, with which he represents all Russians who are not positive fools and grotesques as being endowed. His central figure is usually a person in a false position, general-

ly not of his own making, which, according to the peculiar perversity of
fate, is only aggravated by his effort to right himself."[33]

Unlike Turgenev's hero though, Hyacinth begins life in an uncertain
rather than a false position, and a part of the novel concerns his attempts to
identify his status, to audit the "account between society and himself." In
so far as he is intent upon this goal, Hyacinth becomes increasingly entangled in the world of words that we learn to mistrust in all these political
novels. At a certain point he goes to the British Museum to read the
account of his father's murder and his mother's trial in *The Times*. Even its
"facts" do little to clarify Hyacinth's position, and still less to put him in
any settled relation with the two worlds he comes from. In his interviews
with Lady Aurora, "there were times when he couldn't withstand the
perverse satisfaction of insisting on his lowliness of station, of turning the
knife in the wound inflicted by such explicit reference, and of letting it be
seen that if his place in the world was immeasurably small he at least had
no illusions about either himself or his species" (172). Like Rosy Muniment, who lies in her invalid bed imagining the world outside, Hyacinth
too is engaged in the effort to "describe things [he] has never seen. And
they're just like the reality" (112). "Explicit reference" gives the color of
life to the unseen of Hyacinth's past and future, but it is not enough for
him; "just like the reality" is not the reality itself.

The world represented by his father presses on Hyacinth's imagination
more strongly, simply because it is less immediately available to him than
his mother's heritage of poverty and squalor. His approach to both worlds
is reactive, negative. He gets into connection with the "Duke" and legitimate society by enlisting in the opposition, devoting himself by "a tremen-
dous solemn vow" (273) to the destruction of that society, and in particular, to the annihilation of its symbolic representative—another *duke*—in
what would be a "repetition" of his mother's act. This vow, which is
Hyacinth's chief political act in the novel, his "social contract" if you will,
"had altered his life altogether—had indeed as he might say changed the
terms on which he held it. He was aware that he didn't know exactly what
he meant by this last phrase; but it expressed sufficiently well the new
feeling that had come over him" (273).

The remainder of the novel works out the meaning of "this last phrase"
for Hyacinth, the implications of his inverted allegiance to society, "the
terms" of the contract of destruction. Relations having been established
with society in its abstract, authoritarian manifestation (in Freudian terms,

the mysterious Hoffendahl would stand for the unknown, unapproachable father), the way is now open for exploration of the world thus made psychologically accessible. The position of the hero is "false," as James says, because (1) it does not give genuine access to the goods of the world, but only the opportunity for "exquisite consciousness" of what might be available if one had authentic right to it, and (2) it is a self-defeating position, a vow that leads, in the circumstances, to its own betrayal.

To understand the terms of Hyacinth's false position more thoroughly, we must first put a new construction on his situation up to the moment of the vow. As regards the plot itself, there is little to say. He grows up under the anxious gaze of Pinnie and Mr. Vetch, pries into his parentage, is apprenticed as a bookbinder, attracted to a childhood playmate, meets the Poupins and Paul Muniment and others through his job and later through his frequenting of the Sun and Moon. These connections express Hyacinth's attempts to establish himself in the world—to ground himself in his past, find his vocation, marry and contribute to the ongoing community. But preventing his realization of any of these goals is his lack of commitment, and his uncertainty of the legitimacy of any claims he might make on society. In all his pursuits other people make Hyacinth's decisions for him. As Mr. Vetch tells the Princess later in the book, "Fond of him? Pray, who can doubt it? I made him, I invented him!" (394). Like Stavrogin in *The Possessed*, Hyacinth is whatever others demand that he be, whatever they *say* he is, and thus in danger of becoming another "plausible fiction." But like Razumov (when he betrays Haldin) Hyacinth makes a commitment to Hoffendahl (Councillor Mikulin's counterpart) which changes everything and offers him an escape from the drift of his fate. To be political, one must be able to act on one's own, and this is now the possibility that Hyacinth embraces. His vow accomplishes this because it takes precedence over all other obligations and makes all other future decisions contingent, not ultimately binding. Thus the responsibility of choice is avoided, and he need no longer be afraid of a false step, of engaging in anything that would commit him irrevocably. His earlier uncertainty vanishes because now he *is* committed irrevocably.

Perversely, in typical Jamesian fashion, the result is freeing, and things begin to happen to Hyacinth immediately upon his swearing his oath. Having foresworn everything in order to free himself from the limits of his meager life, he starts at once to engage himself in life—which is what he wanted—and of course becomes committed to whatever he takes up (art,

Paris, the Princess), all of which, both as it represents the world he has sworn to destroy and as it comes to seem more deeply obligating than the vow that gave him access to it in the first place, is in direct conflict with his vow. He cannot renounce his vow, because, like Razumov and others, he now *is* his vow; his newly developing character utterly depends on it. This is the crux of his false position and his exquisite consciousness of it. Like Nejdanov nothing remains for him in this fully undermined existence but to end it absolutely with suicide, the only way of resolving the claims of his vow and the society he has joined by vowing its destruction.

The playing out of these scenes, once his vow has been sworn, also has a characteristic structure. Just as the vow establishes his (negative) relations with his father and society, so now he begins to build similarly inverted relations with his mother and her underworld of passion and sensuality. Hoffendahl is the pole of the first orientation, the Princess is the pole of the second. I need not review here the history of Hyacinth's attachment to Christina, beyond mentioning that as it deepens, the reader becomes increasingly aware that it can lead to nothing for the hero, the premise of whose love is its impossibility of fulfillment—not only because of the vow, but also because, like Frédéric Moreau, Hyacinth is actually in love with an "ideal" mother-figure, imaginable but not realizable. His relation with this figure has its symbolic formula parallel to the vow. This we may call an "avowal." It is to be distinguished from a simple "declaration" in that it encompasses more and less. Since Christina interests Hyacinth only as an unattainable ideal, he cannot declare himself in any conventional sense. On the other hand, representing as she does the whole realm of unattainable possibilities opened up to him by his sworn renunciation of them, his avowal will be more than an expression of hopeless desire. It will in fact be a sort of counter-vow, a confession of the defection of his will from the earlier, still-binding vow that had seemed at first to free him.

We have already seen one expression of such an avowal in Nejdanov's confession to Mariana that he no longer believes in the cause. Ordinarily this avowal is put in writing, however, and in *Virgin Soil* the conversation with Mariana is led up to by Nejdanov's reading poems to her, which in turn grows out of his journal-letter to Vladimir Silin, his slowly developing avowal of all his misgivings. This use of the journal is the characteristic method of making avowal in these books: Stavrogin's confession is another case, and the clearest is Razumov's diary. In *The Princess Casamassima* Hyacinth's letter from Venice is the document of avowal, as in the other cases, less a confession of hopeless love (though that too moves under the surface of them all) than a revelation of all that has become exquisitely conscious as an undermining consequence of the original oath:

> You can't call me a traitor, for you know the obligation I supremely, I immutably recognise. The monuments and treasures of art, the great palaces and properties, the conquests of learning and taste, the general fabric of civilisation as we know it, based if you will upon all the despotisms, the cruelties, the exclusions, the monopolies and the rapacities of the past, but thanks to which, all the same, the world is less of a "bloody sell" and life more of a lark—our friend Hoffendahl seems to me to hold them too cheap and to wish to substitute for them something in which I can't somehow believe as I do in things with which the yearnings and the tears of generations have been mixed.
>   . . . I don't know what it comes from, but during the last three months there has crept over me a deep mistrust of that same grudging attitude—the intolerance of positions and fortunes that are higher and brighter than one's own; a fear, moreover, that I may in the past have been actuated by such motives, and a devout hope that if I'm to pass away while I'm yet young it may not be with that odious stain upon my soul.   (334-335)

This avowal, like those of Stavrogin, Nejdanov, and Razumov, moves inexorably to the decision for suicide.[34] The moment of action is postponed until the delivery of the fatal note from Hoffendahl, which is the documentary counterpart of the avowal, reasserting the claims of society on its sworn destroyer. Viewed most schematically, and in modern idiom, the note Schinkel delivers is a kind of perverse "draft notice" served on a man who has just put in writing his formal statement of conscientious objections to war. The political significance of the vow and the call to action is clear enough. The avowal has its political meaning too, which helps explain why these novels concern themselves with anarchists rather than other kinds of revolutionaries: the avowal is formal notice of disaffiliation, of alienation, or renunciation of the State and its authority. That the State in these cases is ironically represented by the anarchist central committee shows that deeply, probably unconsciously, the novelist recognizes what the best anarchists themselves acknowledged, that the central committee is itself only another version of the State, precisely like it in its distance, anonymity, absolute power, all opposed mirror-like to the recognized authority. Politically speaking, then, at the deepest structural levels of these novels, the antagonists are seen as identical, change is viewed as impossible in revolutionary terms, and the only solution is renunciation—of the social contract and of life itself. What begins as the hero's attempt to establish his own legitimacy (and by implication, the authority of the legitimizing agency) ends with a personal avowal that precludes any further involvement in society on such terms, and undercuts the very idea of legitimacy.

V

In 1884, while he was planning *The Princess Casamassima*, James might have read John Rae's translation of the famous "Revolutionist's Catechism," which began: "The revolutionist is a man under a vow. He ought to have no personal interests, no business, no sentiments, no property. He ought to occupy himself entirely with one exclusive interest, with one thought and one passion: the Revolution."[35] In the story of Hyacinth Robinson, James made such a vow the center of revolutionary politics, and whether or not he had ever come across the "Catechism" he understood enough of the psychology and politics of revolution to see that to be "under a vow" was to be "lost" or "doomed," as later translators would render the phrase.[36]

Historians have never agreed whether the "Revolutionist's Catechism," presented in evidence at Sergei Nechaev's trial in 1871, was the work of that strangely charismatic figure, or perhaps of Bakunin himself. It is fairly certain, however, that Nechaev was such a revolutionist as the "Catechism" invokes—so obviously one of the "possessed" that Dostoyevsky used him as a model for Peter Verkhovensky. The connection between Verkhovensky, Nechaev, and Hyacinth Robinson is that, as revolutionaries, they are all self-destroyers, devoted to a cause that is seen as self-defeating. Dostoyevsky's characters, as his title proposes, are like the swine of Luke viii: 32-33, possessed by devils: "and the herd ran violently down a steep place into the lake, and were choked." In 1869, the year that Dostoyevsky began work on *The Possessed*, James wrote to his mother from Paris: "Oh the tumult, the splendor, the crazy headlong race for pleasure—and the stagnant gulfs of misery to be seen in two great capitals like London and Paris. Mankind seems like the bedevilled herd of swine in the Bible, rushing headlong into the sea."[37] This early "imagination of disaster" is noteworthy not merely because it demonstrates similar perceptions in James and Dostoyevsky, but also because it is an early version of Hyacinth's "revelation" that people "know nothing and suspect nothing and think of nothing; and iniquities flourish. . . . All that's one-half of it; the other half is that everything's doomed!" In Hyacinth's view at this point of his career, the catastrophe is still taken as an impersonal event, worldwide but not quite touching Hyacinth himself. He does not yet understand how his being "under a vow" means that *he* is the one who is doomed. Only when he has seen "everything" for himself, as he writes in his letter from Venice, does the truth dawn fully. And then his position is like that described by James as his own, many years later, on the eve of war in 1914:

> What one first feels one's self uttering, no doubt, is but the intense unthinkability of anything so blank and so infamous in an age that we have been living in and taking for our own as if it were of a high refinement of civilisation—in spite of all conscious incongruities; finding it after all carrying this abomination in its blood, finding this to have been what it *meant* all the while, is like suddenly having to recognise in one's family circle or group of best friends a band of murderers, swindlers and villains—it's just a similar shock. It makes us wonder whom in the world we are now to live with then—and even if with everything publicly and internationally so given away we can live, or want to live, at all.[38]

As in Hyacinth's letter of avowal, we are led from the recognition of "what it *meant*" to the contemplation of suicide. From 1869 to 1914, James's formulation of the situation changes very little; it is not a formulation to respond to national or international politics, insurrection or world war, but at once a personal and a universal politics, such as one finds in Dostoyevsky or Camus.

The chief concern of James, throughout his career, is the possibility of full experience, and the limitations imposed upon its fullness by the conditions of experiencing anything at all. His continuing view is a pessimistic one, that the price of awareness is the loss of any advantage one might gain by it. If one enters into experience actively, one is sure to make mistakes, to miss significances, to arrive finally at full awareness only when it is too late to "do" anything except savor one's sensitivity. Alternatively, one may hold back from experience, play the part of an observer of the "drama" of life, renouncing the advantages of participation in favor of an earlier awareness of what one is missing. This latter seems to have been James's notion of the artist's choice, and most of his writing poses the choices in such a way as to favor it—the implication being that "fullness" in experience is "awareness" rather than "participation," and that the two are mutually exclusive. *The Princess Casamassima*, and to a lesser extent *The Tragic Muse*, are James's big treatments of the first alternative, viewed as a political choice—participation in political life examined as a means of educating the hero's awareness of the possibilities life offers. But James does not allow Hyacinth—does not believe life would allow him—any easy perceptions. Simply considered, the path of renunciation protects the hero against false steps by restraining him from any steps at all. All is mere observation and report on the careers of others, witnessing, even voyeurism. The path of participation, on the other hand, cannot be entered without a commitment just as absolute as total renunciation—that is, a vow which seems to have the opposite force, committing one to act, but which actually amounts to the same thing as renunciation, namely, an irrevocable resignation of one's freedom to choose.

What must have attracted James to the anarchists was their formulation of this same dilemma, in terms that cannot much have appealed to him but surely presented themselves as relevant to his chief themes. The theory of propaganda by the deed was repeatedly phrased as an opposition between words and deeds, watching and acting. Bakunin in 1871 set up these alternatives in a way that strongly suggests Nejdanov's predicament in *Virgin Soil* (1877):

> . . . individual propaganda, even when carried on by the most revolutionary people in the world, cannot exercise too great an influence upon the peasants. They do not respond much to rhetoric, and words, when they do not come as a manifestation of force and are not accompanied by deeds, remain mere words to them. A worker who would simply confine himself to haranguing the peasants, would risk being made the laughing stock of any village, and being chased out of it as a bourgeois.[39]

In a book published in London the same year as *The Princess Casamassima*, Stepniak (the revolutionary *nom de guerre* of Sergei Kravchinsky, himself an ex-assassin) further explained:

> To shake the secular torpor of the Russian masses we had nothing but

the whisper, the secret propaganda addressed with circumspection to private men. Such a propaganda is too inadequate for its task. To rouse the spirit of our masses deeds were required; words served only to explain and bring home to people's understanding that which had struck their mind and excited their spirit.[40]

Already framed by the anarchists themselves in linguistic terms, the phrase "propaganda by the deed" must have seemed to James an apt expression to match against the "deeds of speech"[41] to which he had committed himself in his own career. No doubt it was easy for James to distinguish the violence and terrorism of men like Nechaev and Stepniak from the reflective talk that he himself produced. There was, however, one sort of speech that seemed intimately related to the *Tat* and yet might be more on the side of mind than muscle, thought than act: this was the vow, the ultimate political speech-act. We have already seen how the plot of *The Princess Casamassima* undercuts any simple optimism about this sort of political commitment. On the other hand, James does not attack all such deeds of speech, as Dostoyevsky does in *The Possessed*, nor does he go so far as Tolstoy's Christian-anarchist condemnation of "every vow, and especially every oath of allegiance." Whether or not James would have understood Tolstoy's view that the vow was the very foundation of the State, absolutely necessary "for the organization of the terrible evil which is produced by violence and war," he never came explicitly to such an absolute formulation as Tolstoy's: "Never take an oath to anyone, anywhere, about anything. Every oath is extorted for evil ends."[42] But if James did not fully comprehend what might be at issue, his novel works out a sample case with painstaking fidelity to his own ambiguous sense of the conflicting claims of conscience involved. The implication of Hyacinth's story is that one should not make vows or commit oneself so long as one can avoid it. All the while, however, the counter-motif keeps presenting itself—that one is not open to experience (the sorts of impressions that lead to writing, for example) unless one has already over-committed oneself somehow, or what may be the same thing, had lost all stake in active life—as with Strether in *The Ambassadors*. Total commitment vs. total abnegation, vow vs. renunciation: just as we may identify Hyacinth's vow as his linguistic act of engagement in political life, we may also recognize his avowal of disenchantment as a renunciation not only of the vow itself but also of the participation in life effected by it. That this sequence springs from James's view of his own situation, the choices he felt his vocation imposed upon him, would seem apparent enough—for example, in the way he talks about "experience" and the "impressions" to be gathered from it, both in "The Art of Fiction" in 1884 and in the earlier "Notebook II" which he used as a stock-taking device when he found himself at loose ends in 1881. On the one hand, we can sense the cost of these impressions, their dependence on a notion of the self as primarily a receiving instrument, that does not enjoy or enter into experience so much as "salvage" something from it. On the other hand, the effort of "taking notes" and "rendering" impressions is not really passive. The writer is not a mere esthete, all talk and no action. As James wrote late in life to Henry Adams, "You see I still, in presence of life (or of what you deny to be such), have reactions—as many of them as possible—and the book I sent you is a proof of them. It's, I suppose, because I am that queer monster, the artist, an obstinate finality, an inexhaustible sensibility. Hence the reactions—appearances, memories, many things, go on playing upon it with consequences that I note and 'enjoy' (grim word!) noting. It all takes doing—and I *do*. I believe I shall do yet again—it is still an act of life."[43] The dichotomy between talk and action was perhaps false after all, as if one could do nothing with words, could say nothing with acts. The anarchists had for their part proved that there was a language of action; that was what propaganda by the deed was all about. And James showed how the vow was not merely a promise to do something in the future, but more importantly a deed in the present—*engagement* in both senses of that word. Neither *Tat* nor vow was a perfectly satisfactory compromise for him. Of the former he had an absolute horror, and it would wait for a Camus to inquire into its grammar and meaning. Hyacinth's fate notwithstanding, the vow had more appeal, especially to a writer trying to cut himself loose from a theory of language that insisted on finding the meaning of words only in the things they named. For a vow named nothing; it did something. Laid out on a referential model of language, it would have to be understood as creating its own referent, making itself "true"—as a legislative act becomes the law, as a declaration of independence makes men independent, as all authentic political language binds reality into words specially shared among us.

To understand how such language operates, and what relation it bears to the writing of the novelist himself, we must turn again to the anarchists, in this case to an anarchist of a very peculiar sort—James's friend Henry B.

Brewster, the author of *The Theories of Anarchy and Law*, published in London the year after *The Princess Casamassima*. Brewster was not a political anarchist at all, nor is it quite satisfactory to call him a philosophical anarchist. In *The Theories* his spokesman Wilfred is an advocate of what Brewster called "syntactisme,"[44] a kind of anarchist linguistic epistemology, interesting in its resemblances to Wittgensteinian language theory. Attacking traditional views of language as primarily referential, Brewster proposed the following analysis:

> I prefer to use the term "speech" instead of "language," and though the definition may seem arbitrary, let me for the sake of clearness distinguish the two. . . . Take for example a newspaper. In some of its columns you will find many bits of information [that are merely "language"]: political telegrams, the state of the weather, crimes and accidents, the rate of exchange, fashionable movements, and so forth. In all these cases language serves merely as the interpreter of things that have been previously seen, heard, felt, counted, or measured; of things, in short, that interest us because they represent the play of one of our senses, or of several of them in combined action. . . . [For an example of "speech,"] consider the leading article. You will perhaps not find in it a single remark that would interest us were it detached from the surrounding ones, or that could not be met by some counter-proposition equally trustworthy. Yet all the remarks may stand in such a relation one to the other that the entire article becomes a powerful performance capable of stirring public opinion, and possibly of influencing the destinies of the nation. . . . It owes its strength to a structure independent of the sentiments it appeals to. It subsists in virtue of an interdependence of its parts far more subtle than the gross and lifeless connections pointed out by logic. . . . [D]isconnected utterances conveying information owe their strength to a previous work of some of our senses, simple or combined, which they translate into words. Connected utterances bearing strength with them owe that strength to the fact that they embody, instead of translating, a primary reality. They express nothing, they *are* something.[45]

According to Brewster, referential language and its function, "faithful representation" or "truth," are much overrated, while "speech" or "poetry" is undervalued. "Truth itself, however much you may get of it, is but a factor in a larger work, and its greatest value is not in that which it declares, but in that which the declaration is ignorant of, but tends to fashion and form. Whatever you may express, you are at the same time co-operating in the growth of a reality of a quite different kind, you are making something different to what you express. Truth is but a parcel of some becoming reality. . . ."[46]

In these ideas about "speech" as opposed to "language," we may recognize our notion of political language, especially the vow, which creates its own reality instead of referring to any external, named thing. Brewster makes the connection himself when he says, "our great work in life is not translating or expressing truth, but building or fashioning forms. What is our social and political activity else?"[47]

Presumably Brewster would also have included novels in the category of "speech," although he did not care for them very much. Obviously they create a reality that was not there before, something more than truth. And so a connection may be made out between politics and fiction, between vows and stories of vows, both of which are "building or fashioning forms"—"deeds of speech."

That James had already written *The Princess Casamassima* before he read Brewster's book is not important; he could have found similar ideas (less precisely distinguished as linguistic) in the work of more typical and prominent anarchists like Tolstoy and Bakunin in the 1880s.[48] Most likely he came to his views—and they are much less settled than Brewster's—on his own. What is important to understand is that the ideas are anarchist ideas, and that they lie behind the political novel's formulation of the problem of language.

No anarchist could doubt that a language of action was preferable to a language of reference. The institutions of civilization could be distinguished good from bad according to their dependence on linguistic superstition. Strip away the magical authority of constitution and scripture, state and church would dissolve, leaving room for more authentic religious and political life, grounded in natural and spontaneous speech acts. It did not disturb the anarchists to perceive that there could be no truth-value for a "deed of speech," that for every "single remark" there would always be "some counter-proposition equally trustworthy." Brewster cheerfully points out that even this last "truth" is vulnerable to its own contrary. Man must learn to enjoy this freedom from settled formulations. He must accept the responsibility for creating reality through speech, and must refrain from the fetishism of names that embalms life in words.

The appeal of such a theory to a novelist might be problematic. A professional writer would know the tricks of rhetoric and propaganda, and understand the tenuous relation between words and things. In "The Art of

Fiction," James had likened the activities of the novelist and the historian, with implications for the idea of "truth" that are scarcely comforting to any believer in history as non-fiction. He pointed out how an "illusion of life" might be achieved by mere "solidity of specification," that is, by treating words as if they infallibly betokened something in reality. Any skillful propagandist might create a world of fiction—like Peter Verkhovensky's "legend" of the crown prince—that would be taken for "truth" by a gullible political audience. Moreover, it was no comfort to recognize that if language could express credible lies it could also state the truth. For "how," as Razumov asks, "can one tell the truth from lies?" The reply he gets, a placid appeal to verisimilitude and honesty, must be taken ironically since the narrator who answers him is at that very moment a dupe of just such trust as he advises.

Searching for an infallible means of holding words to their referents or enforcing the truth of propositions, men might retreat into either behaviorism or skepticism. A behaviorist reduced speech to neurological events whose significance was merely a matter of laws of association. A thing was connected to its name as a stimulus to its response. In *Nostromo* Conrad identified political language as crudely conditioned behavior of this sort:

> They had stopped near the cage. The parrot, catching the sound of a word belonging to his vocabulary, was moved to interfere. Parrots are very human.
> "Viva Costaguana!" he shrieked.[49]

Political language like parrot language has no truth value, only symptomatic relevance for the state of the organism.

The opposite alternative, skepticism, is also illustrated in *Nostromo*, in Decoud's fate on the island. It is the particular temptation of the verbally-oriented man—like Decoud or Razumov—to locate reality in the mind alone; the words generated there create a systematic delusion that is the only reality there is. Because these words must be part of a private language, they can refer to nothing in reality; there are no other users of the same words with whom to agree on their denotation, and thus no way of ever deciding whether or not any word is properly applied, no criteria for truth. Skepticism thus is fatal even to the single consciousness the skeptic begins with: once alone on the island, without anyone to talk to, Decoud's individuality "merged into the world of cloud and water, of natural forces and forms of nature." "He beheld the universe as a succession of incom-prehensible images . . . , senseless phrases . . . , an ironical and senseless buzzing." To depend on a private language for one's illusion of reality is, ultimately, to have no language at all. Moreover, this chaos is just another form of parrot gabble. Behaviorism and skepticism both lead to the loss of linguistic significance.

A third alternative was to regard language as in some relation with reality other than referential. Both behaviorism and skepticism were attempts to protect the referential theory of language by throwing the weight on one of its two terms, words-in-the-mind or things-in-the-world. To escape this subject-object dualism, it was necessary to give up the no-tion of truth, a relation of words to things, in favor of the notion of the creative speech act—bringing together words and deeds. Perhaps a novelist could understand this reorientation better than others, because it was so clear that the words in novels did not refer in the ordinary way to things in the world. Verisimilitude or truth-to-life in fiction, if it was to be more than a trick of pseudo-reference, must depend on some capacity of language other than mere naming things or stating facts. Although the words of a novel had no truth value, they seemed to tell about life in a manner that lost little if any of its human importance merely because the author invented rather than reported what he saw. Nor was there any great difficulty in making the shift from enjoying stories that were true to enjoy-ing those that were only true-to-life. Obviously no story, true or fictional, was ever the same thing as experience itself. The essential elements of stories apparently had less to do with accuracy of imitation than with other values—among them the inner consistency and connectedness that Brewster noted as primary in deeds of speech. Even "solidity of specifica-tion" might not really have to do with reference after all, since the things specified existed only in the novel itself. The verisimilitude of an account would be a matter of seriousness rather than honesty, precision rather than accuracy, probability rather than factuality, authenticity rather than truth. The notebooks in which James stored his materials are filled with plots and the makings of plots—relationships, encounters, sketches of action. There is little interest in facts or truths observed from life, and the stories he hears at dinner-parties are chiefly regarded as "germs" for his imagination to work with, the less of the actuality known the better.

Language in James's novels is tentative and exploratory. Words are utilized to loosen and expand experience, not to crystallize or hypostatize it. Even at the end of a novel, ambiguities are reluctantly dispelled. Hence the pains taken in *The Ambassadors* or *The Wings of the Dove* to hold open and undeclared the meanings of the relations between the characters. Like Densher, who refuses to open Milly's last letter, or like Strether, who "recognised at last that he had really been trying all along to suppose nothing," the reader is encouraged to take note of everything but to suspend judgment as long as possible, for the sake of further complication, significance, reality. Only this postponement allows James to fill out his case, while the "truth" is held in abeyance; it makes the difference, for instance, between a cheap little affair and *The Ambassadors*.

The price James and his characters pay for the freedom to create their own linguistic reality is the nagging suspicion that if reality can be created, it perhaps has no substance independent of the creating consciousness. Henry Brewster might be able to sit easy in a world that owed its existence to syntax, but James was not eager to embrace the solipsism that seemed to be implied.

Either there was a nameable reality independent of men and language, or there was not. If there was, it was too narrow to support the fictive imagination; if there was not, everything was fiction. Between these alternatives he found it hard to choose. So long as he could believe that his language was shared, not the private language of the extreme skeptic, he was at liberty to suppose that the reality he created might exist outside his own mind. Illusion or not, reality depended on linguistic solidarity among men. For a writer such solidarity would have its base in his audience, and after the failure of *The Bostonians* James was particularly sensitive to the difficulty of finding readers who "spoke the same language." This is perhaps reflected in Hyacinth's career in *The Princess Casamassima*. In the early part of the novel, Hyacinth is "other-directed": insecure about whether or not he "belongs" to society, he bends every effort to attach himself—that is the force that pushes him towards Paul Muniment and the anarchists. By means of his new "social contract" he expands his reality, moving through an enlarging world with his vow as passport, but finally he is left alone with his discoveries and finds himself merely a name on a letter, a character in Hoffendahl's plot, an "invention" of Mr. Vetch, a minor figure in Christina's fantasy, at the center only of his own sordid tale—which he can affirm only by concluding. His career is that of the typical anarchist described by Brewster in *The Theories of Anarchy and Law*:

> What have we this time at the beginning? A man who looks around him, and not within. And what have we at the end? A man in whose eyes the proper form of society is one which supposes, and tends to promote, the highest degree of inward organization, the most complex and centralized type of moral individuality. On this field he will seek to realize the unity of a perfect federation, and he rejects, as a dream of Utopia, the hope of bringing human beings into any such cohesion. His first interest turns away from the solitary being, towards the fellowship of men; and his last word is that this fellowship is both to be promoted and to be limited by the virtues that make a distinct, well-entrenched individuality.[50]

The ending Brewster imagines—"a distinct, well-entrenched individuality"—is available to Hyacinth only as death and disaster, because he cannot afford to be alone in a world that others have no part in. Brewster at least leaves the possibility of "fellowship," promoted and limited by the individual; for Hyacinth, only limitation remains, since his individuality has itself been totally mediated by fellowship now fast dwindling. Finalities like these are what James really meant when he spoke of the "imagination of disaster." It is worth recalling the context of that phrase in his letter of 1896, for it does not apply narrowly to his political novels, but sums up much of what we have been saying about the larger uncertainties of his art:

> Well that's one way of living—treating life as not *all* solitude and syntax—that has much to be said for it. But I have the imagination of disaster—and see life indeed as ferocious and sinister.[51]

The tone of these sentences, coming as they do in a relatively light-hearted letter, may stand as the final ambiguity of James's position. Stoically—and to a certain extent even complacently—James sees himself like Hyacinth driven to the wall. But the solitude and syntax that were not enough for Hyacinth *must* be enough for James, whether or not that is all there is to life. There is something in James's acceptance of this lot that reminds one of Nechaev's "Catechism," only substituting the word "artist" for "revolutionist" and the word "creation" for "destruction." The task James set for himself was to create reality through language, to *do* what he feared might not simply *be*. He knew that, according to the premises of such an enterprise, the only important reality that could exist for human beings was a shared reality, a "fellowship," as Brewster had it, that "is both to be promoted and to be limited by the virtues that make a distinct, well-entrenched individuality." The promotion of a shared reality was the function of syntax, the mediation between consciousness and consciousness; its limitation was the solitude out of which one necessarily spoke to and for others, if one were to speak at all. The imagination of disaster was the other side of James's fierce determination to create, for if reality must be continually "said" into existence, then disaster, chaos, silence would be always imminent, not as a threat from without so much as an apprehension from within. At the end of "Notebook II" there is a passage expressing one side of this anxiety:

> If I can only *concentrate* myself: this is the great lesson of life. I have hours of unspeakable reaction against my smallness of production; my wretched habits of work—or of un-work; my levity, my vagueness of mind, my perpetual failure to focus my attention, to absorb myself, to look things in the face, to invent, to produce, in a word.[52]

This was disaster imagined as a personal failure of creative power. Projected as world cataclysm, the vision became all the more "ferocious and sinister," but it was no less a matter of individual responsibility; that was the way James characteristically viewed all life's crises and opportunities. This is not to say, then, that he was apolitical, except perhaps in the narrowest sense of the word, for his fiction brought him in touch with other people, on issues of social and moral importance. True, his insistence on the loneliness of his situation sometimes seemed to be more of a comfort or justification than a price paid for experience and awareness, but with that qualification noted, one may admire his willingness "to look things in the face"—and above all, "to invent, to produce." These are social as well as artistic virtues. For James, all life "comes back to the question of our speech, the medium through which we communicate with each other." The deed of speech—his fiction—was the most serious business of life. If sometimes his terminology reduces the question to a matter of "good breeding" or "good manners," we may allow him these touchstones, realizing that he never spoke lightly of them. Whatever the lapses in his work, his ideal was clear: to speak "as people speak when their speech has had for them a signal importance."[53] There was no other guarantee of authenticity or truth, and no other defense against the "uncreating word" of the propagandist or the "universal darkness" of the terrorist.

5

"Mentalized Sex" in D. H. Lawrence

"And I, who loathe sexuality so deeply, am considered a lurid
sexuality specialist."

I

D. H. Lawrence is probably the most notoriously censored author in all of
literary history. His very first novel, *The White Peacock*, had to be toned
down, words like "mucked" and "passionate" changed to "dirtied" and
"infatuated." From then on it was one suppression after another. When the
police confiscated the first edition of *The Rainbow* in 1915, Lawrence
automatically became the inspiration (though not quite the spokesman) for
a new generation of writers who wished to establish sex as a legitimate
subject of literature—with what effect everyone knows.

Lady Chatterley's Lover, his last novel, was Lawrence's major effort in
this struggle. "I always labour at the same thing, to make the sex relation
valid and precious, instead of shameful. And this novel is the furthest I've
gone. To me it is beautiful and tender and frail as the naked self is, and I
shrink very much even from having it typed. Probably the typist would
want to interfere—."[1] In 1928 he had it printed in Florence, privately,
having first explained all the dirty words to the Italian printer—who said
he knew of such words himself and saw no reason to be squeamish about
setting them in type. At first Lawrence had thought that he might do an
expurgated edition for his British and American publishers, but it proved
impossible. He said the book bled when he tried to clip it.[2] No legitimate

97

publisher dared to bring out an uncensored edition until 1959 in the United States and 1960 in Great Britain—that is, thirty years after Lawrence's death. One wonders what he would have thought of the way publishers and readers have finally made use of his "frail" classic.

Lawrence said that he had "put forth" *Lady Chatterley* "as an honest, healthy book, necessary for us today."[3] He wanted "men and women to be able to think sex, fully, completely, honestly, and cleanly."[4] He was not so much advocating any sort of action as he was undertaking a cleansing of men's minds. "The mind has to catch up, in sex. . . . Balance up the consciousness of the act, and the act itself. Get the two in harmony. It means having a proper reverence for sex, and a proper awe of the body's strange experience. It means being able to use the so-called obscene words, because these are a natural part of the mind's consciousness of the body."[5]

Unwelcome as *Lady Chatterley* and its purpose were in polite circles of the late twenties, there was a large underground public waiting for the many pirated editions of the book with open arms. No doubt some of its readers misused the novel just as the censors said they would, but others embraced it for more respectable reasons. Edmund Wilson ended his review of the contraband Florence edition with a characteristically shrewd prediction: "All serious writers in the English-speaking countries are much in Lawrence's debt, for even the limited circulation of *Lady Chatterley's Lover* cannot fail to make it easier in future to disregard the ridiculous taboo that the nineteenth century imposed on sex."[6] Long as it took to get *Lady Chatterley* legally in print, it was widely read among young literary people during all those years, and probably did exert the influence Wilson said it would. Whether or not it had quite the effect that Lawrence himself intended is a more complicated question, for he was after more than merely opening up the genre to frank descriptions of lovemaking. He wanted to reform the lovemaking itself.

Some readers of *Lady Chatterley* have supposed that Lawrence was an advocate of sexual promiscuity, if not himself lewd. The truth is that he was a faithful and even a puritanical husband, though he had come by the role rather dishonorably, having run off with his French professor's wife. He believed in lifelong monogamy, and he never wrote approvingly about any sexual practice that went against it. "Nothing nauseates me more than promiscuous sex in and out of season."[7] Of course in *Lady Chatterley* his heroine twice commits adultery, but in the first instance she is condemned for it, and in the second she is only forgiven because her own marriage is both loveless and sexless, while she and her new lover intend to marry as soon as possible. "I realize," he said in his defense of the book, "that marriage, or something like it, is essential, and that the old Church knew best the enduring needs of man, beyond the spasmodic needs of today and yesterday. The Church established marriage for life, for the fulfillment of the soul's living life, not postponing it till the after-death."[8] So Lawrence's advocacy of more honesty and more genuine passion in sexual life should not be read as a defense of all sexual activity. Indeed, he thought that until the mind "caught up" with the body, in sexual matters, it might be reasonable for people to refrain from intercourse altogether.[9]

What then did Lawrence believe the sexual life of man ought to be, once the catching up was accomplished? What was the ultimate advice of *Lady Chatterley's Lover*?

One answer might be hinted in the famous scene in which Connie Chatterley and her lover weave forget-me-nots in one another's pubic hair. Some readers have found that idyllic interchange ridiculous, but I suppose even they recognize the accents of innocent fun-in-bed that Lawrence was attempting:

> He fastened fluffy young oak-sprays round her breasts, sticking in tufts of bluebells and campion: and in her navel he poised a pink campion flower, and in her maidenhair were forget-me-nots and woodruff.
> "That's you in all your glory!" he said. "Lady Jane, at her wedding with John Thomas."[10]

Successful or not as a literary effect, its charm is not lost on all readers. What complicates matters is the juxtaposition of such frolics with heavier moments. Could the following equally well-known passage in *Lady Chatterley* be an example of Lawrence's ideal of sexual encounter?

> It was a night of sensual passion, in which she was a little startled and almost unwilling: yet pierced again with piercing thrills of sensuality, different, sharper, more terrible than the thrills of tenderness, but, at the moment, more desirable. Though a little frightened, she let him have his way, and the reckless, shameless sensuality shook her to her foundations, stripped her to the very last, and made a different woman of her. It was not really love. It was not voluptuousness. It was sensuality sharp and searing as fire, burning the soul to tinder.
> Burning out the shames, the deepest, oldest shames, in the most

secret places. It cost her an effort to let him have his way and his will
of her. She had to be a passive, consenting thing, like a slave, a physical slave. Yet the passion licked round her, consuming, and when the
sensual flame of it pressed through her bowels and breast, she really
thought she was dying: yet a poignant, marvelous death.[11]

This was one of the scenes that the prosecuting attorneys in the British trial
of *Lady Chatterley* saved for trumps in their summation speech. They
quoted still more of it:

> In the short summer night she learnt so much. She would have
> thought a woman would have died of shame. Instead of which, the
> shame died. Shame, which is fear: the deep organic shame, the old,
> old physical fear which crouches in the bodily roots of us, and can only
> be chased away by the sensual fire, at last it was roused up and routed
> by the phallic hunt of the man, and she came to the very heart of the
> jungle of herself. She felt, now, she had come to the real bedrock of
> her nature, and was essentially shameless. She was her sensual self,
> naked and unashamed. She felt a triumph, almost a vainglory. So!
> That was how it was ! That was life! That was how oneself really was!
> There was nothing left to disguise or be ashamed of. She shared her
> ultimate nakedness with a man, another being.
> And what a reckless devil the man was! really like a devil! One had
> to be strong to bear him. But it took some getting at, the core of the
> physical jungle, the last and deepest recess of organic shame.[12]

"What does it mean?" the prosecutor coyly asked. "I do not know, I do not
suggest. There is more than one meaning which you can put to those two
pages, if you want to take offense. Who knows what is the effect on the
young man or woman reading those two pages? What is he or she going to
think? Is it going to be a good influence, or can it only corrupt and de-
prave? What is the tendency of it? Where is the justification contained?
Where again is the good that a book can do, any book which contains a
passage such as that?"[13]

Did the prosecution blunt this particular bullet in order to do more
damage, or simply out of an unwillingness to be more precise about so
unmentionable an act as Lawrence was apparently describing? However
the authorities might come to terms with it, at least in part the passage must
be intended symbolically, to suggest Lawrence's own activity as a
writer in searching out the secret places, "the last and deepest recess of
organic shame," just as in part it is a description of Mellors buggering

Connie. How could he not have known what he was saying, on both scores? But supposing Lawrence to have known what he was saying, why do we suddenly have these evasive terms to describe matters surely just as deserving of plain Anglo-Saxon as other comminglings of these same lovers? Why mince words here if not there?

The trouble with the forget-me-not passage—if there is any trouble with it—must come down to its being too cute. And the problem with the "deepest recess" passage—if there is anything wrong with it—is that it is too suggestive, too teasing, too discreet. There is something dangerously posed and poised about both passages, something that goes against the unguarded speech and act that Lawrence was advocating.

Several years before writing *Lady Chatterley* Lawrence had stated the case for frank expression with admirable clarity, in a letter to a female friend: "The word penis or testicle or vagina doesn't shock me. Why should it? Surely I am a man enough to be able to think of my own organs with calm, even with indifference. It isn't the names of things that bother me; nor even ideas about them. I don't keep my passions, or reactions or even sensations *in my head*. They stay down where they belong." [14] The argument was carried further in another letter, to another woman, at the time of *Lady Chatterley*:

> I want, with Lady C., to make an *adjustment in consciousness* to the basic physical realities. I realise that one of the reasons why the common people often keep—or kept—the good *natural glow* of life, just warm life, longer than educated people, was because it was still possible for them to say fuck! or shit without either a shudder or a sensation. If a man had been able to say to you when you were young and in love: an' if tha shits, an' if tha pisses, I'm glad, I shouldna want a woman who couldna shit nor piss—surely it would have been a liberation to you, and it would have helped to keep your heart warm. [15]

All this seems reasonable enough until one begins to notice the repeated denial of any room "in the head" for sexuality. The notion that "uneducated" people were able to keep their lives "warm" longer than others is obviously false—worship of a primitive, unconscious, "natural" man who never really existed. The short-circuiting of the head that Lawrence advocated as an ideal of sexuality is not really bestial—despite the opinions of his enemies—so much as it is simply impossible; and impossible not merely to educated, modern men, but to all men. The mind and the body are not separable in the way Lawrence seems to imagine. "Passions," "reactions," "even sensations" do not "belong" somewhere "down" below the waist, but transpire in the entire organism.

Lawrence argued that "thought and action, word and deed, are two separate forms of consciousness, two separate lives which we lead." [16] He admits the need "to keep a connection" between these separate lives of mind and body. "But while we think, we do not act, and while we act we do not think. The great necessity is that we should act according to our thoughts, and think according to our acts. But while we are in thought we cannot really act, and while we are in action we cannot really think." [17]

Whatever common sense may seem to reside in these theories, they are at best metaphorical, simply a means of distinguishing attitudes and values. There are different kinds of mental activity, and different kinds of physical activity, but they are not necessarily opposed, only different aspects of existence—or different ways of describing what life is like. Lawrence put his objections to "mentalized sex" much more intelligibly a little further on in the same essay when he said: "When people act in sex, nowadays, they are half the time acting up. They do it because they think it is expected of them. Whereas as a matter of fact it is the mind which is interested, and the body has to be provoked." [18] It is true that sometimes people think and act according to prescriptions rather than feelings or desires; and of course prescriptions have a sort of "mental" cast to them, since they get formulated and passed around in language. "How different they are, mental feelings and real feelings. Today many people live and die without having had any real feelings—though they have had a 'rich emotional life' apparently, having showed strong mental feeling. But it is all counterfeit. . . . Our education from the start has *taught* us a certain range of emotions, what to feel and what not to feel, and how to feel the feelings we allow ourselves to feel. . . . The higher emotions are strictly dead. They have to be faked." Lawrence's point, although obscured even here by his mental/physical dichotomy, comes across with plenty of force: sexual life has become conventionalized, trivialized, commercialized. "The radio and the film are mere counterfeit emotion all the time, the current press and literature the same. People wallow in emotion; counterfeit emotion. They lap it up: they live in it and on it. They ooze with it." [19] What Lawrence wants is a new sexuality, freed from the self-indulgent pattern of popular romance. But how does he imagine his own work—also popular and romantic, though perhaps not so obviously—how does he imagine *his* novels effecting the changes he wants? Long before *Lady Chatterley*, Lawrence wrote an elaborate satire on such faked feelings and counterfeit emotions, in the form of a burlesque novel called "Mr. Noon." The satiric manner was not really suited to his talents or message, and so Lawrence never finished this book, but the one hundred pages he wrote are interesting. To get the full effect, one must take a pretty strong dose; here are several paragraphs from the chapter called "Spoon," in which the hero goes in for some heavy necking with the heroine:

> Ah, dear reader, you don't need me to tell you how to sip love with a spoon, to get the juice out of it. You know well enough. But you will be obliged to me, I am sure, if I pull down that weary old scarecrow of a dark designing seducer, and the alpaca bogey of lust. There is no harm in us any more, is there now? Our ways are so improved; so spiritualized, really. What harm is there in a bit of a spoon? And if it goes rather far; even very far; well, what by that? As we said before, it depends *how* you go, not where you go. . . .
>
> Mr. Noon was a first-rate spoon—the rhyme is unfortunate, though, in truth, to be a first-rate spoon a man must be something of a poet. With his mouth he softly moved back the hair from her brow, in slow, dreamy movements, most faintly touching her forehead with the red of his lips, hardly perceptible, and then drawing aside her hair with his firmer mouth, slowly, with a long movement. She thrilled delicately, softly tuning up, in the dim, continuous, negligent caress. Innumerable pleasant flushes passed along her arms and breasts, melting her into a sweet ripeness. . . .
>
> A deep pulse-beat, a pulse of expectation. She was waiting, waiting for him to kiss her ears. Ah, how she waited for it! Only that. Only let him kiss her ears, and it was a consummation.
>
> But no! He had left her, and wandered away to the soft little kiss-curls in the nape of her neck; the soft, warm, sweet little fibrils of her hair. She contracted with a sharp convulsion, like tickling. Delicious thrills ran down her spine, before he gave her the full assurance, and kissed her soft, deep, full among the fine curls centred in the nape of her neck. She seemed to be lifted into the air as a bit of paper lifts itself up to a piece of warm amber. Her hands fluttered, fluttered on his shoulders; she was rising up on the air like Simon Magus. Let us hope Mr. Noon will not let her down too sharp.
>
> No! No! Even as she rose in the air she felt his breath running warm at the gates of her ears. Her lips came apart; she panted with acute

anticipation. Ah!—Ah!—and softly came his full, fathomless kiss; softly her ear was quenched in darkness. He took the small, fine contours subtly between his lips, he closed deeper, and with a second reeling swoon she reeled down again and fell, fell through a deeper, darker sea. Depth doubled on depth, darkness on darkness. She had sunk back to the root-stream, beyond sight and hearing. . . .

His mouth was coming slowly nearer to her mouth; and yet not approaching. Approaching without disclosing its direction. Loitering, circumventing, and then suddenly taking the breath from her nostrils. For a second she died in the strange sweetness and anguish of suffocation. He had closed her nostrils for ever with a kiss and she was sleeping, dying in sweet fathomless insentience. Death, and the before-birth sleep.

Yet, not quite. Even now, not quite. One spark persisted and waited in her. Frail little breaths came through her parted lips. It was the brink of ecstacy and extinction. She cleaved to him beyond measure, as if she would reach beyond herself. With a sudden lacerating motion she tore her face from his, aside. She held it back, her mouth unclosed. And obedient down came his mouth on her unclosed mouth, darkness closed on darkness, so she melted completely, fused, and was gone.[20]

What Lawrence hates in all this is the scripted quality of the lovemaking, the self-consciousness and the posturing, as if the whole thing had been written out by a playwright, cast by a director, and were now being played by rather indifferent actors: ". . . all the time, of course, each of them had a secondary mundane consciousness. Each of them was aware of the entry, the other spooners, and the passers-by outside. Each of them attended minutely when one pair of spooners crept through the gap in the big doors, to go home. They were all there, mark you. None of your bestial loss of faculties."[21] Later on, when the heroine makes plans to get married, she thinks of it this way: "She decided, if possible, to open the last long chapter of a woman's life, headed Marriage. She intended it to be a long and quite banal chapter, cauliflower and lovey-doves."[22] It is this that Lawrence calls "acting up" to sentimental myths of sexuality, love, and marriage.

Obviously, one must agree with Lawrence that such self-dramatizations are loathsome. The difficulty comes when we try to understand the difference between honest and dishonest accounts (fictional or not) of such matters. How, for example, do we distinguish the self-indulgent quality of

"The Spoon" in the passages just quoted, from a description such as the following in *Lady Chatterley's Lover*?

> And it seemed she was like the sea, nothing but dark waves rising and heaving, heaving with a great swell, so that slowly her whole darkness was in motion, and she was ocean rolling its dark, dumb mass. Oh, and far down inside her the deeps parted and rolled asunder, in long, far-travelling billows, and ever, at the quick of her, the depths parted and rolled asunder, from the centre of soft plunging, as the plunger went deeper and deeper, touching lower, and she was deeper and deeper and deeper disclosed, and heavier the billows of her rolled away to some shore, uncovering her, and closer and closer plunged the palpable unknown, and further and further rolled the waves of herself away from herself, leaving her, till suddenly, in a soft, shuddering convulsion, the quick of all her plasm was touched, she knew herself touched, the consummation was upon her, and she was gone.[23]

Is not Connie Chatterley just as self-regarding in this scene as is Emmie Bostock as she waits for her ear to be "quenched" in the Co-op entry? What precisely is the difference between "she knew herself touched, the consummation was upon her, and she was gone" and "darkness closed on darkness, so she melted completely, fused, and was gone"? As it turns out, of course, we are to understand that Connie's orgasm is genital, not to say vaginal, while Emmie's is merely literary—but anatomy aside, who can tell them apart? In "Mr. Noon" the author comes round on the reader from behind and nudges him: Aha, caught you having lascivious thoughts there, didn't I? Or, no less sneaky, Lawrence and the reader tut and gloat together over the foolish girl in the entry, whom we knew all along was just titillating herself, not really letting go. Again it is necessary to ask whether either of these passages is consistent with Lawrence's desire to open up the novel, and the minds of his readers, to frank and unselfconscious sexuality.

The problem goes deeper even than this. Were it only a matter of inconsistency—passages that seem to go against the spirit of his announced values—we could write them off as lapses or confusions that Lawrence, like any prophet, had to risk. But the difficulty really lies in the medium itself, the form that Lawrence chose to work in—the novel. Is it possible to render a scene of sexual feeling in fiction without indulging in "mentalized sex" of the kind that he despised?

II

In "Pornography and Obscenity," his chief manifesto on the subject of
sex in literature, Lawrence begins with the obvious point, that pornography "is an invariable stimulant to the vice of self-abuse, onanism,
masturbation," and goes on to assert that "there is an element of pornography in nearly all nineteenth-century literature," while "the mass of our
popular amusements just exists to provoke masturbation." "And this," he
insists, "is, perhaps, the deepest and most dangerous cancer of our civilization."[24] The trouble with pornography and masturbation, according to
Lawrence, was the "desire to spite the sexual feeling, to humiliate and
degrade it." As a result, "the sex flow is dying out of the young, the real
energy is dying away."[25] Masturbation was supplanting healthy sexuality,
pornography was usurping the true novel.

The novel might yet reform itself, and survive. If so, that would make a
difference to civilization. The idea of *Lady Chatterley's Lover* was that it
would function as anti-pornography. What was needed, as Lawrence put it
in the title of an essay, was "Surgery for the Novel—or a Bomb." The
"serious novel" was dying. "'Did I feel a twinge in my little toe, or didn't
I?' asks every character of Mr. Joyce or of Miss Richardson or M.
Proust. . . .The audience round the death-bed gapes for the answer. And
when, in a sepulchral tone, the answer comes at length, after hundreds of
pages . . . the audience quivers all over, and murmurs: 'that's just how I
feel myself.'"[26] Lawrence had good reason to include Proust in his rogues'
gallery of "serious" new novelists who took more pleasure in art than life,
for not only was he the worst offender in the sin of prying into his own
sensations and thoughts, but he was also a self-conscious defender of
fantasy, worse than any of the nineteenth-century romanticists in this
regard. Lawrence justified the novel as a means to life, a sort of shock
treatment to wake readers up. Proust thought of it rather as access to
dreams more real than life:

> Alas, it was in vain that I implored the dungeon-keep of Roussain-
> ville, that I begged it to send out to meet me some daughter of its
> village, appealing to it as to the sole confidant to whom I had disclosed
> my earliest desires when, from the top floor of our house at Combray,
> from the little window that smelt of orris-root, I had peered out and
> seen nothing but its tower, framed in the square of the half-opened
> window, while, with the heroic scruples of a traveller setting forth for

unknown climes, or of a desperate wretch hesitating on the verge of self-destruction, faint with emotion, I explored, across the bounds of my own experience, an untrodden path which, I believed, might lead me to my death, even—until passion spent itself and left me shuddering among the sprays of flowering currant which, creeping in through the window, tumbled all about my body. In vain I called upon it now. In vain I compressed the whole landscape into my field of vision, draining it with an exhaustive gaze which sought to extract from it a female creature. . . . And if she had appeared, would I have dared to speak to her? I felt that she would have regarded me as mad, for I no longer thought of those desires which came to me on my walks, but were never realised, as being shared by others, or as having any existence apart from myself. They seemed nothing more now than the purely subjective, impotent, illusory creatures of my temperament. They were in no way connected now with nature, with the world of real things, which from now onwards lost all its charm and significance, and meant no more to my life than a purely conventional framework, just as the action of a novel is framed in the railway carriage.[27]

Proust describes here his first experiments with masturbation, and then his subsequent withdrawal from ordinary life and "nature," and his growing dependence upon imagination for both sexual and emotional gratification. He is clearly one of those perverts of self-analysis who according to Lawrence prefer fantasy to reality, the pleasures of imagination to health and nature:

The only positive effect of masturbation is that it seems to release a certain mental energy, in some people. But it is mental energy which manifests itself always in the same way, in a vicious circle of analysis and impotent criticism, or else a vicious circle of false and easy sympathy, sentimentalities. The sentimentalism and the niggling analysis, often self-analysis, of most of our modern literature, is a sign of self-abuse. . . . There is hardly a writer living who gets out of the vicious circle of himself—or a painter either. Hence the lack of creation, and the stupendous amount of production. It is a masturbation result, within the vicious circle of the self. It is self-absorption made public.[28]

According to Lawrence, the secret but widespread practice of masturbation was part of a general movement away from free and natural sexuality which, so far as Englishmen were concerned, "began only in the nineteenth century."[29] There is some reason for accepting at least part of this view, for it is fairly clear that the nineteenth century was indeed the first period during which masturbation was so thoroughly feared and outlawed as to produce reactions like Lawrence's. Thus, for example, in the long history of male infibulation—the use of various artificial constrictions of the foreskin to prevent erection—apparently the first suggestion of its use to inhibit masturbation did not occur until 1786.[30] But of course this does not mean that no one masturbated before that date, only that not so many worried about it. As it happens, it was that same year that the eminent British surgeon, Dr. John Hunter, gave it as his professional opinion that masturbation "in itself does less harm to the constitution in general than the natural" act of intercourse.[31] By the time (1810) his *Treatise on the Venereal Disease* had reached a third, posthumous edition, his editor felt impelled to announce his own belief "that Onanism is more hurtful than the author imagined."[32] Later writers went so far as to allege, falsely, that Hunter had "recanted in his future editions," because he finally realized "that the solitary masturbator can repeat his crime as often as he pleases . . . [while] the compliance of a female is not always to be obtained."[33] After Hunter the Victorian medical establishment closed ranks on masturbation for a century.

Lawrence's attitude toward masturbation, although in one sense an attack on nineteenth-century practice, is also very much indebted to official Victorian opinion on the subject. It is not surprising therefore that Lawrence sometimes sounds like the generation of prigs he despised for their anti-sexuality. Here, for example, is the typical opinion of a physician in 1839: "every one will admit that, he who is addicted to the unmanly habit of masturbation or onanism, is isolated from society, concentrates all his affections on himself, exerts none of the mutual sympathies of the different members of society, which contribute most powerfully to the good of all."[34] Compare Lawrence's own theory of the bad effects of self-abuse: "The great danger of masturbation lies in its merely exhaustive nature. In sexual intercourse, there is a give and take. A new stimulus enters as the native stimulus departs. Something quite new is added as the old surcharge is removed. And this is so in all sexual intercourse where two creatures are concerned, even in the homosexual intercourse. But in masturbation there is nothing but loss. There is no reciprocity. There is merely the spending away of a certain force, and no return. . . ."[35]

As everyone knows, masturbation is frequently accompanied by sexual fantasy. Laws against pornography are typically based on formulations of a relation between imaginative experience and sexual activity—and what the mealy-mouthed legislators have in mind when they say "sexual impurity" is simply masturbation. Thus the trial judge in Roth v. the United States instructed the jury: "the words 'obscene, lewd, and lascivious' as used in the law, signify that form of immorality which has relation to sexual impurity and has a tendency to excite lustful thoughts." [36] The prosecution in Regina v. Penguin Books Limited—the trial of *Lady Chatterley* in 1960—asked the jury in its opening remarks: "Does it suggest—or, to be more accurate, has it a tendency to suggest—to the minds of the young of either sex, or even to persons of more advanced years, thoughts of a most impure and lustful character?"[37] Victorian authorities had also made these obvious connections between masturbation, pornography, and the abuse of the imagination. The manuals they put out for parents and teachers (*What a Young Man Ought To Know, Good Morals and Gentle Manners, Dr. Foote's Plain Home Talk, Home-Treatment of Sexual Abuses, Lectures on Chastity*) invariably contained similar analyses of the dangers of reading improper literature, and the results of an inflamed imagination:

> Many a young person indulges his imagination in wandering, where in person, at present he can not follow; in hearing what he dare not tell; in seeing what shame would forbid him to disclose; and in seeking what modesty would blush to reveal. These flights of unbridled fancy can not be indulged in with safety. They are the prolific source of all crime, and sin, and shame. . . .
>
> Everything that excites the imagination, inflames the passions, stimulates the curiosity, and corrupts the heart by unchaste suggestions is to be shunned. Impure thoughts, vulgar language, vicious company, obscene books, and lascivious pictures are the bane of good society. No one who is subject, in any degree, to such influences can remain pure.[38]

It should be especially noticed that the Victorian enemies of self-abuse did not suppose the impure exercise of the imagination was limited to young readers. To blame for the pollution of others, writers in particular—as professional *fabulateurs*, like Proust—were themselves most obviously in masturbation's hot grip. Rousseau, who in his *Confessions* had frankly discussed the origin of *Julie* as a masturbatory fantasy, was the horrifying example everyone fixed on, until his very name began to be used instead of Onan's: "Have I not often told you that I was another Rousseau?" Ruskin confessed in a letter to a friend.[39]

Partly this susceptibility was a function of the sedentary habits of writers, which made their minds and genitals irritable and inflammable (the cold water douche, followed by brisk towelling, was recommended for the body, while the mental equivalent was "getting out more" in polite society). Rousseau was noted for the "disproportionate increase of the mind to the body," resulting "from inaction and a continued sitting posture"—and the psychosomatic medicine of the day postulated a set of interconnections between "languid circulation," "obstruction in the liver," "excite[d] . . . imagination," and "melancholy character." [40] One need only add the universally accepted linkage between masturbation and insanity to arrive at a full etiology of the Victorian novelist's occupational disease.

One early symptom of this sort of madness—Rousseau provided the example again—was the upsetting discovery that masturbation could apparently "afford . . . greater gratification than intercourse with the other sex, the idea of whom, after all, creates the excitement. . . ."[41] This anomaly was accounted for by the power of the imagination: "as the masturbator has not a material object for the beginning and end of his pleasures, his imagination must supply and invent one. . . . Prints, statues, public exhibitions, and a variety of other subjects, are fixed on by the imagination; and the mechanical force employed is more stimulating than the natural."[42] Here is the Proustian thesis once again. The question was especially intriguing to a generation fascinated with the mind/body problem: How could a mere fantasy excite someone more than the living embodiment of that fantasy? It was a central concern of psychologists from Coleridge to G. H. Lewes, and gave rise to a separate literary manner, from *The Monk* to *The Picture of Dorian Gray*.

At this point, of course, the terms of the discussion need no longer be exclusively sexual. The issue was the issue of consciousness itself. For all his fixation on sex, Lawrence himself saw this deeper layer: "It is no good being sexual. That is only a form of the same static consciousness. Sex is not living till it is unconscious; and it never becomes unconscious by attending to sex. One has to face the whole of one's conscious self, and smash that."[43] It was not a crisis of sexuality but of consciousness, or as he sometimes formulated it, of will. The Proustian consciousness, the Noonian consciousness, the Chatterley consciousness—in short, the consciousness of masturbation, of spooning, of impotence—all seemed to Lawrence part of the fatal self-consciousness of the nineteenth century.

"Today practically everybody is self-conscious and imprisoned in self-consciousness. . . . Fight the great lie of the nineteenth century, which has soaked through our sex and our bones." [44]

On the personal level Lawrence must have felt that his marriage somehow protected him from any charge of masturbatory solipsism. But at the very least it is problematic whether he did not invest so much of his emotional life in Frieda, as he had earlier in his mother, that she became the "world" for him—every other relationship in abeyance, overshadowed, or translatable into this one, leaving him with only a projection of himself (like Emmie in the entry) and not a social relationship at all. This possibility is hinted in a dialogue between his surrogate Somers and his wife in *Kangaroo*:

> "I intend to move with men and get men to move with me before I die," he said. Then he added hastily, "Or at any rate, I'll try a bit longer yet. When I make up my mind that it's really no good, I'll go with you and we'll live alone somewhere together, and forget the world."[45]

This was hindsight, of course, for Lawrence had already given up Australia and moved on with Frieda to New Mexico by the time he wrote this. Later in the same novel, he analyzes his hero's situation still further: "he had an ingrained instinct or habit of thought which made him feel that he could never take the move into activity unless Harriet and his dead mother believed in him."[46] This, as one might have expected, he cannot convince himself of. The female figure seems to represent the world, the "all-in-all" to him, and precludes any social "activity."

Monogamy, exclusive love—the institutions Lawrence championed as bulwarks against masturbation and the isolated consciousness—may not have been quite the defenses he hoped. Although monogamy obviously does not necessarily interfere with social or communal life, it is not an infallible sign of it either. There can be too much adjustment and accommodation in romantic love, so that the partners play into one another's fantasies (if only by preserving their privacy), and the supreme susceptibility for Lawrence, to be touched by the "other," may be faked in the mirror of sexual intimacy.

At some level Lawrence probably knew all this too. Both *Kangaroo* and *The Plumed Serpent* are full of reservations about love as a means to mutuality: ". . . human love as an all-in-all, ah, no, the strain and the unreality of it were too great."[47] "Though a woman be dearer to a man than his own life, yet he is he and she is she, and the gulf can never close up."[48] Indeed, the collection of little newspaper essays published in 1930 as *Assorted Articles* is largely comprised of attacks on the modern conception of love, much in the old vein of "Mr. Noon."

Lawrence wrote two books—*Psychoanalysis and the Unconscious* and *Fantasia of the Unconscious*—in an attempt to rehabilitate "consciousness" by dementalizing it, discovering new "centers of consciousness" that have nothing to do with the enemies, knowledge and reason, but divide up the realm of the traditional unconscious into provinces and estates, known by mystic names like "blood consciousness." In *Fantasia* there is an especially interesting treatment of dreams—which, oddly enough for an anti-rationalist, Lawrence thought much over-emphasized in psychoanalytic theory. "Most dreams are purely insignificant, and it is the sign of a weak and paltry nature to pay any attention to them whatever."[49] He argued that dreams—even the more authentic "soul-dreams" that return over and over to "haunt the soul"—are largely mere mechanisms of the psyche, without relevance or truth to the waking life, "sheer automatic logic."[50] At first glance, Lawrence's attitude might seem inconsistent, for after all dreams are "the royal road to the unconscious," and it is the unconscious that Lawrence is always urging us to enter. But of course the "royal road" Freud had in mind was a well-lighted thoroughfare, and the point was to illuminate the irrational with theory and analysis. Lawrence wanted to plunge into the darkness.

In *Kangaroo* there is a passage of autobiography that helps explain his attitude:

> In his full consciousness, he was a great enemy of dreams. For his own private life, he found his dreams were like devils. When he was asleep and off his guard, then his own weaknesses, especially his old weaknesses that he had overcome in his full, day-waking self, rose up again maliciously to take some picturesque form and torment and overcome his sleeping self. He always considered dreams as a kind of revenge which old weaknesses took on the victorious healthy consciousness, like past diseases come back for a phantom triumph.[51]

Lawrence fears dreams, one suspects, for the same reasons that he fears masturbation, and indeed all flights of fancy, from William Blake to James Joyce. Like the rest of imaginative life, dreams were too self-indulgent, too close to one's secret sins.

The Victorians also understood these connections, for they saw the same danger of sexual arousal inherent in dreams as in waking fantasies or "imaginative" literature. Some authorities went so far as to maintain that dreams should be suppressed, just as pornography: "Patients will tell you that they *cannot* control their dreams. This is not true. Those who have studied the connection between thoughts during waking hours and dreams during sleep know that they are closely connected. The *character* is the same sleeping or waking. . . . A will which in our waking hours we have not exercised in repressing sexual desires will not, when we fall asleep, preserve us from carrying the sleeping echo of our waking thought farther than we dared to do in the daytime."[52]

Lawrence's own attitude is not far from this. "To sleep is to dream: you can't stay unconscious," he wrote in one of his essays—not quite convinced perhaps, certainly not pleased about it, but seriously.[53] Dreams then are not unconscious at all, but, as I think Lawrence saw, the purest state of consciousness; consciousness and fantasy are thus crucially linked in their deepest nature.

Consciousness is symbolically mediated awareness. When we speak, for example, of "feelings" and "emotions," using metaphors of control and isolation such as "harbor," "cherish," "nurse," or, in another direction, "stifle," "smother," "fan," "air," "erupt," we reveal our sense of being locked in our mental space, so that it seems as if we "have" the feelings, possess rather than experience them. Similarly with other mental activity, at the level of conscious awareness. Feelings are a good example because we tend to think of them as antithetical to consciousness, as in the cases of Connie Chatterley and Emmie Bostock. In fact Emmie remains conscious all along, as Lawrence complains, and this is because she focuses her awareness on the symbolic significance rather than losing herself in the simple pleasure of what she experiences. Connie, on the other hand, is supposed to "lose consciousness" through giving herself to unmediated rhythmic activity, becoming at one with her physical present. The distinction is between feelings attended to by the self-conscious "I," and passions engaged in at the surface of awareness, in the motions and chemistry of the appropriate parts of the body. This is not a mind/body distinction, though it may sound like one. The mind is engaged in the passions too, but not self-reflexively, "watching itself." Mind and consciousness are not identical—that is the key to the distinction. But in spite of *Fantasia of the Unconscious* Lawrence wanted his categories lined up in the military formation of traditional psychology, so that he could take his stand for passion over feeling, for unconscious against conscious life, for the deep rhythms of sleep instead of the rapid play of dreams on the surface of awareness. The irony was that this stand was also a stand against the novel.

III

We have already been introduced to Lawrence's opinion that "there is an element of pornography in nearly all nineteenth-century litera-ture"—that is, in the novel as a genre—and that there is something "slightly indecent . . . in *Pamela* or *The Mill on the Floss* or *Anna Karenina*."[54] This "indecency" comes from "a desire to spite the sexual feeling, to humiliate and degrade it," and the examples chosen are obvious cases of the exploitation of sexual subject matter, whatever we might think of the various codes of sexual ethics they present. Lawrence pushes his attack on his predecessors rather unfairly, not to say recklessly, but nonetheless, from a certain point of view, *Pamela* probably is somewhat indecent—a story of a pure virgin successfully resisting seduction until finally her would-be seducer agrees to marry her—and even *Anna Karenina* is not totally free of such teasing "puritanism," nor *Jude the Obscure* nor *Middlemarch* nor many nineteenth-century novels. So there is a truth in Lawrence's judgment—one that even helps to explain why his own experiments with the "frank" description of sexual activity fail to avoid self-consciousness.

It is worth keeping in mind that *Lady Chatterley's Lover* itself was acquitted of being pornographic barely one generation ago, and that the continued sales and the favored spot on the drugstore racks must depend on its reputation if not its actual usefulness as a dirty book. How then does it differ from novels that, by Lawrence's lights, deserve the reputation *Lady Chatterley* has unfairly acquired?

Lawrence thought the sexuality of Boccaccio and similar Renaissance storytellers might be a healthy antidote to the pornographic tendencies he saw in modern fiction. We can see from this opinion at least one side of Lawrence's intentions in *Lady Chatterley*—namely, to "talk dirty" and to describe sexual "bouts" without allowing the reader to "get involved." But the vagueness of these concepts and intentions can be seen in the quotation marks blurring that last sentence. Even more or less graphic descriptions of "bouts" may be chaste so long as the aesthetic distance is preserved, and the encounter remains on the page instead of in the reader's imagination. To call a sexual encounter a "bout" is one way of distancing oneself from it; another is to treat it as a "bout," in the manner of Boccaccio. So long as "getting involved" is more a matter of amusement or enlightenment than of the willing suspension of disbelief, a reader is protected from his own viciousness. Thus Lawrence naturally prefers Fielding to Richardson, the distanced classicist to the absorbed gossip. And yet, taste aside, Lawrence is willy-nilly in the tradition initiated by Defoe and Richardson—since that is the mainstream of the novel. The genre could not take the direction that Fielding tried to lead it in, simply because the open, hearty mode of epic satire did not confront the problem of consciousness, merely laughed at it—as if you could reverse the tide of literacy and get people to stop reading and writing in their "closets" or "under the stairs." The new audience was not simply an economic phenomenon, nor was its new form of literature merely a symptom of the "privatization of experience," as social historians have sometimes supposed. These new readers were offering up their imaginations to imitations of life with peculiar zest. Fielding satirized the vulgar playgoer who takes the actors for real people, and the scenes for real events; but behind such naiveté lay a newly sophisticated literary consciousness, a new desire to enter seriously into the thoughts and feelings of characters whose lives made ordinary existence seem an adventure. Dr. Johnson, that morbid solitary, saw the matter clearly enough, though with jaundiced eyes, when he pronounced for Richardson's combination of realism and sentiment; and these virtues proved inextricable as well as indispensable in the novel.

Dr. Johnson's formulation was revealing: we do not read novels for plot but for sentiment. The implication, of course, was that nothing happens until Pamela's letters produce their remarkable effect on Mr. B. Pamela's self-analysis, her probing and recording every vibration of her consciousness as it tingles to Mr. B.'s thrusts of will—*that* was the novel, as Richardson conceived it. The hero-villain wants something to happen, but Pamela's virtue, ingenuity, and duplicity balk him at every turn, and these failures provide a series of occasions for the expression of sentiments—that is, feelings brought to consciousness, to verbalization—dealing with the actions proposed and frustrated in the plot. The epistolary novel offers a medium especially suited to such a structure, since the sentiments that are the by-product of these frustrations can have a dual existence, both as the literal novel under the reader's eyes, and also as the packet of letters that becomes a major prop in the plot as it unfolds. The connection between sexuality and self-conscious writing is perfectly defined when Pamela sews her "papers" in her petticoats. The emphasis on imaginative mediation of sexual excitement is made clear in the structure of the episodes: Pamela hastens to pen and paper after each attack by Mr. B.—so quickly indeed that verisimilitude is strained for the sake of urgent and hot response to event. Her experiences must give the sense of immediacy, but are also something to be rolled on the tongue, at leisure and in retrospect. It is the most intense case possible of dramatic irony—the reader knowing something that a character does not know—for the reader has the coveted letters in his hands throughout, and is in intimate touch with Pamela's consciousness at every moment—the ultimate end of Mr. B.'s desire. Perhaps the situation is best summed up in the fact that her adventures are recounted to her parents, who cannot do anything but look on, horrified, after the fact—the primal scene reversed.

In a novel like *Clarissa* a number of points of view are laid before the reader in this way—seducer, seduced, friends and relatives—and in later sentimental novels, for example Flaubert's *Sentimental Education*, this variety of response is again exploited, though usually with more or less focused attention to the sentiments of the hero, who is typically the frustrated sentimentalist. Marcel in *Remembrance of Things Past* is the classic case, a "giant of sentiment" as he has been called. Pamela is a more complicated instance since she is apparently not the frustrated party in the novel; there is no structural reason for her to have sentiments, which are little more than unacted desires, the whiff of language as they dissipate, or the path of thought around the impasse of will. In so far as *Pamela* ignores Mr. B.'s feelings, while exploiting Pamela's, it is the author's novel, its events being manipulated by Richardson for the sake of the thrills of sentiment he can extract from an essentially voyeuristic situation. It is from this point of view that Lawrence's accusation of pornographic intent is most justified. In the usual sentimental novel the hero's inability to act, with its consequences in verbal consciousness, is a result of ambiguity or conflict within his own character—thus the *Bildungsroman* is based on the hero's progress through a series of self-discoveries and consolidations, more or less dialectically structured as: desire, conflict or inhibition, impasse, sentimental commentary, reorganization of character, newly emergent desire, and so on. The structural necessity of allowing the reader relatively free observation of the hero's consciousness is obvious. But Pamela is less a developing sensibility than a trapped mentality, and our interest in her thoughts has, unfortunately, less to do with any growth or maturing of her character than it does with her plight—at best the reader is in the position of moral investigator, and of course there are more derogatory terms available for such roles and tastes.

Lawrence's own novels are typically sentimental in their structures, and their heroes are afforded many opportunities to vent desires that circumstances of character and plot prevent them from enjoying except in words. Plots themselves, in his novels, tend to consist of little more than the movement of the hero's disposition from relatively self-conscious aimlessness and indecision (for example, in *The Plumed Serpent*, Kate Leslie's restless tourist's attitude toward Mexico, or in *Lady Chatterley*, Connie's dissatisfaction with her life, and her experiment with a lover), through a period of elaborately contemplated and rationalized encounters with parts of the self that must be exorcised (Kate's struggle with her own feminine will, Connie's passing "beyond shame"), in order to arrive finally at a mature and undivided character, one which acts on desire directly and immediately, does not raise obstacles or consider alternatives for itself. The focus is usually on the hero as he works at disciplining his consciousness toward its silent perfection. He is never a victim, as Pamela has to be regarded.

All this is consciousness as a phenomenon of inner life, but consciousness had its social aspects as well. "A man must be self-conscious enough to know his own limits, and to be aware of that which surpasses him," Lawrence admitted in "Pornography and Obscenity." The effect of *this* awareness was to undermine the self-consciousness that gave rise to it, and to turn the soul outward, toward society. "What surpasses me is the very urge of life that is within me, and this life urges me to forget myself and to yield to the stirring half-born impulse to smash up the vast lie of the world, and make a new world. If my life is merely to go on in a vicious circle of self-enclosure, masturbating self-consciousness, it is worth nothing to me."[55] So, to combat self-consciousness, the prescription was to come to its limits, whatever that might mean. "Smash that."

Sometimes the smashing seemed to be a fairly traditional revolutionary goal, as in a letter to Bertrand Russell during the period when Lawrence thought he and Russell might join forces against the war and the establishment:

> Now either we have to break the shell, the form, the whole frame, or we have got to turn to this inward activity of setting the house in order and drawing up a list before we die.

But we shall smash the frame. The land, the industries, the means of communication and the public amusements shall all be nationalized. Every man shall have his wage till the day of his death, whether he work or not, so long as he works when he is fit. Every woman shall have her wage till the day of her death, whether she work or not, so long as she works when she is fit—keeps her house or rears her children.

Then, and then only, shall we be able to *begin* living. Then we shall be able to *begin* to work. Then we can examine marriage and love and all. Till then, we are fast within the hard, unliving, impervious shell.[56]

It was during this same period that Lawrence was most serious about getting a small group of friends together in an utopian community he called Rananim, to be set up in Florida, or some other distant "island." But he was continually sorting and sifting his friends, so that the lists of potential Rananimians changed as fast as its prospective locations. Years later, when-ever Lawrence felt that he could break through to a Jungian "social uncon-scious," he would revive this utopian fantasy. But it faded quickly: "Myself, I suffer badly from being so cut off. But what is one to do? One can't link up with the social unconscious. At times, one is *forced* to be essentially a hermit. . . . One has no real human relations—that is so devastating."[57] Or again, "What ails me is the absolute frustration of my primeval societal in-stinct. The hero illusion starts with the individualist illusion, and all resis-tances ensue. I think societal instinct much deeper than sex instinct—and social repression much more devastating. There is no repression of the sexual individual comparable to the repression of the societal man in me, by the individual ego, my own and everybody else's. I am weary even of my own individuality, and simply nauseated by other people's."[58]

These last letters, written toward the end of his life, express more of Lawrence's personal fears and loneliness than he was usually willing to reveal. Lawrence had spent his life wandering, rootless and often friendless, from cottage to cottage, country to country. He collected experiences, but never gathered friends or planted roots. He allowed no place to become his locale, but botanized everywhere. Thus his best nature poems are like "Humming-Bird," fantasies totally abstracted from the natural scene, part of a bestiary of the imagination. It was no different with people. He had followers of course, who would camp on his trail, but they could count on being turned away at some early juncture, if not by Lawrence himself, then by Frieda. To any ordinary observation, it would seem that he was searching for something, some ideal or culmination like his Rananim. But so much of his failure to find it seems willed, that some other interpretation must be necessary. The "social unconscious" that he thought might satisfy him was never achieved, even in his novels. Instead there were struggles among individual wills for mastery, in life with friends such as Russell or J. Middleton Murry and Katherine Mansfield, or in fiction between characters such as Birkin and Ursula, Gerald and Gudrun. The implication is that his real goal was to rehearse these struggles over and over, to reaffirm whatever truth it was that they held for him.

In *Kangaroo*, perhaps his most self-revealing novel, the social unconscious is explored in its traditional terms, as a movement toward a total state, an identification of every person with the group will. But the long central passage of the novel, the "Nightmare" chapter, in which Lawrence recounted all his personal difficulties with the state and the state-mentality in 1915, interrupts him from settling comfortably into a unanimous fascist movement. By the end of the novel the flirtation with totalitarianism seems to have never been more than another struggle of wills, between "Kangaroo," the leader of the fascist movement in Australia, and the hero, Somers, a recalcitrant "writer" whose longings for a religiously organized world are only less strong than his instinctive pan-individualism, his sense of the "dark gods" within himself.

> That was now all he wanted: to get clear. Not to save humanity or to help humanity or to have anything to do with humanity. No—no. Kangaroo had been his last embrace with humanity. Now, all he wanted was to cut himself clear. To be clear of humanity altogether, to be alone. To be clear of love, and pity, and hate. To be alone from it all. To cut himself finally clear from the last encircling arm of the octopus humanity. To turn to the old dark gods, who had waited so long in the outer dark.[59]

Self-consciousness of Somers's type wins out over the social unconscious of Kangaroo. There is a sort of wan and wistful sense of impossibilities, but the final choice is made clearly enough for the private, inward life. "Man's isolation was always a supreme truth and fact, not to be forsworn. And the mystery of apartness."[60]

Having brought his hero to this crisis in *Kangaroo*, Lawrence suddenly reveals a terrible impatience with the demands of denouement that must follow. "Now a novel is supposed to be a mere record of emotion-adventures, floundering in feelings," he sneers. "We insist that a novel is, or should be, also a thought-adventure, if it is to be anything at all complete."[61] But the adventure is not so engaging from this point on, and Lawrence cannot repress a growl of annoyance as he begins the next chapter: "Chapter follows chapter, and nothing doing. . . . To be brief. . . . "[62] In other words, the important part of the novel is apparently over, and the rest— a fourth of it— is merely tidying up. The texture of verisimilitude is pulled back together, though never again so tightly as it was in the "Nightmare" chapter just preceding the unravelling. This impatience with "emotion-adventure" is really an impatience with "thought-adventure," that is, with the need to clothe his theoretical resolution in narrative garb once he had recounted the memories of 1915 that lay behind the novel's political passion. In other novels, where the resolution is less clear by this point in the plot, Lawrence maintains his interest in his characters and their doings until the end. But here, having allowed a huge hole of flashback to gape in the center, giving a view back into his own political past, Lawrence has exhausted himself in dramatizing the remembered reality, and seems to have no energy left for fantasizing a present to conclude his story. In a way it is the opposite of the structure of *Pamela*, in which, once the long fantasy siege laid to Pamela's conscience has been raised, and the impasse removed by allowing her consciousness to come into contact with Mr. B's, through her letters—once these climaxes have occurred, there is suddenly an overwhelming access of dramatic energy in the novel, in the confrontation of Pamela and Mr. B.'s sister Lady Davers, and the excitement seems strangely healthy, as if we had finally gotten out in the fresh air of social life, out of the closet of Pamela's imagination. In *Kangaroo*, the denouement is stifling, a corridor whose turnings are only too well known in advance. This is interesting, because it suggests just how deeply Lawrence's hatred of the novel went: so long as he could keep his characters struggling toward each other, throwing themselves upon one another in an effort to blot out their individualities, just so long could he maintain his own excitement in the "adventure." But at some point in most of his work—and it comes quite early in *Kangaroo*—the failure of such efforts to permanently obliterate consciousness must be faced, and that is the moment that the heart goes out of the fiction. It is as if the goal of the typical sentimental hero—to achieve a fixed character, to fulfill his disposition to a moral nature and take his place as a mature individual in a social world—is precisely what Lawrence most desires to avoid. But he cannot avoid it, for he writes novels, novels quite as much in the mainstream of English fiction as those of Richardson. He may not have been satisfied with the genre, but he could neither change it nor abandon it.

Whatever their differences in resolution and energy, the interest of Lawrence's novels, as of *Pamela* and other examples of the genre, chiefly lies in the experience of becoming totally absorbed in the movement of another person's thoughts and emotions, those of the author or of his hero, to the exclusion of any awareness of extra-literary reality. It is in this respect that the conditions of the novel approach those of fantasy and dream—and of course the emphasis in the mainstream of the genre, on the sentimental display of the hero's consciousness, is clearly a development fostered by the peculiar combination of abstractness and closely-textured concreteness afforded by the medium. Thus it is that Lawrence's complaints about most novels, as well as all sorts of self-conscious fantasy experiences, must seem odd to us, coming as they do from a man who exploits the very modes and structures he attacks, and who heats the imagination in his fiction no less than Richardson or Tolstoy do in theirs. Lawrence was shrewd enough to see that a heated imagination might come as easily from eavesdropping on the mental life of, say Lambert Strether, as on that of Pamela Andrews. But we must add Connie Chatterley, Kate Leslie, Rupert Birkin, and others, to the list. It is extenuating perhaps that their author's brightest hope for them is that they may achieve wholeness, unconsciousness, and silence, but to tell the story of their successes Lawrence must use words. And a further irony is that he cannot really communicate to us any very helpful notion of the goal he has in mind, since it is itself pure experience, unmediated by language. As Kafka said, experience cannot be written, only lived.

Of course much modern fiction, including that of Lawrence and Kafka, has had as its chief aim the expression, or indication, of this inexpressible, the breaking of the bounds of the medium, in order to spill over into real life and provoke readers into some non-literary response, some incommunicable living of their own. Indeed this last is even the presumed intention of the pornographer Lawrence despised, to throw a verbal net over the reader's consciousness and to drag it into the darkness and oblivion of orgasm. Lawrence tries for a less momentary consummation, to help us back to the "dark gods" within us, but the means he takes to bring us there are necessarily part of consciousness, appealing to our reason, caressing our sympathies, provoking our feelings—whatever it takes to move a reader to give up his own verbal world and risk the ego in an unformulated terrain.

6

Pornography, Masturbation, and the Novel

At an early point in his "study of sexuality and pornography in mid-nineteenth-century England" (*The Other Victorians*, Basic Books, 1966) Steven Marcus announces that "psychology is the one mortal enemy of pornography." After Marcus has had his say and is drawing conclusions in his final chapter, among them that "we are coming to the end of the era in which pornography had a historical meaning and even a historical function," the reader is constrained to agree, that for Marcus at least, "pornography has lost its old danger, its old power," and that psychology, or one school of psychology, is responsible for this loss.

Although he never says it in so many words, Marcus obviously dislikes pornography. One can sympathize to a certain extent, for the vaults of the "Kinsey" Institute for Sex Research in Bloomington are hardly the ideal surroundings, nor is the job of reading through thousands and thousands of pages the proper mode of enjoying dirty books. Still, it seems something to account for, that Marcus does not quote a single licentious passage for the pure sake of prurience. I do not mean to suggest that his quotations will not tempt some readers to fold down the corners here and there, but only that Marcus himself seems to take no pleasure in the salacious, and will not join the reader in a time-honored complicity. There is a bit of sniggering, sometimes (but not often) infectious: "This passage teaches us that masturbation was unquestionably at the bottom of all Uriah Heep's troubles," or "In short, he represents Europe as seen through the eye of a penis," or "It is all rather like 'The Solitary Reaper' written in a sewer." But of simple bawdy pleasure, there is none.

The puzzled reader who, with some embarrassment, nonetheless *likes* his pornography, will do well to study the epigraph to *The Other Victorians*, a passage from Freud which gloomily begins, "However strange it may sound, I think the possibility must be considered that something in the nature of the sexual instinct itself is unfavorable to the achievement of absolute gratification . . . ," and which concludes with grim optimism, "This very incapacity . . . becomes the source, however, of the grandest cultural achievements, which are brought to birth by ever greater sublimation of the components of the sexual instinct. For what motive would induce man to put his sexual energy to other uses if by any disposal of it he could obtain fully satisfying pleasure? He would never let go of this pleasure and would make no further progress."

If psychology has finally killed pornography as Marcus hopes, it is Freud's work. "For the first time in human history it became possible to discuss sexuality in a neutral way; for the first time a diction and a set of analytic concepts or instruments were established through which men could achieve sufficient intellectual distance from their own sexual beliefs and behavior so as to be able to begin to understand them." For Marcus this work is a "retrieving of human sexuality," in part a retrieving of it from pornography. Although "the impulses and fantasies of pornography . . . will always be with us, . . . [it is] after all, nothing more than a representation of the fantasies of infantile sexual life, as these fantasies are edited and reorganized in the masturbatory daydreams of adolescence. Every man who grows up must pass through such a phase in his existence, and I can see no reason for supposing that our society, in the history of its own life, should not have to pass through such a phase as well."

Ignoring the obvious inconsistency in the two views of human nature and history presented here, let me move directly to what Marcus's attitude toward sexuality really comes to, stripped of the ameliorating historical consciousness. Speaking of the "truly and literally childish" character of flagellation literature and behavior, at one point Marcus lets slip the following: "For if it is bad enough that we are all imprisoned within our own sexuality, how much worse, how much sadder must it be to be still further confined within this foreshortened, abridged, and parodically grotesque version of it." He might well have been thinking of pornography instead of flagellation, for such is precisely his sense of the relations between actual and pornographic sexuality: "if it is bad enough . . . , how much worse . . . ."

Here is the emotional (*not* "neutral") framework of *The Other Victo-*

rians. The first two-thirds of the book are devoted to Victorian sexuality (bad enough), the last third to Victorian pornography (much worse). Chapters are devoted to official sexual doctrine, as represented in William Acton's *The Functions and Disorders of the Reproductive Organs*, to Henry Spencer Ashbee's incredibly ambitious bibliography of pornography, and to the anonymous eleven-volume sexual autobiography, *My Secret Life* (since brought out in its first public edition by Grove Press). Then there are chapters on pornographic fiction, on flagellation literature, and finally on "pornotopia," that is, the genre (if it is a genre) as genre.

In thus dividing up his book, and distinguishing Victorian sexuality from Victorian pornography, Marcus makes special use of two key terms, "authenticity" and "fantasy." These are indices of value for him, the former signifying plus, the latter minus. The term "inauthentic" is not used, nor is this a phenomenological vocabulary, whatever the title of the book might lead one to expect. Authenticity is what rings true for Marcus, whatever he feels one can trust as accurate to the Victorian facts of life—not, be it emphasized, as *they* understood them, but as Marcus and presumably his reader understand them. Fantasy, contrariwise, is whatever does not ring true, whatever cannot be trusted as more than an obsessive symptom of sexual disorder, interesting only in that light. As it turns out in this scheme, pornography is never authentic (when it seems so, it transcends itself), while other accounts of Victorian lust, as *The Functions and Disorders of the Reproductive Organs* or *My Secret Life*, may sometimes be authentic, though they too are primarily fantasy.

Since authenticity is good and fantasy bad, it follows that pornography is absolutely never "Literature," although it is sometimes "literature" as in "the vast literature of flagellation," and usually fiction. In pornography, according to Marcus, "whenever there is a choice to be made, the pornographic convention or mode [that is, fantasy] triumphs over the literary, and triumphs over its reality and reality itself." No doubt whenever the same choice presents itself in literature, reality triumphs.

Clearly, with distinctions and definitions like these, we are not going to learn very much about authenticity and fantasy, pornography and literature, beyond what we already stubbornly know. Marcus begins by saying that he will "use the word 'pornography' as the general descriptive term for most of the material discussed," but he is soon speaking of it as a "genre." Positive criteria for inclusion as "material discussed" seem, in the preface, to boil down to covert or illegal publication, and as soon as the term shifts from "descriptive" to denotative function, a negative criterion begins to operate, excluding works whose publication was contested or otherwise scandalous because of obscenity or licentiousness *if* they happen to be what Marcus calls Literature. This, of course, is precisely the way the Supreme Court views such matters, with what nicely discriminating consequences for the education of public taste we all know. Thus we hear little or nothing of such variously outrageous books as *The Mill on the Floss, Ruth, The Ordeal of Richard Feverel, Griffith Gaunt, Tess, Lesbia Brandon, Esther Waters*. If there is something interesting to be learned from the difference between pornography and literature, as Marcus has the distinction, one would imagine that the borderline cases which barely make it into print would be of some importance. Instead, we get comparisons of Dickens and *My Secret Life*, and a paragraph on *Ulysses* and *Madame Bovary*.

Assuming that pornography, however we define it, does have interesting relations to literature, perhaps even *is* a form of literature, how shall we go about discovering these? Let me offer as an alternative starting-point the sensible remark of Geoffrey Gorer, from his contribution to *Does Pornography Matter?* (London, 1961): "The object of pornography is hallucination. The reader is meant to identify either with the narrator (the 'I' character) or with the general situation to a sufficient extent to produce at least the physical concomitants of sexual excitement; if the work is successful, it should produce orgasm." Marcus cannot help but know this—though he is long in withholding any explicit statement on it. On page 185 he mentions Genet's "masturbatory fantasies," but he has in mind their genesis, not their goal. On page 204 he finally brings the matter into the open, as if too obvious to merit any special recognition: "Pornography, which is a fantasy, regularly tries to extinguish its awareness of that circumstance, for the most obvious reason—a person engaged in an autoerotic fantasy is not aided in his undertaking if he permits himself consciously to reflect upon his state while he is involved in it." The point Marcus is edging into here is, I think, more crucial than he knows; it is, in fact, the missed opportunity of his book, for much as he recognizes the uses of pornography for masturbation fantasies, he never explores the nature and necessities of pornography from this point of view. He spends most of his time isolating a few characteristic fantasies (all he believes exist) and pointing out how "unliterary" they are. Although it is perfectly clear that the underlying and compelling fear of Victorian sexologists, including those Marcus quotes in the first part of his book, is the fear of masturbation, and although it is equally obvious that the pornographic fantasies which are his main concern in the remaining parts of his book are written primarily for masturbators, by masturbators, and are themselves structurally and functionally very much like masturbation, Marcus is curiously uninterested in this significant relationship between the two divisions of his subject. Indeed, when tantalizing evidence of the large correlations offers itself, it goes begging. Marcus states that pornography "is a historical phenomenon . . . [which] begins to exist *significantly* sometime during the middle of the eighteenth century . . . ," but he makes no attempt to correlate this occurrence with the history of masturbation and attitudes toward it, not always what they were in the nineteenth century. At another point, in one of his rare footnotes, he refers us to E. J. Dingwall's *Male Infibulation* (London, 1925) for an "account of the history of mechanical devices used to prevent masturbation. . . ." If Marcus had more than glanced at Dingwall's book, which he calls "slightly eccentric but preternaturally learned and precise," he would know that it is not about the prevention of masturbation at all, but the prevention of intercourse, especially in the cases of actors and athletes of antiquity. This mistake might not be so bad, were it not for the lost connection to be established between the rise of pornography and the first recorded attempts to prevent masturbation. For although Dingwall does not even include the heading in his index, he devotes a few pages to it where he draws our attention to the earliest suggestions that infibulation might prevent masturbation, in 1786 to be precise.[1] The date is a lovely coincidence, since that year also saw the publication of John Hunter's *Treatise on the Venereal Disease*, the most reasonable and permissive statement on the masturbation question by an English physician (and a very great one) before the twentieth century, thus fixing some probable limits to the rise of concern and the development of Victorian delusions about masturbation that correspond rather remarkably with the rise of pornography. Moreover, since Marcus himself throws out hints regarding the simultaneous and "inseparable" growth of pornography and of the novel, associating these with "the development of private experience—sociologists call the process 'privatization,'" one would expect some revelations, if not about *Moll Flanders* and *Clarissa*, then about *Henry Esmond* or *Bleak House* or *The Ambassadors* or other nineteenth-century variations in the Richardsonian tradition. Is pornography as

Marcus says merely a "parody" of the private experiences which such
novels render and foster, or—given the changes in attitudes toward masturbation—are there perhaps deeper structural connections than he is willing to admit, on the model of the masturbator's own experience, including
his fear and guilt as well as his secret pleasure?

To answer this question we will have to know more than Marcus tells us
about the "official" Victorian attitudes toward sexuality, especially
masturbation. Another useful hint furnished by Dingwall is his mention of
J. L. Milton's *Spermatorrhea*, a book that in a little over a dozen years
went through ten editions warning Victorians of the dangers of what seems
to have been the nineteenth century's sexual version of mononucleosis
(related to "the vapours").[2] Although he has apparently not read Milton,
Marcus knows enough about spermatorrhea from his own source, Acton,
to understand it (the words are Acton's) as "a state of enervation produced,
at least primarily, by the loss of semen." The conclusion Marcus jumps to,
however, that spermatorrhea is the "opposite [of] ungratified sexual excitement," is misleading. It allows Marcus his irony ("Whichever way one
turns, then, things are terrible. Sex is thought of as a universal and virtual-
ly incurable scourge") but at the expense of accuracy about what the Victorians actually believed. The fact is that spermatorrhea—as Milton explains
the various disorders that come under that heading, nocturnal emission,
gleet, the passing of seminal fluid in the urine—is not ordinarily accompanied by sexual excitement. Even the "wet dream" is devoid of erotic
pleasure, is not even a dream, in spermatorrhea; Acton quotes the French
authority Lallemand: "Little by little, the phenomena of excitement which
precede the orgasm diminish, and at last completely disappear; the emission then occurs without dreams, without erection, without pleasure."

The Victorians identified a number of factors as causes of spermatorrhea, especially youthful masturbation. Marcus makes light of the fact that
the authorities believed spermatorrhea could "be the result of sexual excess, but then it can just as well be the result of intellectual excess, mental
exertions having apparently the same consequences as sexual athletics.
. . . In one respect, at least, self-help and self-abuse seem indistin-
guishable." Marcus to the contrary, these apparently opposite causes have
something very significant in common. Both overtax the will, exhaust it so
as to leave the victim open to *involuntary* loss of semen, the loss of control
over the sexual organs. Even those authorities who did not include mental
exertion among the causes of spermatorrhea nevertheless agreed to the im-

portance of the will in preventing it. They argued with one another about the ways and the degree to which the mind could control the body, but almost all concurred in the view that the will ought to hold desire in check. Hunter in 1786 had thought sexual intercourse as much a mental as a physical act, and ascribed impotence to a want of "harmony" between mind and body, will and desire. Acton, whose psycho-physiological theories are largely derived from William B. Carpenter's *Principles of Human Physiology* (1844), was also anxious to preserve some prominent part to volition, though now at the expense, if possible, of desire.

Milton takes issue with all three, trimming down Hunter's view of sexual desire to "an instinct in man's natural state, *as certainly called into action by its normal exciting cause as the expulsion of the contents of the bowels and bladder is brought into play by the presence of faeces or urine*, but more capable of being subjugated by the will, especially when the desire is feebly developed, as sometimes happens in men of very weakly frame or great mental capacity." Carpenter, Acton, and Acton's other favorite source Lallemand, play "mentalists" to Milton's "behaviorist." They seem, according to Milton, to think that "secretions are very much under the *control of the nervous system.* Such obscure expressions as these have ever been the bane of medicine. . . . I have yet to learn that any amount of mental activity directed to the liver, stomach, or pancreas will increase the secretion of bile or gastric or pancreatic juice." As to Lallemand's idea that mental exertion may cause spermatorrhea, "I submit with all deference that he is wrong, and that the biographies of eminent men afford no warrant for such a supposition; for I do not consider the revelations of that filthy wretch, Rousseau, any criterion." On the other hand, Milton will allow a certain degree of psychic influence, especially in cases of impotence. Here he agrees with Hunter on the "want of harmony" which is "very common among spermatorrhea patients, and there is a form of it peculiar to them; that is, when men become alarmed, and attempt connexion just to see whether they are impotent or not."

As one reads further, the central interest that begins to emerge as underlying such discussions of the claims of will and desire in sexuality, is a concern which engaged nineteenth-century scientists and pseudoscientists alike, namely the mind/body problem,[3] here especially as it complicated what sexologists had noted as the characteristic relations between lustful thoughts, including those induced by pornography, and lustful acts, including those performed unconsciously, such as wet dreams, and those performed involuntarily, such as erections and ejaculations. Acton, "considering these phenomena," quotes Carpenter on "the very obscure subject of dreams," and ends up maintaining that "the modified power of control by the will does, I believe, almost invariably exist in lascivious dreams." Not only can the will control thought, but even apparently involuntary physiological events are somewhat susceptible: "not that, after the orgasm itself has commenced, the will has much power to check the continuation of the muscular spasms and the ejaculatory efforts of the vesiculae, though even over these it has, when honestly exerted, no little control, being able to shorten as well as prolong the ejaculatory act." "But," Acton concludes ruefully, "to put an entire stop to it, when once commenced, is apparently impossible."

In Marcus's analysis, these ideas lead to an "anal-economic" theory of Victorian sexuality. "The sexual hygiene of continence is unmistakably founded on the idea of bowel control, and the connection of this with the fantasy of semen as money is self-explanatory. . . . [T]he youth who has learned to control his sphincter should by the same token be able to constipate his genitals." There is good evidence for such an interpretation, not only in passages Marcus quotes from Acton, but throughout the literature—as in my quotation from Milton on the relations of secretion and the nervous system. In this connection too, Marcus makes much of the metaphor "to spend," which he says "had not yet been displaced by the modern 'to come.'"[4] But however neatly it all falls into place at this level of analysis, there is something to be gained from postponing such simplifications until more of the confused Victorian beliefs about the relations of sexuality to will, imagination (fantasy), desire, and other mental activities (especially memory) have been sorted out. In particular, one wants to know why the Victorians were so afraid of masturbation and its fantasies, why they were so anxious to put the realm of fantasy—in masturbation, reverie, and even dreams—under the tight discipline of the will.

Of course the Victorians understood well enough the masturbatory use to which pornographic materials were put; what is curious and perhaps revealing is the connection they saw between lascivious thoughts and other kinds. The universal hatred of Rousseau among our authorities was no accident. Not only did he masturbate and *tell* about it (if not shamelessly, at least brazenly), but he also *thought* about it. As Marcus says, "however much Acton is for the consciously willed direction of life, he is unequivocally against turning it inward." There is much to follow up in this remark. The habit of prying "into his mental and moral character with a despicably morbid minuteness," of which Acton accuses Rousseau, is just the turn of mind that the masturbator is often assumed to possess, as another expert, D. H. Lawrence, has also affirmed in similar language already quoted in the foregoing chapter: "The only positive effect of masturbation is that it seems to release a certain mental energy, in some people. But it is mental energy which manifests itself always in the same way, in a vicious circle of analysis and impotent criticism, or else a vicious circle of false and easy sympathy, sentimentalities." Rousseau himself would have accepted much of this description of his own peculiarities. The "mental energy" Lawrence speaks of is, of course, pornographic energy, the "furtive, sneaking, cunning rubbing of an inflamed spot in the imagination."[5] It is the energy which produced not only classics and junk like *The Memoirs of a Woman of Pleasure*, and *The Amatory Experiences of a Surgeon*, and autobiographies like *My Secret Life* and *The Ups and Downs of Life*—but also works like *Julie*, *Pamela*, and a thousand other novels, variously adapted versions of the materials that feed more explicitly into *Our Lady of the Flowers*. That is to say, in Marcus's terms, it is the energy that creates fantasy rather than that which labors at authenticity. Here is Rousseau in Book IX of the *Confessions*, conceiving *Julie*:

> How could it be that with such inflammable feelings, with a heart entirely moulded for love, I had not at least once burned with love for a definite object? . . .
>
> I was meditating on this subject in the finest season of the year, in the month of June, beneath cool groves, to the song of the nightingale and the murmuring of the streams. Everything combined to plunge me once more into that too seductive indolence to which I was naturally inclined. . . . Unfortunately I started remembering the dinner at the Chateau de Toune and my meeting with those two charming girls, at the same season and in country more or less similar to the country I was in at that moment. This memory, which was the sweeter for the innocence associated with it, recalled others of the same kind to me. Soon I saw all around me the persons I had felt emotion for in my youth: Mlle Galley, Mlle de Graffenried, Mlle de Breil, Mme Basile, Mme de Larnage, my pretty music pupils, and even the enticing Guilietta, whom my heart can never forget. I saw myself surrounded by a seraglio of houris, by my old acquaintances a strong desire for whom was no new sensation to me. My blood caught fire . . .
>
> What then did I do? My reader has already guessed, if he has paid

the least attention to my progress so far. The impossibility of attaining the real persons precipitated me into the land of chimeras; and seeing nothing that existed worthy of my exalted feelings, I fostered them in an ideal world which my creative imagination soon peopled with beings after my own heart. Never was this resource more opportune, and never did it prove more fertile. In my continual ecstasies I intoxicated myself with draughts of the most exquisite sentiments that have ever entered the heart of a man. Altogether ignoring the human race, I created for myself societies of perfect creatures celestial in their virtue and in their beauty, and of reliable, tender, and faithful friends such as I had never found here below. I took such pleasure in thus soaring into the empyrean in the midst of all the charms that surrounded me, that I spent countless hours and days at it, losing all memory of anything else. No sooner had I eaten a hasty morsel than I was impatient to escape and run into my woods once more. When I was about to set out for my enchanted world and saw wretched mortals appearing to hold me down to earth, I could neither restrain nor conceal my annoyance. . . .

I saw nothing anywhere but the two charming girl friends, their man [that is Rousseau himself], their surroundings, and the country they lived in, nothing but objects created or embellished for them by my imagination. I was no longer master of myself even for a moment, the delirium never left me. After many vain efforts to banish all these fictions from my mind I was in the end altogether seduced by them, and my only occupation was to try and impose some order and sequence upon them, to turn them into a sort of a novel.

This is a description, from the writer's point of view, of an obsessive masturbation fantasy, turned to typical pornographic purposes. The account even includes the familiar special attention to the look of the manuscript: "I wrote and copied [it] out during that winter with indescribable pleasure, using for the purpose the finest gilt-edged paper, with blue and silver sand to dry the ink, and blue thread to sew my sheets together." And the effect on the reader, although not directly sexual, is nonetheless intended to be physiological: "The return of spring had redoubled my amorous delirium, and in my erotic transports I had composed for the last part of *Julie* several letters that betray the ecstatic state in which I wrote them. . . . Whoever can read those two letters without his heart softening and melting with the same emotion which inspired me to write them, had better close the book: for he is incapable of judging matters of feeling." Behind these metaphors of "softening and melting" is the tradition of various euphemisms for orgasm, and Rousseau's whole account reads like an amateur pornographer's notes on his avocation.

According to Marcus, pornographic writing, because it is private and self-indulgent, obsessive, fantasizing, and so on, is not literature. It cannot be authentic, because its autoerotic aims are necessarily hedged in with secrecy and self-deception. While it may produce orgasm, it is never really moving because the true emotions must depend on an "other," and the pornographer is the solipsist par excellence. Like Emerson, the pornographer aspires to be a "transparent eyeball" (substitute "penis"); he yearns for an impossible transcendence—"totality."

Although pleasure is his presumed object, the pornographer has no conception of true pleasure because "the idea of gratification, of an end to pleasure (pleasure being here an endless expression of retentiveness, without release) cannot develop." But all the items in this catalogue of pornography's "mad-parody" of the novel are, in fact, genuinely applicable to the mainstream of fiction from Rousseau and Richardson to Joyce, Kafka, and Genet. If pressed, Marcus might admit as much, so long as he could save Dickens, George Eliot, and a few other Victorian masters from the tradition, but it seems to me that almost all the major novelists since Jane Austen have been in the Richardsonian camp, and that, indeed, the novel has defined itself historically in just the terms Marcus uses to condemn pornography.

In any case, Rousseau is boldly guilty—in the passage I have quoted—of most of the sins of masturbation fantasy. He yearns for the "totality" Marcus accuses the pornographers of imagining. He desires "infinite pleasure," but has no idea of "gratification, an end to pleasure"—unless it is the very totality Marcus believes impossible. He is the solipsist Marcus despises, preferring his fantasies to real people. And his fantasies are secretive, self-indulgent, obsessive, even psychopathic. Obviously I do not think that is all there is to be said for Rousseau (or the tradition), but let us limit the question to these "vices."

There is, I grant, something in Rousseau's preference for fantasy over reality (or better, characters over people) that makes one uneasy. The sexual interpretation must be that the masturbator prefers his imaginary partners to any actual ones. The possibility that masturbation might provide more pleasure than ordinary copulation was familiar to the Victorians, and their explanations are worth noting. Acton says something on the subject, and seems even to associate the phenomenon with Rousseau; but Michael Ryan has the most interesting account:

> It is admitted by the most enlightened physiologists of modern times, that masturbation causes much more excitement in the whole system than sexual intercourse, and that it is more frequently repeated, and is consequently more injurious to health, and more productive of disease.
>
> M. Deslandes, a late elaborate author on the subject, is of opinion, that as the masturbator has not a material subject for the beginning and end of his pleasures, his imagination must supply and invent one, and that this mental exertion very much contributes to his subsequent depression. In such cases the mind is occupied with a lover, a married or single woman, a former wife or mistress, or some amorous vagary which greatly excites the nervous system. Prints, statues, public exhibitions, and a variety of other subjects, are fixed on by the imagination; and the mechanical force employed is more stimulating than the natural.
>
> It is also to be recollected, that this solitary vice may be perpetrated by either sex, as often as the person pleases, while the compliance of the opposite sex is not always, or so frequently, to be obtained.

Implicit in this account is the quite correct opinion that the excitement peculiar to masturbation (in *some* ways more intense than *some* fornication) derives from the imagination of persons, real or fanciful, about whose images cluster, as we learn from Rousseau or Proust, deeply attached and often extremely ambivalent emotions. These images, for good or ill, are like the powerfully affecting images of dreams. Although consciously cultivated and transformed—memories converted into fantasies—they nonetheless express unconscious organizations of fear and desire. I suppose what makes us uneasy about Rousseau is that we recognize something of our own experience in his. In any case, he forces us to consider the way in which we all "play authors" of our own past, choosing and distorting our memories according to feelings rather than facts:

I have only one faithful guide on which I can count: the succession of feelings which have marked the development of my being, and thereby recall the events that have acted upon it as cause or effect. I easily forget my misfortunes, but I cannot forget my faults, and still less my genuine feelings. The memory of them is too dear ever to be effaced from my heart. I may omit or transpose facts, or make mistakes in dates; but I cannot go wrong about what I have felt, or about what my feelings have led me to do; and these are the chief subjects of my story.

Implicit in Rousseau's words is the recognition that the memories he most desires to retain and transmit are largely fantasy, not a matter of dates and facts but of feelings and the structures of human relationship that both excite and represent feelings. In pornography as in masturbation, the same pattern of memory and fantasy feeds into the solitary imagination, giving expression to deep and often conflicting emotions. Even more than Rousseau's visions, the usual pornographic and masturbatory scenes are extremely schematic, having been imagined so many times and, in the case of pornography, by so many minds that most of the nuances have rubbed off.

The obsessive impulse in question here is not that which leads to the writing of history or historical fiction, but rather that which, in combination with other impulses already identified in Rousseau—secrecy, self-indulgence, self-absorption, willfulness—issues in confession literature generally, including all those fictional varieties which have in common the need to ground their "revelations" in supposed or actual memories, no matter how bare of remembered or invented detail they turn out to be. The excitement of the imagined is, as the Victorian medical authorities understood, much greater for these authors and their readers than that of actual encounters with life. Memories themselves are stimulating not as fragments of a loved certitude that something has happened, but as gritty, irritating uncertainties about which the secretions of emotional life build layers of fantasy, like a pearl. Such memories even lose their identity as memory, and become the bare and abstract fantasies boringly reiterated in the trashiest pornography.

Memory, screened as Rousseau seems almost to recognize, is crucial in the masturbator's fantasy, whether structured as memoir or as fiction. Perhaps the memories involved are most deeply those of childhood (the typical voyeurism of pornography is no doubt, in Freudian terms, peeking at the primal scene), but in literature the content is rarely so important as the medium or mechanism of imagination. Thus many sorts of content may minister to sexual stimulation—as fetish literature strongly proves. Proust has a classic statement of this emphasis:

But none of the feelings which the joys or misfortunes of a "real" person awaken in us can be awakened except through a mental picture of those joys or misfortunes; and the ingenuity of the first novelist lay in his understanding that, as the picture was the one essential element in the complicated structure of our emotions, so that simplification of it which consisted in the suppression, pure and simple, of "real" people would be a decided improvement. . . .

The novelist has brought us to that state, in which, as in all purely mental states, every emotion is multiplied tenfold, into which his book comes to disturb us as might a dream, but a more lucid, and of a more lasting impression, than those which come to us in sleep.

In the process of "recapturing the past" the sorts of "real" things that give pleasure are not potent until disembodied by their pastness. We should compare the similar preference of Rousseau for the non-physical, and the testimony of Acton et al. on the problem of mind and body. The great paradox of masturbation is the ability of the masturbator to excite himself by non-physical means. Of course, there are usually physical means used as well, but that seems of less interest to all contributors to the discussion, whether for or against the practice. Thus the Victorian physicians focus on the nocturnal emission (compare Proust's emphasis on dreams) as the most difficult case needing treatment, where the mind alone produces orgasm. These authorities are also fond of enumerating cases of erection and ejaculation brought on by horseback-riding, walking fast, sitting on hard chairs, and the like. What essentially fascinates them is any case of "involuntary emission," the chief symptom of spermatorrhea. One suspects the real meaning—or at least the best metaphor—for all these concerns is the simplest occurrence in sexual life, the erection. The "involuntary" onset of erection might seem particularly puzzling—even frightening to the childish imagination—because, unlike breathing or other similar physiological events, it is not regular or cyclic. Most important, it is ordinarily accompanied by related mental activity, if not volitional then at least causal. In this subject we have already seen the nineteenth-century sexologists displaying the keenest interest. The enemies of masturbation and pornography (including Lawrence and Marcus) quite rightly realize that the battle must be fought against the imagination (fantasy, the pleasure principle), which must be kept strictly under the control of the will (authenticity, the reality principle) if it is to be prevented from giving rise to irrevocable physical acts. Pornographers and masturbators, on the other hand, have as their ideal a fantasy so powerful that it results in orgasm without any "physical" stimulation. Here too the will enters in, but not antagonistically: the ideal is, in fact, "voluntary emission"—orgasm at will.

Pornographers are frequently moved, or so they assert, by their own descriptions. Marcus quotes an instance from *The Amatory Experiences of a Surgeon*: "What an orgy of lust we enacted that night. It seemed heavenly to me at the time, and even now as I write these lines my old cock stands at the remembrance of it." Marcus comments, "the possibilities suggested by this device, and the assumption of identity it makes between the author and his readers, do not require further discussion." The device does tempt remark, since it epitomizes so much of what pornography has in common with the whole tradition of sentimental fiction. Given our discussion so far, some things are immediately apparent—for example, the perfectly appropriate use of the erection as the symbol of the power of fantasy-memory to provoke response. But there are further aspects of the device, considered as characteristic, to be explored. Marcus himself has some instructive ideas on the subject elsewhere in his book, though he seems not to make the connection here: "in [pornography]—as in the mind of a child—no distinction is made between thought and deed, wish and reality, between what ought to exist, what one wants to exist, and what does in fact exist. It is a fantasy whose special preconditioning requirement is that it deny, delay, and stave off for as long as possible the recognition that it is a fantasy. Recognition dispels the dream of omnipotence and returns one to oneself, alone and palely loitering on the cold hill's side." It is hard to understand Marcus's objection to pornography in these terms, since the attempt to bridge the gap "between thought and deed, wish and reality . . . what ought to exist . . . and what does in fact exist," is quite thoroughly established as the great heroic exploit of the nineteenth century—the central effort of *Daniel Deronda*, Mill's *Autobiography*, *Alice in Wonderland*, of Melville and Tolstoy, of Emerson and Kierkegaard and Marx, wherever one looks. It was precisely the formulation of Blake and Wordsworth that the loss of the child's ability to *not* make the distinction was the disastrous beginning of the modern world. Many Victorians could go no further than to advise that we learn to live with the disjunction, but our own century's favorite heroes of the past are those who refused to embrace the simple "fact and fancy" dichotomy of *Hard Times*, a novel Dickens grew beyond. And in particular it was the novelists who plotted the characteristic nineteenth-century solution, the reuniting of "reality" and "fantasy" in fiction itself.

None of this is especially newsy, nor is the failure of the nineteenth-century effort, at least in so far as it has led to the modern predicament, likely to be disputed. The point rather is that the pornographer's contribution, a certain blend of realism and fantasy, memory and desire, is hardly to be dismissed as irrelevant or un-literary or vicious, on *these* grounds, shared with most of the novelists. Moreover, it is an oversimplification to say that the pornographers do not distinguish "between thought and deed, wish and reality." There are degrees of awareness among writers who work in the tradition of Rousseau, but even the most self-conscious and articulate, like Proust, are not in their methodology so far removed from the stupidest retailers of smut, and none are fooled by their own fantasies, nor do their readers imagine that the things described are actually happening—any more than the author or reader of a recipe is fooled into thinking he is eating when his mouth waters at the thought of it.

Presumably one might establish levels or stages of effect on a reader according to how these effects are apparent in his physical condition: heavy breathing, tears, a lump in the throat, smiles, erection, orgasm. To distinguish simply two classes, mental and physical effects, is to fall into the mind/body problem the Victorians were trying to clamber out of, a mistake which I suspect lies behind Marcus's insistence that pornography is not literature, is indeed anti-literary. "There is, on the face of it, nothing illegitimate about a work whose purpose or intention is to arouse its readers sexually. If it is permissible for works of literature to move us to tears, to arouse our passions against injustice, to make us cringe with horror, and to purge us through pity and terror, then it is equally permissible—it lies within the orbit of literature's functions—for works of literature to arouse us sexually." This is Marcus's most generous concession, and he makes it to save *Ulysses* and *Madame Bovary* as literature; but he immediately qualifies: "Literature possesses, however, a multitude of intentions, but pornography possesses only one." What these other intentions are, Marcus is not here obliged to say, but one gathers that, at their "most literary," they are chiefly mental effects, while "pornography falls into the same category as such simpler forms of literary utterance as propaganda and advertising. Its aim is to move us in the direction of action." In fact, as any reader of pornography knows, there are many combinations of purposes to be found in the dirtiest books, even if we limit criteria to the uses they are put to by readers. Moreover, these same readers often use "Literature" for similar purposes. And finally, even limiting the case to those purposes we might think of as sexual, there is still a wide range of effects, from the low level, "soft-core" pornography of the sensibility school (as Paul Krassner says, it "gives you a soft-on"), to the sexualized reverie of Rousseau, the self-conscious and self-indulgent sublimation of Proust, or the anti-sexual sexuality of, say, Kafka and Genet—not to mention the concomitant result, orgasm, which may or may not occur in any of these varieties.

According to Marcus, who does not recognize any of these varieties or degrees, the literary genre to which pornography is most akin is "the utopian fantasy." His catalogue of the paradigmatic features of "pornotopia" includes elements that do indeed appear in some utopian fiction—the isolated setting (castles, islands, etc.), the animated landscape (as in dreams, a body-image, here invariably female), the "abstract" nature of the relations between the characters (and their sexual organs), the "compulsion to repeat," the impatience with the limitations of language, in general the "projective" characteristics of all fantasy—but we do not get a dynamically conceived account of the genre, an analysis of how the parts are necessary to each other and to the whole. To be fair to Marcus's insight we should say that, although pornographic fiction is not like all utopian fantasy, it does share with it the status of sub-genre, both being varieties of the gothic novel.

It is too far off our present track to show in any detail how utopian fantasy differs from its sister or parent genres, nor do I have space here to develop the theory of the gothic novel very far, but some of its outlines may be sketched in, to show its relation to pornography—and, by the way, to the confessional literature we have already linked with pornography. I hope thereby to explain at least part of the meaning of pornography as a genre, the interrelation of its parts, and perhaps even something of its genesis and its attraction. So that I may abbreviate more conveniently, I will avoid full examples, but I have in mind as models Hoffmann's *The Devil's Elixirs*, Lewis's *The Monk*, Maturin's *Melmoth the Wanderer*, Emily Bronte's *Wuthering Heights*, Hawthorne's *The House of the Seven Gables*, and Kafka's *The Castle*.

The gothic novel has an episodic structure, and as in pornography, the episodes are repetitive. This combination of episode and repetition produces (or represents), in the gothic, an ambivalence toward history:

events repeat themselves in succeeding generations, thus undercutting ideas of duration, sequence, temporal cause and effect. The typical formula is the family curse, which is worked out over long periods of time as if in a single moment. Theoretically the novel could continue forever repeating this moment: in fact, the family usually dies out, or is rescued from the curse by the author allowing a symbolic dying-out to occur. In Marcus's example from pornography, *The Lustful Turk*, the symbolic conclusion of the "curse," and the book itself, is the castration of the hero—the end of the generation.

In the most sophisticated cases, the characters must concern themselves with the nature of memory, history, and fate, since these are the terms in which their problem is set. The question of free will plagues either characters or author, generally without resolution. The hero is supposed to be his own victim as well as the victim of his ancestors, and his demons are figments of his imagination "dreamed into" actual existence. In this way, history is "made" by its heroes. Time and space are "inner" and dreamlike, and the plot is not a narrative but a tableau continually reimagined and relived. As in dream, the action is visual, and the meaning hinges on juxtapositions of symbolic content. A characteristic tableau is Oedipal: two men, one with a knife, standing on the threshold of a woman's bedroom, all three related by blood.

Several methods of structural representation are common. The interpolated story provides a convenient way of giving repetition the illusion of progression—as in the "infinite regress" of *Melmoth the Wanderer*. This method is a favorite with pornographers too. A more revealing technique is the generational chronicle as in Hoffmann, who combines it with the interpolated story (as do Hawthorne and Emily Bronte). In both methods, the heroes of the repeated tableaux nearly always resemble each other, and are frequently doubles. In the generational chronicle, family inheritance accounts for the likeness and also enforces the symbolic point, that the same man (scion) is being afflicted by (is inflicting upon himself) the same recurrent nightmare. Genetically, this is to be explained as the author's own obsession, the characters being projections and fragmentations of the self. Audience reaction would be analyzed similarly.

What is "gained" by this repetition? In some instances it is cathartic, but in the usual case it is merely expressive, a repeated acting-out which does not come to thinking-out. Typically there is a kind of problem posed, but this is a screen for the real intention, namely, to bring repressed matter to the consciousness. The problem is: what would happen next (say, at the threshold of the room)? The answer is usually a given: it is what has already happened, to set the curse going. This throws the answer into the infinite regress. All such "narrative" problems and solutions are a screen, as Kafka discovered, for problems of perception and will (see the climax of *The Castle*, where K falls asleep). For the most sophisticated gothic novelists, the question is not one of what will happen next, but what is real, and what is the author/hero's responsibility for reality.

One answer to these last questions is implicit in the system of surrogates that the gothic makes use of, different characters standing in for the author/hero in the repeated scenes. Reality, the argument would go, is my dream. It is this wish/fear that the novelist is testing. The very common threat of the "abyss"—a fall into oblivion, as in Poe—seems to be a corollary structure. If the character relaxes his watchfulness, reality will disintegrate. From the genetic point of view, the author must *will* reality (his story) into existence: when he stops exerting his imagination, reality stops too, and then there is nothing. This danger lies behind all gothic terror. Equivalents in pornography are willed sexual play, with the emphasis on control of the foreplay, which may lead either to orgasm (oblivion, courted and feared) or to impotence (symbolically the same loss of power and control). A further twist, in both the gothic and pornography, is the frequent sense that the will is helplessly in the hands of fate (merely the other side of the coin, another symbolic equivalency): thus the awe at the phenomenon of involuntary erection, the fear of loss of control, the ambition of "orgasm at will" (*choosing* oblivion).

In the ordinary novel the end comes when the possibilities of combination given at the beginning have been exhausted. In the gothic, since there is only one possible combination, given in tableau, the end comes only with physical exhaustion pure and simple, or with a leap (as in *The Castle*) outside the realm of the given. In every case, this leap is a *deus ex machina*, since to abandon the given is to admit to being the author, and to refocus attention on what it means to write (imagine, dream). In pornography, the leap is similar, from the world of the projected reality to the author/reader's own body and act of ejaculation. If the end is thus non-literary in one way, it nonetheless says something about literature, a phenomenological comment on the relation of imagination and reality (in Victorian terms, mind and body). This comment is essentially different from that which the endings of other novels suggest, since in most gothic fiction and pornography there is no true plot (only a tableau) and therefore can be no buildup of probabilities for the leap; rather there are continual and equally unsuccessful attempts, suddenly ended by climactic success, through a shift of the attention, a relaxation of the will and watchfulness. The experience of masturbators fantasizing (with or without pornography) is similar. Success is intentional but not part of a predictable sequence. The sequence *is* predictable (repetitive, not really a sequence), but the moment of success (relaxation, orgasm) is not. Of course, in most gothic and pornographic fiction (*as* fiction), the leap never comes at all, or (curiously) is not recognized when it does come. Usually the novel goes on regardless. I confess I do not understand this failure of recognition, but one thing is clear, that the line between fantasy and reality in reading gothic and pornographic fiction is a torn and ragged edge, as compared with the careful knitting-up of loose threads of probability in other genres.

Given this structure—there is a good deal more to be said about it—certain facts about the language of pornography and of the gothic begin to cohere systematically. The concrete/abstract paradox noted by Marcus in pornographic language is, of course, a favorite observation of readers of Kafka. The problem centers around the referential theory of language, which has been the bane of most linguistic philosophy from Locke to Wittgenstein. Marcus says of the characteristic cliches of pornography, "such words function as non-specific abstractions—they can all be filled with the same general content. On the other [hand], to the extent that they become verbally non-referential, they express an important tendency in pornography." In particular, Marcus says that "the forbidden, tabooed words" of pornography "are minimally verbal, that they are still felt as acts, that they have not been dissociated from the tissue of unconscious impulses in which they took their origin." Behind Marcus's observations here lies the referential theory of language, constructed on the paradigm *noun* equals *name* equals *thing*. Not only is this paradigm inadequate to the ordinary operation of verbs, adjectives, etc., but it is equally misleading as an account of the way most nouns function in the usual forms of discourse. Marcus is correct to suppose that pornography moves away from the referential use of language toward an expressive, or "active" use; moreover, he is also right (following Ian Watt) in thinking that the tradition of realism in the novel has often justified itself by appeal to the theory of reference, intimately tied up for the realist with the theory of mimesis. The mistake is to suppose that one use (or theory) of language is more "authentic" or true than the other. Each is limited to saying what it can say. In the gothic, as in pornography, language "says things into existence," as in Poe's "The Power of Words," and if this is a linguistic function akin to advertising and propaganda, it is not less literary for that, only less bound to a certain set of conventions about the relations of words and things. The language of pornography and of the gothic novel is closer to the oral tradition (the dirty joke, the ghost story), which has more successfully preserved speech-as-act than has the "Gutenberg" tradition.

Even the realistic convention has as one of its aims *moving* the reader, but the gothic and pornographic modes go further, directly involving the reader less as observer than as participant. To put it another way, the sort of writing Marcus admires as "authentic" is chiefly concerned with *describing*, a matter seemingly of mentioning, naming, referring. Pornography and the gothic—Marcus's "fantasy"—are rather concerned with *creating*, a matter of talking about what does not exist in order to bring it into being (as, for example, Pickwick—a favorite instance of the linguistic philosophers who discuss the subject). Obviously, realistic fiction, so far as it is fiction at all, is also dependent on the creating power of language; the most sophisticated pornographic and gothic fiction, however, tends to shift this power into the center of attention, so that method becomes subject matter. This tendency fits in with the stake these genres have in memory, imagination, and the will. Caught, as they often are, between the referential and the creative theories of language, these authors are struggling toward a synthesis such as that of Proust or Kafka, a kind of "authentic fantasy" to use Marcus's terms.

Before leaving the subject of the relations of pornography and the gothic, I would like to treat one aspect of their conjunction in more detail. I have alluded more than once to the idea or condition of "totality," which Marcus condemns the pornographers for aspiring to. I have also spent a good deal of time discussing the conflict of will and desire as understood by Victorian physicians, and especially as reflected in their belief that lascivious fantasies, waking or dreaming, could be controlled by the will. We have seen how the pornographer similarly attempts to control the imagination by the will, although his ends are quite different—voluntary orgasm rather than continence. Let me now bring these matters together, in order to see what light the theory of the gothic novel may shed on them.

Victorian authorities on sex point out that masturbation is more exciting (and thus dangerous) than copulation, because the imagination is more powerful a stimulus than the senses themselves. Rousseau and others agree, in their terms, with this priority. It follows, for those who desire the strongest excitement, that even in actual copulation, the imagination and will should be exercised as in masturbation, in the production of fantasy.

Masturbation fantasies are typically visual, and the imagination of pornographers and gothic writers is typically spatial and visual, as the structural principle of the tableau demonstrates. It follows for the case of the "masturbator" who is actually copulating that his greatest pleasures will be voyeuristic—often a matter of adjusting the positions of his partners to his favorite visions. The multiplication of such posturings, by increasing the number of partners, by mirrors, and so on, is also familiar. Masturbating by means of a partner is, then, not simply a matter of having a fantasy, but of regarding an actual, physical and visual, situation as if a fantasy. (Much "normal" sexual intercourse follows this pattern: thus our partners are often more beautiful than familiar, more agitating than sooth-ing; the well-known psychotic extreme is "Romantic Love.")

We have already seen that the power of fantasy largely derives from the attachment of deep feelings to certain "core" memories, as in Rousseau. These memories are the material for the tableaux of the gothic, "family memories," in the form of a curse handed down from generation to genera-tion. Repetition is preferred to novelty in these obsessive fantasies because the emotion attached to the past (structured into the character) does not so much arise from the fantasy as give rise to it. The fantasy expresses the feelings. The reality is brought into existence by the desire for it. Or, to put the matter in terms that confront the Victorian problem of will and im-agination, the mind imagines the world necessary to its wishes. That world then exists.

None of these relations are reciprocal or mutual. They are "one-way," like the infinite regress. In gothic fiction, this is often perceived as fate: how can the hero break the chain of fantasies-growing-into-reality when they arise out of his own deepest wishes (the family curse)? In pornography the equivalent is what Marcus most objects to, the "letch"-ridden hero's return again and again to the "same" keyhole or cunt, the impossibility, as Marcus puts it, of gratification—an end to pleasure. Of course, the point is that there are, in pornography, innumerable ends to pleasure, an infinite series of orgasms. I cannot believe that what Marcus wants is some final orgasm—but then I do not know what else he can mean. In any case, it does seem to me that something of the sort *is* what the pornographer wants—not an end to desire (though perhaps that is implied) but an endless orgasm, the oblivion or loss of self that Freud calls "absolute gratification" and that Marcus calls "totality."

The striving for totality manifests itself in pornography and in gothic fiction in a characteristic way. Given the repetitive structure of these genres, no buildup can grow in the narrative. Yet to achieve totality, each repeated version of the same scene would seem to require some increase of power. Generally this is accomplished by the multiplication (fragmentation) of characters, so that either the descendants of the original hero become more numerous, or if not actually, then symbolically they multiply—in Hoffmann the family breeds in, incestuously, so that each character represents the whole family, while in Hawthorne the ghosts of the dead ancestors hover in the room or the memory. In pornography, familiar bodies from the earlier portions of the novel begin to turn up, or the hero begins to reminisce about old times with new lays. Since the power of the fantasy depends on the accumulation of feelings clinging to a single repeated and remembered scene, the multiplication of characters (each representing an earlier representation of the scene) increases the excitement. In pornographic, gothic, and confessional literature, this multiplication is often symbolically represented by an *affair à trois*— usually two men and a woman, as most commonly in *My Secret Life*, sometimes one man and two women, as in Rousseau's fantasy for *Julie*. The underlying model for such *affaires à trois* is not the triangle, which implies a return of the self and thus a sort of reciprocity (Marcus thinks of the daisy chain as the appropriate model), but is rather the infinite regress we have recognized as a familiar motif, in which there is no mutual stimulation, only unilateral, essentially voyeuristic pleasure. A number of variations occur, but few seem genuinely triangular—mutually pleasurable to all three parties. For example, the author of *My Secret Life* has a particular fondness for intercourse with a woman who has just left another client. Or, frequently in pornography, the narrator describes mounting someone who is mounting someone else. Female narrators, for instance Justine, are often at the other end of the same broken chain, being mounted by two persons at once, an equally unilateral situation from the narrator's point of view.

The symbolic meaning of such an infinite regress is complex. The situation is essentially voyeuristic, as descriptions of such orgies make clear. The excitement comes from watching, either the other or oneself—and this watching is a fantasy, a memory wrapped in sentiment. The other in these cases is representative of *all* the others and thus a convenient means of rendering the central attraction of such fantasy, the accumulation of past feelings and reliving them all at once. This is one reason why pornography generally delays the orgy until late in the book, when there is more to recall. Finally, the fact that the narrator is always at one or the other end (the opposite end is nowhere, the longed-for totality) gives the sense of absolute control by the will of the narrator, who typically (as the author of *My Secret Life*) settles the order and duties of those "in line" himself, whose penis is the initial energizing force, all the other organs beating to his time. Sometimes this is thought of as "giving pleasure," but at bottom it is most evidently the desire to control the other, to produce (and watch) an effect, simply to exert the will (with the concomitant fear of relaxing one's watchfulness—that is, orgasm).

Often (perhaps always) the infinite regress scene just described is not only the culminating fantasy of the book (pornography or gothic tale) but also the very fantasy which, in some limited or disguised way lies behind all the previous ones. In gothic fiction that attempts to give the illusion of plot, the action usually amounts to a progressive uncovering of this final scene (for example, at the outset we do not know of what the curse consists, but at the conclusion we discover, in an old manuscript, that it was *this*, and all intermediate scenes have been approximations of it). Furthermore, while the meaning of the scene is rather obviously Oedipal on the surface of it (the threesome equals parents plus child), its deeper meaning seems to me not sexual but metaphysical (or epistemological)—a representation of the relation of self and other. That both pornography and the gothic tradition conceive this relation as unilateral seems not necessarily a failing of those genres (in spite of Marcus's Christian humanist complaints), but rather an indication of the nature of fiction and of the fictive imagination—the subject of the most sophisticated gothic novels. Ultimately gothic and pornographic fictions drive the reader back out of fantasy, however much they may seduce him to it in the meantime, for the effects of terror or orgasm, especially the latter, most obviously take place in the world of everyday reality, unreal and total and absolute as they may seem in that world. That they also take place in private, in the absence of others, is less significant than it may seem—for the orgasm, as other bodily experiences, is always a private experience no matter how its achievement is managed.

The gothic and pornographic writers, in one degree or another, are concerned with the brute fact that man is trapped in his own skin, and the fantasies of these genres explore the possibilities of escaping the prison of the senses, through the agency of the imagination. The failure of the genres is not in their refusal to recognize or allow for the other, but in their inability to reach it (at the opposite end of the infinite regress) despite every effort to believe that they will or do. This failure is given in the nature of the attempt. I would point again to *The Castle*, where K most nearly approaches his goal when he allows himself to recede furthest from it, to give up the striving of the wakeful will. (Compare Aphorism 23: "There is a goal, but no way; what we call the way is only wavering.") This is the "leap" I spoke of earlier, which is the only delivery there is from the infinite regress. It is not something which the hero can accomplish as an exploit, or the author as a tour de force; it is achieved only by "letting up," by an act of faith that the other is there, and need not be proved or attained. (This was the very sensible advice many Victorian physicians gave to victims of impotence.) The pornographer and the gothic novelist attempt to be the voice of God, to say the *logos* that brings the other into being; but the other is the voice of God, which must be listened to, not created. These are not the limits of pornography, but the limits of literature, and of all saying, which cannot call into being an answering voice. Our words make a world, but that world passes with those words. It is willful exercise, dependent on the continual exertion of the mind. It is the nature of writing, to make something of experience, to give it meaning. Books and libraries are man's determined effort to create meaning and hold it in existence, by force of will. One does not find anything but the elaboration of self—no matter how admirable—in this realm, humility, love, prayer, notwithstanding. For the rest, it is well to remember that there are possibilities in life quite beyond literature, and not even to be imitated in it. Such literature as we have been discussing so reminds us.

7

Adam and Everyman:
Paul Goodman in His Stories

I

Paul Goodman lived just short of sixty-one years. He began writing stories in high school (poems much earlier), and produced a book a year for the rest of his life—fiction, poetry, drama, social criticism, literary analysis, psychoanalytic theory, etc. He called himself "a man of letters" to account for the range of his interests, but he valued the poems and stories above all his other work. They would last.

He composed in pencil and always had some stub in his pocket, along with the scraps and used envelopes on which he wrote most of his poems. His stories were written in longhand on the cheapest newsprint, now brown and crumbling; he used every inch right to the edge of the paper. The second draft was typed, expertly, and he sometimes made further corrections in pencil before sending it to an editor. After publication he sometimes revised again, on the printed pages, whether or not there was any likelihood of a new edition. Manuscripts were discarded like husks, so that there was rarely more than one version, always in process, alive, the cambium layer of his imagination.

Eager as he was for publication, he did not work for the sake of final products. A few stories were still being retouched a full generation after writing; readers complained that he spoiled their favorites, "The Lordly Hudson" and *The Grand Piano*, with second thoughts. All this goes to show a passion for writing itself, the act rather than the result. It was, as he

149

frequently bragged, his vice, or more affirmatively, his "way of being in the world."

During different periods in his life he fell into different habits; up to the age of about thirty-five he was a night-owl, and told people he did his best work between two and four *a.m.* But morning, afternoon, or night he had one inviolable rule of thumb: write at least a page a day. This was enough to become involved with the material, so that on good days he might continue working well beyond that minimum. Since he threw very little away, this means that his average output should have been about a book a year—just as it was.

One is reminded of the stories about Trollope, writing by the clock and breaking off for luncheon in the middle of a sentence. In Goodman's case, however, the crucial factor was not discipline but method—or better, rhythm. That is to say, it was not the daily stint that produced so much, but the daily temptation to do what he loved to do, to lose himself in his work. There was something almost physiological about it. In his style, in his very character, there was a flow that fed this rhythm, so that if the first page went well, he was likely to complete an entire section in a sitting. His typical unit of composition was just that long—what he could write in a sitting. It was like breathing to him, second nature.

The enormous advantage of such a combination of habits and intentions is obvious. The act of authorship is thereby rescued from the tediousness and drudgery of all long-term, open-ended pursuits, where the moment of completion lies at some ultimate point, not known till it suddenly arrives, little solace for the pleasures and frustrations buried along the way. Perhaps especially for a writer like Goodman, who never quite let go of his works but kept on tinkering with them even after they were printed, this potential for daily achievement and closure was indispensable. I think it was the secret of his productivity.

Goodman's prose rhythm developed out of his devotion to the short story. In that genre he could always work with episodes of the right length. The manuscripts that survive are scarcely smudged or interlined, and many of them have a rhapsodic quality, almost chanted, with little trace of any pause longer than the time it might take to whittle a pencil sharp. In his long works these episodes were easily accumulated into larger wholes, loose structures of emotion and event that often seem like prose poems.

Although from the beginning he preferred the rhapsodic episode, he also wrote "scenes," somewhat in the manner of Maupassant. Much of his juvenilia struggles in this straitjacket, and one can watch the progressive releasing of his powers as he discovered models that encouraged him to follow his own bent. His creative writing teacher at City College accused him of imitating Joyce, but he had darker corners to explore: Ring Lardner and Sherwood Anderson, Cocteau and the obscure surrealist Pierre MacOrlean. Most of all, he learned from Hawthorne, who taught him that a story was like a dream.

Hawthorne was Goodman's favorite writer of stories, and he borrowed so heavily from him, and was in some ways so similar, that it helps to keep him in mind while considering Goodman's career. Like Hawthorne, he wrote an undergraduate novel which he then suppressed, turning instead to a genre that allowed for youthful experiment at less risk. When Hawthorne finally returned to the novel, after twenty years, he did so more or less by accident, and he never really abandoned the episodic method. Goodman did not wait so long to try out the possibilities of the novel-in-stories: he began his first, *Johnson*, soon after he graduated, and his second, *The Break-Up of Our Camp*, followed in a few years. These books were experimental, for Goodman never stopped trying out different forms, but though more complex and ambitious than his stories, the same raw materials went into them, and they were composed according to the same pattern of small units. A number of their chapters were published in magazines as separate stories—obviously part of the plan, another idea he may have gotten from Hawthorne.

Like most of his early fiction, these books were based on Goodman's own experience. *Johnson* was part of a campaign to win the affections of the "black-blond sea-lion" who inspired its fantasies, and *The Break-Up of Our Camp* was also written in the midst of its scenes, the Jewish boys' camp where Goodman worked as dramatics counselor in the mid-thirties. He seems often to have preferred to write about the things going on around him, as if they might still be soft to the impress of the imagination. The history of love poetry is full of precedent for the conversion of sexual longing into literature, but *The Break-Up of Our Camp* is not about love at all. By the time he wrote it, Goodman was so confirmed in his art that, through a curious twist of the usual order, all experience had been potentially eroticized for him. He was not an ambulance-chaser, looking for stories to tell, but everything that happened to him was doubly quickened, like living at risk or under a vow; if it came to nothing in life, it might in art.

This was not all to the good. Life could become too artful, while art stared and ogled shamelessly. One result was a strong tendency toward symbolism, of the self-examining sort found in those tales of Hawthorne that deal with the temptations of the imagination, "Young Goodman Brown," "Wakefield," or *The Scarlet Letter*. All through the *Johnson* stories Goodman plays with these possibilities of watching the self from the perspective of its other avatars, like Chillingworth gazing rapt into the soul of Dimmesdale. But for Hawthorne it was the unpardonable sin, while for Goodman it was simply a fact of life for the artist, to make the self an object of contemplation.

The short story format lends itself to such interests by not setting up complex narrative expectations; one is alone with the author and his thoughts. Dedicating his last book of stories in 1968, Goodman acknowledged his debt not only to Hawthorne's tales but also to Beethoven's piano sonatas, a model that suggests something of the almost abstract self-communing that his stories facilitate with their harmonies of tone, symmetries, formal rhythms independent of any threads of plot. More like dreams than anything else, these patterns are only partially in the control of the artist—which is why in his best work they seem to express character rather than mere attitude or tone. It was to this level of the self he wanted to dive. Sometimes, as in most of the *Johnson* stories, he merely arranges his motifs without finding this stronger current, but then he will strike upon it in the midst of formal exercises, in the breathtaking surges of "The Tennis-Game" or "Out of Love." It cannot be an accident that these are occasions when Johnson himself is suddenly translated out of his ordinary consciousness to a new state of awareness, where everything is luminous. One begins to understand Goodman's addiction to writing, and its reciprocation with his everyday life.

The Break-Up of Our Camp is also a formal *tour de force*, and in touch with deeper sources of feeling. Not that there is anything flashy or even very dramatic in it. Most of the moments one remembers come in passages of quiet prose: the survey of the crowded mess-hall, when the dramatics counselor's eye falls on the camper "Winkie, who did not yet know—but I knew—that he was going to be Macbeth"; or the comical departure of the camp owner, "Huffski Puffski Ben Tumpowski," just a hop-skip-and-jump ahead of the sheriff; or the laconic exchange between the narrator and a Vermont farmer looting the premises before the last occupants have left.[1] One by one these little unveilings have a mild, almost picturesque turn, but their lasting effect is disturbing rather than calming. For one thing, these are merely odd moments, unimportant events, not the hinges of action. Why remember them? And after all, what *are* the important events? This is a vision of the last days, collapse, decay, and the saving remnant. Again comparison to Hawthorne is hard to resist, for the shadowy unease engendered is precisely that of *The House of the Seven Gables*.

Where were all these habits and pleasures leading him?—the rhapsodic method, the toying with experience, the addiction to risks, the incessant experimenting, and the drift away from realism into symbolism. It was all part of a general decision to follow impulse at any cost, soon to surprise him in the turn it took.

II

In March 1936, not long after finishing the first draft of *The Break-Up of Our Camp*, Goodman began a new story with the unpromising title "Prose Composition." Its subtitle was more descriptive—"sustained—rapid—jokes—slow—forthright—and disturbed"—but scarcely adequate to the revolution it represented in his literary method. During the next four years Goodman wrote another dozen like it, and all the rest of his fiction in the late thirties shifted more or less drastically in style and manner depending on just where in the wake of these "prose compositions" it lay.

Goodman quickly realized that it was a turning point for him. Before long he had given his new literary manner a more prepossessing name—cubism. Four years later he was thinking of it as his "cubist period"—though he never quite said it so pompously—and was planning a collection of stories to commemorate it, including a preface in which he provided the following theory of his own practice:

> Now by literary *Cubism* let us here understand not abstraction from subject-matter, but in the presentation of subject-matter an accompanying emphasis and independent development of the signifying means. And in effect this means, if the work hangs together, that the relations of the characters, thoughts, and acts will seem to be partly advanced by the mere literary handling, apart from their natural or imaginary relations. In a scientific work this is of course a dangerous fallacy, the "literary fallacy"; but in literary works it gives a literary, formal quality to the subject-matter which is to my taste excellent.

Goodman's theory of literary manner was really a theory of art and alienation. The various manners—realism, naturalism, symbolism, cubism, and so forth—were analyzed according to their formal characteristics, and these in turn were correlated with "author-attitude," the social and psychological interaction of a writer with his world. *Realism* was accepted as a sort of norm of fiction, representing the "harmony between the author's sense of what is meaningful and at least the potentiality of the scene accurately described." There is no alienation here, and whatever "problems" come into focus—for instance, as in Jane Austen—are seen against a background of tolerable institutions and reasonable conventions. *Naturalism* however begins to express "latent alienation by a malicious or indignant selection of the pointless or unsavory, tho usually relieved by youthful compassion." Goodman's own early work fell in this category, the tradition of Dreiser and Ring Lardner. The formula of *Symbolism* goes a step further: "it is intolerable that the scene should be merely what it seems, it must contain also some other meaning." This was what he discovered in *The Break-Up of Our Camp* when he came to revise it in the early forties: his uneasiness with the naturalistic presentation led him to explore beneath the surface—not so much to causes as to "contexts of causes," the hidden psychic contents looming larger than mere chains of event or even the motives and dispositions of his characters. Finally, the *Cubism* at which he had arrived in 1936–1940 represents a further retreat from conventional subject matter, to "inventive play in the literary medium itself, more or less abstracted from the represented scene. . . . One can easily see genetically how the passage from method to method described above would lead to abstraction, if (a) the art seemed more and more worth the trouble and (b) the scene seemed less and less worth the trouble."

Such theorizing can help a reader understand what Goodman was up to in his "prose compositions," but the analysis was very much after-the-fact, and too schematic to do justice to his own case. It is important to know that he first began self-consciously reconsidering his approach to fiction at the same time that he was preparing the most dramatic and far-reaching changes in his own way of life. In 1936 he left home for good, uprooting himself from his beloved Washington Heights, the neighborhood in which he had been born and raised, to seek his fortune (starting at $900 a year) as a research assistant in English literature and a graduate student in philosophy at the University of Chicago. It would be a mistake to think of

Goodman as embittered or out-of-touch during his Chicago years, or of his cubist stories as slipping into the rhetoric of alienation. Indeed, the story from this period that made the biggest stir among critics, "A Ceremonial," was lauded for qualities that were just the opposite. Klaus Mann (the novelist's son no less) singled it out from all the stories in *New Directions 5*: "The tone of this young American voice reminds me, admitting the infinite differences in style and scope, of certain venerable accents long-known and ever-loved—the accents of Goethe's mellow wisdom and fatherly confidence." Hardly a description of alienation. Was it pure spite when Goodman replied that Mann had missed the point, that imaginary celebrations are "the cruellest form of satire"?

We must take Goodman's word for it, that alienation was what he saw when he confronted the work of his late twenties, but surely Mann was not *that* far off when he heard serenity in Goodman's voice. The objective facts of his life also indicate a happier relation to the world, and every photograph that survives from this period shows an irrepressibly beaming face. Perhaps alienation *suited* him? This is an important ambiguity in a man who twenty years later suddenly gave up writing fiction in order to devote himself to social criticism, appointing himself society's scourge and healer simultaneously. *Growing Up Absurd* was not merely the work of an alienated artist.

III

At the beginning of the forties it had looked as if Goodman's career was assured. Back from four years in Chicago with several dozen new stories in his famous trunk, he was making a splash on the New York literary scene. Two of his books were scheduled for the end of 1941. *Partisan Review* was printing him regularly, *Kenyon Review* and *Poetry* only a little less often, and New Directions included him in its *Annuals* for 1940 and 1941 and in the *Young American Poets* series. The University of Chicago Press was interested in his dissertation. When he applied for a Guggenheim, his references included not only academic bigwigs like Richard P. McKeon and Ronald S. Crane, but also the young moguls of avant-garde publishing and criticism, John Crowe Ransom, Philip Rahv, Dwight Macdonald, and James Laughlin. He was also looking around for a teaching job. Friends at several colleges would put in a good word for him; at the age of thirty he already had disciples.

But he did not get the job he wanted at Queens, he did not get the Guggenheim, and the University of Chicago Press would print his dissertation only if Goodman came up with $895 to pay for typesetting. The fate of his books was still more ominous. *Stop-Light*, his imitations of Japanese Noh plays, came out a week after Pearl Harbor. His antiwar novel *The Grand Piano* coincided with the fall of the Philippines. They got scarcely a review. Meanwhile Goodman was digging his literary grave deeper by composing diatribes against his strongest backers, James Laughlin and John Crowe Ransom, for supporting the war. And he got into a vicious fight with Phil Rahv at *Partisan Review* over the issues of pacifism, the draft, and sedition.

By the middle of 1942 things looked black. Although Laughlin and Ransom continued to publish him in New Directions and *Kenyon*, the *Partisan Review* closed its doors, as did the literary establishment in general. In 1943 he published no stories or books, nothing but two poems and an essay written with his brother on "Architecture in Wartime." Some of his friends wondered where he was living, and on what. He managed to get a job at a little progressive school in upstate New York, but was fired at the end of the school year for seducing his students. Instead of becoming famous he was becoming notorious.

He continued to write at a furious pace. Just as in the late thirties he had flourished in alienation, Goodman now seemed to thrive on adversity. If anything, his troubles improved his style, by giving him something to write about. It was impossible to remain aloof from a world that battered him so thoroughly. His response was to offer his views on education, community planning, anarchism, psychoanalysis, religion. He wrote one major book after another, a dozen between 1940 and 1950. These works took the brunt of Goodman's collision with reality, though he also wrote well over one hundred stories, plays, essays, reviews, and prefaces—not to mention the steady flow of poems. His new relation to society is apparent in their topics—political, psychosexual, religious—the prickly areas of his previous alienation.

After the nadir of 1943 Goodman began to be printed again, by tiny avant-garde houses no one had ever heard of —Vanguard and New Directions were his gilt-edged publishers. By the end of the decade he was perhaps the most-published unknown author in America, as he ruefully put it. "During this period," he wrote to the Guggenheim Foundation in

1949, "very many persons in my ambience, including several close friends, have received aid from you. But very few seem to have done as much work as I, have published as much, or received as little remuneration. Could you answer me, frankly, what it is I do that is wrong?" However others might account for this seesaw of success and discouragement, notoriety and obscurity, it is evident that Goodman's self-image as a writer on the outs with society was hardening into a stance— and *that* was becoming his career.

At the same time that his social thought was unfolding in books like *Communitas* and *The May Pamphlet*, his fiction was developing in somewhat different directions. On the one hand there was his grand project *The Empire City*, explicitly begun as "An Almanac of Alienation" but soon bursting the mold of schematic satire on "that error, America 1940," to become a strange, panoramic inward vision of his times. On the other hand, there was his shorter fiction, now almost completely stripped of the conventional realistic façade—plot, character, setting—so that one hesitates to call some of them stories at all.

At first Goodman tried to fit both his new novel and his stories into the theory of literary manners he had worked out. The larger project was "expressionistic naturalism," a sequence of heroic portraits in which the larger-than-life characters were really only abstractions from "sociological and psychological causes." The shorter pieces were called "dialectical lyrics," a Kierkegaardian label for the old-fashioned familiar essay, as in *Mosses from an Old Manse*, except that the handling was cubist, with much more emphasis on the formal means than in Hawthorne's sketches.

But as he became more confident about his place in literary history, Goodman lost interest in theorizing about the stages of his career. And anyway, much as the theory of literary manners elucidates his earlier work, these new categories are inadequate to the remarkable feats of imagination they christen. *The Empire City* was afloat far beyond its moorings. Already in *The Grand Piano* a "world" had begun to develop. In spite of their origin as mere abstractions from "the true causes of events," Goodman's characters had come to life; they stood for something, not in the sense of representing causes or powers, but in the sense that virtue inhered in their lives. All the characters were heroes, all their acts exploits. Rather than terms like "expressionistic naturalism," one does better to recall the examples of medieval romance and classical epic, *Don Quixote* and *Candide*.

Similarly the short stories of the forties go beyond their initial conception as further experiments in manner and genre. The main development began in 1944, after Goodman was fired from his schoolteacher's job. His stories grew polemical in self-justification. "The Knight" indignantly defended his Greek notion of pedagogy: "the teacher patiently hour by hour awakens him, teaches him boldness toward the girls, and sets him free; then they think that the teacher will not have been in love with the boy." In "A Goat for Azazel" Goodman's provocative lifestyle was summed up as a kind of Dionysian self-sacrifice: "Jimmy dared and did those things that we did not even know we desired."

Whatever one feels about these moral acrobatics (the actions are easier to defend than the exculpations) there is no doubt that his embattled stance was beginning to turn in on itself in peculiar ways. Both these stories have loose, episodic structures, with a few thinly realized characters wandering through moral and psychological fogs too privately conceived to be penetrated without the biographical key. This was the last gasp of verisimilitude.

As narrative structure gave way to personal exegesis, the mood became increasingly self-critical—though it seems always to have surprised Goodman to find himself under attack in his own work. Finally, in "On the Question: 'What is the Meaning of Life?'" he came to the point all his stories had been circling near: "In every work I return to the one theme, of disparaging the ego; shall I not direct it home, to hatred of myself? and stop escaping into generalities?"

In "Incidents of the Labyrinth" he found an allegory of the self's search for the soul in the myth of Theseus and the Minotaur. Every thrust and parry of this dialectical lyric betrays self-doubt. As he says, a person who asks questions like "What is the meaning of life?" is not likely to be happy, and one who merely wants to know what sort of question it is, or what sort of person would ask it, is in a still worse way.

One reason Goodman was writing such stories in 1946 is that he had gone into therapy with Alexander Lowen, then one of Wilhelm Reich's trainees, and after four or five months of learning the exercises, was continuing self-analysis on his own. In 1947 he met Fritz and Lore Perls, and for the next few years he worked with Fritz on *Gestalt Therapy* (1951) and with Lore on his character problems. All his writing in the forties bears the mark of psychoanalytic ideas, but after 1946 his fiction is often best understood *as part of* his own analysis. Some of his stories, like "Little Bert" or "Terry Fleming," are literally attempts to recover childhood memories, and in "Incidents of the Labyrinth" and "The Midnight Sun" he seems to be trying to use the dialectical lyric as a framework for free association. His earlier cubist writing had been highly controlled; now the rhapsodic style, the chanting tempo, are not so much formal devices as propaedeutic exercises, like the Reichian yoga, to open himself to the unconscious. The scenes themselves—wanderings in the labyrinth, voyaging on unknown seas—are obvious analogues of inward search.

From its earliest Reichian beginnings Goodman's psychotherapy seems to have been a struggle against the ego, regarding it as the inhibiting, controlling, rationalizing part of the self, in order to free the instinctual sources of the imagination, which he sometimes called the soul. On the other hand, his work as a theorist of therapy, and later as a therapist himself, showed how the ego's powers of formulation and analysis could be put to creative use, could draw on the soul's energy.

Goodman as therapist, Goodman as patient: obviously this is too pat, yet even before his therapy he was seeing himself in just this checkered light: "As for me, I am expert in formulations. These I can always make and say, 'there'—'that is what it is'—'it is only that, no fear'—'I am safe.' 'Next?'—'am I safe?'. . . let me speak no evil of the creator spirit, listening to whom, over my shoulder, and taking in the scene, I joyfully make them, these true formulations. But it is not meant that I should use them to ward off the world."

He had often used the traditional motif of the divided self or Doppelgänger to pose this dilemma of consciousness and impulse in his fiction. It began in his early twenties with conventional romantic alternatives—Johnson-in-love, Johnson-out-of-love. Under the influence of Reich it was portrayed much more psychoanalytically as the wrestling of the ego with the instincts, Theseus and the Minotaur. Finally, with Gestalt Therapy, he arrived at the paradox of relenting—Kinnison the sailor who brings the message of doom to Mytilene, and Kinnison the sailor who brings the reprieve.

This last phase offered the most hopeful resolution of the dilemma. "Out of Love" had ended with the death agony of Johnson-in-love, scarcely even perceived by Johnson-out-of-love—simple loss and blotting out. "Incidents of the Labyrinth" broke off at an impasse, with Theseus throttling himself—*he* is the Minotaur. But "A Sailor of the *Dolphin*" concludes with Kinnison somehow made whole, no longer divided against himself, and no longer glaring implacably at the society that surrounds him. "Relent, remedy" is the moral of the story, and Part III of "The Galley to Mytilene" shows the sailors methodically working their way through the woods, cutting down the bodies of the suicidal inhabitants and reviving those that still have a breath of life in them. As if to say, after one relents toward oneself, then one may relent toward one's fellows, toward one's "only world"—and go about the business of resuscitating the survivors.

It is easy to see how this pattern might eventuate in *Growing Up Absurd* and the rescue operations of the sixties. How many of Goodman's last stories have this same plot!—not merely "The Galley to Mytilene," but also "The Death of Aesculapius," "Bathers at Westover Pond," "A Lifeguard," "A Rescue," just to name the most conspicuous examples. Of course they are all symbolic representations of Goodman's practice as a therapist; and it was this whole drift, both in vocation and imagination, that led to his undertaking the larger therapeutic endeavor of the sixties. He used to say that he began taking patients because his friends kept coming to him with their problems; why not be professional about it? The same could be said of his career as consulting physician to his country: the patient was on his hands and conscience already. "Relent! remedy."

                                        IV

Although he lived another twelve years (what a twelve years!) Goodman wrote no short stories after 1960. One reason is obvious: he had no time for stories during the sixties, for he was too busy prescribing for his country's ills. Yes, but why choose to narrow himself to a social critic? Hungry as he was for audience and fame, devoted as he was to ideals of freedom and community, it cannot have been easy to give up the art he had lived by for thirty years. Why was it the price of his calling as public therapist?

Goodman wrote two kinds of fiction during the fifties. Although they bear some relation to his earlier categories of literary manner, he had invented less categorical terms for them by 1960, when he wrote the preface to a new collection of stories, *Our Visit to Niagara*: "I suppose my stories and novels are, finally, myths. . . . In principle there are two opposite ways of making mythical stories: to start with the American scene and find the mythical emerging from it, or to start with an ancient foreign myth and discover that it is familiar to oneself."

Goodman wanted to think of these two kinds of fiction as more alike than they actually are. True, their themes are identical; he writes over and over about death by drowning, resuscitation, and the ambivalence of the lifeguard, rescuer, or physician who, although he saves the victim, cannot save himself. He also keeps returning to the theme of paradise lost, often enough to make it clear that he feels a connection there, that it is only by ransoming his own health, his own chance for happiness, that the healer acquires his power—as Aesculapius risks the wrath of Jupiter in reviving Hippolytus. Put it the other way—the ability to remedy depends not only on having relented but also on having resigned oneself—and we begin to see the dim outlines of desire and anxiety, imagination and analysis, the ego and the instincts, in short, all the dilemmas of his previous fiction, looming behind the most prominent themes of the fifties, hope and resignation, resurrection and despair.

These patterns are very differently handled according to whether Goodman begins with his present experience or with ancient myth. "The Death of Aesculapius" and "An Asclepiad" were written in the early fifties, probably back to back. The first is one of Goodman's finest myths, full of power and beauty. He is able to retell the ancient story in episodes that echo his own plight, yet do not seem to be burdened with it. He is the hero, of course, Aesculapius healer and victim, yet Goodman does not usurp the story with his own injured grumbling. The myth does just what myths ought to do: it allows for the expression of universal feeling, draws on instinctual energy, gives a traditional framework in which the artist can tell his dream without feeling obligated to torture a psychoanalytic meaning out of it.

"An Asclepiad" is strikingly different. The myth of Aesculapius is invoked again, but the situation is taken from modern psychotherapy, the episodes are abstracted from Goodman's own practice. Compared with "The Death of Aesculapius" this story is both more candidly self-examining and also more querulous and self-righteous. As a glimpse into Goodman's state of mind in 1951, it is appalling. Here he is, trying to be sensible and resourceful, but turning morose and bitter; he wants to be helpful and openhanded, but his soul is starved and loveless, his spirit dry. The grim fact is that therapists become therapists *because* they cannot be cured, and *in order* not to be cured—it is a defense against as well as a device of preventive medicine. How to cope with this fact?

Next to this pair, set a couple of stories from the late fifties: "Jeremy Owen," which was originally intended as the beginning of a new novel, and either of Goodman's two attempts to create a mythic world for St. Wayward, the would-be hero of the abortive fifth book of *The Empire City*. The fact that both were meant as the protagonists of novels tempts us to read them as trial paradigms for Goodman's revised conception of himself. He was looking for vocation in these figures. But his paradigms were not viable, even as heroes of novels; Goodman could not invent anything for them to *do*.

Between the two it is the plain story of our own times, set in a small-town diner, an automobile salesroom, the Museum of Modern Art, that puts the most life into the idea that one *could* find vocation as a civic healer. After his adventures in New York City, Jeremy Owen was to go back home, where he would get on the local school board and do some good—much as Goodman himself did after publishing *Growing Up Absurd*. In fact Jeremy gets no further than quitting his job and going off to New York in search of something to do; yet at least there is this, his decision to quit, the energy of disgust and the yearning for vocation. At the other extreme, the adventures of St. Wayward are pure moonshine. Riding around on a unicorn, Wayward is looking for dragons to fight, but it is mere pose, and the best that Goodman can think up for him is to fill out the empty space in the center of the frieze above St. Mark's cathedral in Venice.

What are we to make of this second contrast, the unfulfilled American saga and the limping saint's legend? First of all, it is apparent that the content has shifted since the early fifties. Instead of writing about the physician who cannot heal himself, Goodman is now casting about for a worthy action for a younger and more hopeful hero to perform. The difficulty is not that opportunity has lapsed—on the contrary, the *idea* of opportunity, the need for a promising call to action, has only now arisen, along with this rejuvenated protagonist. Nevertheless, if more seems possible now, it is felt only in the realm of the practical, the American scene in its chronic emergency; the mythic past can no longer energize Goodman's imagination—because the story he wants to tell is still to unfold. If he knew what the plot was to be, what action his hero had to perform, he might find a suitable myth to convey it. In the meantime, it is precisely *not knowing* that is his subject.

Obviously these faltering anticipations are leading up to the writing of

Growing Up Absurd, which, as Goodman himself later said, *was* the action he had been trying to find for his heroes. Everything finally conjoined in producing this book: his therapy and theorizing, his failure to win an audience for his fiction, his increasing sense of citizenly responsibility, his restless need to be doing something, stirring things up. Goodman's fiction certainly registers all of these pressures, but it cannot do anything about them. And when he finally wrote the book that did, he stopped writing fiction entirely.

Among the very last of his stories, written just before *Growing Up Absurd*, is an extraordinary combination of the two modes, American and mythic. This was "Adam." As if he knew it was to be one of his last stories, and ought therefore to present some accounting, the amalgamation itself is called to attention, made a theme, as Goodman moves back and forth from the realistic report of his own sufferings and complaints in the fifties, to his vision of eternal Adam, naming the beasts, discovering Eve, encountering the serpent, and so on. At the end Goodman brings the two together dramatically by introducing himself as a character in Adam's story, and speaking with him from the persona of Everyman: "'Adam,' I say, 'I love you and I should be proud to see you happy and great, but I don't know how.'"

Adam replies: "'No, Everyman,' he says, 'you do me a lot of good. And you *do* make me feel that you love me. . . . You make a mistake, Everyman, to search for me so hard as you do. You could really sit quite still and I would know you by your work, how you love me. . . . You have revived my purpose to succeed.'"

I think this curious dialogue must be regarded as the final exchange between the divided selves and Doppelgängers of Goodman's fiction. Adam stands for the deepest nature of man, neolithic, mythic. In the terms of Goodman's self-analysis, he represents primary nature, the instincts, source of all energy and life. Everyman then stands for humanity, civilized, social, carrying the weight of history and culture. He is the ego, the writer, the felt self. Thus we have Everyman addressing Adam, Goodman communing with his soul. What he says, what they say to each other, is remarkable when one remembers this same encounter as it was imagined in the forties, Theseus and the Minotaur locked in a murderous embrace. "Relent, remedy"—that is the lesson of the fifties, and by the time he came to write "Adam" it is poignantly apparent that he had learned it, and was ready for a new challenge. Finally the call came because he was ready for it. Paradise was lost, but Adam survived somewhere in Everyman, if not for art at least for life, for humanity. America was not Eden, but it was "my only world," and in need of rescuing, at sea. If one could not be a famous artist or a warrior saint, one might be a rescuer.

8

Realism and Ethics

It is surprising how, in the argument over realism, the relations between art and life, so little attention is paid to either art or life. Traditional subjects of literary study are studiously ignored in the new meta-criticism, which is only about itself; nor, in many pages of vigorous response, do the defenders of old-fashioned criticism say what *they* think is the proper literary fare for a child, for a citizen, for a moral being. As yet no one seriously thinks that the future of realistic fiction depends on the outcome. Literature, it is believed, will continue to educate our moral sensibilities, refine our tastes, and hearten our spirits.

Of course it is really only a small proportion of the vast faculty of literature that devotes itself to the rarified question of whether stories can or ought to imitate life; most of us, even those who follow the debate with partisan interest, continue to lecture undergraduates on *Paradise Lost* or *The Scarlet Letter* without raising any doubts about their semiotical status. But do not expect, if you slip into the back of the lecture hall, to hear very much about sin and death. Teachers and critics are timid about making moral judgments, whether in the classroom or in the fancy literary journals. The argument over the politics of realism is a good example, for it ought to stir up controversy about the civic function of art, but seems instead to revolve around recondite notions of epistemology. But let us boldly ask the question these polemicists skirt: what has been the effect in our culture of encouraging this propensity in the species to spend so much time day-dreaming to someone else's story?

Emerson warned the PBKs at Harvard that much reading was bad for the soul: "instead of being its own seer, let it receive from another mind its truth, though it were in torrents of light, without periods of solitude, in-quest, and self-recovery, and a fatal disservice is done." He speaks here of serious books, not novels, which he thought beneath notice. The very best books were dangerous if not kept subordinate to life, and the true use of all books was to inspire, that is, to bring us through the imagination back to life. Yet how often we read for opposite reasons, to escape boredom, kill-ing time on the subway or in the airport! It is not to help us while away the hours that great artists create. Whatever the Latin tags may assert, in-formation and entertainment are low aims of a trifling art.

Bookworms (as Emerson called them) are not the only persons who read too much. Whoever reads to avoid life or to compensate for its in-sufficiencies uses books wrongly. The trash that now circulates through the American imagination is perhaps no worse than in Emerson's day, but the sheer amount of time we devote to the surrender of consciousness betrays something terribly wrong with our society. Imagine the jolt if we were to give up our vicarious experience, whether TV or spectator sports or bestsellers. A mass society in which there is so little religion, fraternity, public life, physical labor, or uncorrupted natural beauty needs an enormous addiction to fill the emptiness.

Literacy is therefore worshipped in our society without anyone inquir-ing very far into what it brings with it in the way of alienation, self-consciousness, and passive intelligence. (At least we *ask* the question about TV, though we refuse to answer it.) School teachers and parents congratulate themselves when the bright child is seen off in the corner absorbed in a book while the slower children are noisily playing with their blocks. Sooner or later all the children are in their corners, enjoying the security of giving the mind into some firm grip—if not books then TV or movies. By the period of peer-group conformity, which begins early in our society, everyone has mastered one of these ways of belonging and escap-ing at the same time.

No doubt the propensity is in the genes, but civilizations might exist—have existed—without the compulsory training up of every single consciousness to the habit of such large and regular doses of public reverie. (In Bob Nichols's utopian novel, the first thing we learn is that writing is forbidden in Nghsi-Altai.) Our way of life—urban anomie—probably requires its tranquilizing entertainment and media pap in order to keep people from breaking down altogether. When the world outside is dull and dark, we switch on the lights and all the windows become mirrors, reflecting back our own imaginings. Or somebody's imaginings. We have discovered techniques to make sure the screen never goes blank.

The attack on realism is like the old complaint about "escape literature"—implying that there is some better manner or subject that could not be so easily enlisted on the side of vacuity. The new twist is that the critics no longer believe that *any* literature can be trusted to give an authentic representation of reality; how could there be a trustworthy realism when there is no single reality, no authority, no truth? The function of literature, say these critics, is to dismantle our castles in air, not to build them. This nihilism pretends to be a critique of our passive acceptance of authority (enshrined in the realistic conventions), but in fact it is part and parcel of the despairing relativism that infects the entire society. In dissolving reality into meaning, the enemies of realism seem to think that they thereby free the imagination to make its own truth, but several thousand years of experience go to show that human beings cannot live in such a solipsistic world. The loss of faith in the ground underfoot is fatal to the next step. Even the history-rewriting "Newspeak" of *1984* is not so impious as the positivist existentialism that denies the Creation itself. It is a mistake to think that such a view of language and reality ultimately celebrates the *Logos*, returning from the Sixth to the First Day; on the contrary, the effect is to cheapen every actual sentence while extolling the chameleon virtues of syntax and rhetoric. Poe shows where such theories lead: since in his philosophy language can instantiate every dream with equal validity, he invites us to make ourselves comfortable and enjoy the hallucination. What a debasement of the glorious powers of speech and imagination!

The only literature at all interesting is about life, the acts and fates of human beings. Only these subjects move us, give us joy, inspiration, resolve. A certain regard for probability, at least enough verisimilitude to establish a relation between the story and life, is prerequisite to these effects—or to a novel's making any sense at all. In the spectrum of literary manners, from realism to cubism to purely abstract fiction, there is a cut-off point beyond which most readers will never go. Renouncing subject matter for the sake of form is a temptation only to the theorist who wants to know the limits. Even a great artist bores us to tears when he writes something like "The Burrow," Kafka's monstrous infinite regress of the spirit. Granted, if a work is comprehensible at all it is mimetic, but these funhouse mirrors finally draw attention to themselves alone. Most readers are interested in other lives, not the philosophy of art. Accordingly the history of fiction in the West has developed few literary manners on the formalist side of cubism, whereas realism is crowded by its competition—naturalism, symbolism, surrealism, the gothic, and so on—all sharing a basic commitment to subject matter, narrative continuity, and audience. Writers like Kafka, Genet, or Beckett are often cubist in manner, but no great writers or works are purely abstract.

Formalism is the hair shirt approach to literary experience, keeping the reader alert to his own concerns by frustrating them in page after page. Would it not be just as well to give up reading? It does not follow, however, that realism exacts the opposite price, complete abandonment of consciousness to the author's will. Granted, every narrative of human events, so long as it adheres to conventional notions of time and space, cause and effect, seems to have the power to entrance the reader who wants to go under the spell. No need for "mystic gesticulations" such as Holgrave uses in *The House of the Seven Gables* when he mesmerizes Phoebe by reciting his story of Alice Pyncheon. Most people are like Phoebe's scrawny chickens: chalk a line in the road and we stand bemused. Indeed, for purposes of oblivion any old plot will do, the more routine and unembellished the better; once over the threshold there is nothing in the formula novel to shake the reader back to his senses. But as the old saying about hypnotism assures us, no one can be put to sleep against his will. One chooses the mystery or thriller, so called, in order to be mystified or thrilled sufficiently to forget one's existence.

Here the fascination of realistic fiction most closely approaches the hypnotic power of TV or film. In the latter there is no respite whatever from the march of plot, no moment when we can safely look aside even in the imagination, and compare one reality with another. The "live" or "pseudo-live" medium demands our total attention—if attention is the word for it, for life itself requires a very different sort of awareness. Not even the extreme redundancy of cues saves the illusion from an instant's lapse. The theater is hushed and darkened to blot out every distraction, and one learns to pull the shades in the mind as well.

Although the realistic manner may be adapted to any narrative medium, the illusion of life is a more fragile affair in the visually-oriented arts and therefore, paradoxically, much more rigidly enforced. Fiction also invites absorption in its world, but one goes more at one's own pace; despite Poe's advice few stories are written to be read at a sitting, though many are

meant for the same spellbound audience. With novels there is at least always the possibility that something will jar the reader out of his trance by
moving him or making him think. The paramount rule of realism—*do
nothing to call the façade into question*—has ambiguous force in the greatest literature, where the reader may exclaim in the midst of the most compelling scenes, What a writer! . . . and find himself breathing hard in his
own world again. One risks being brought up short like this in every scene
of *War and Peace* or *Moby-Dick*, not so much by the frequent violations of
realistic decorum as by the extraordinary feats of mimesis. And there are
many other realistic works that not only compel belief but also force the
imagination back to reality, chastened, exalted, satisfied.

The ease with which a reader can move in and out of the fiction-trance
comes of its being a verbal medium, continuous with everything else that
fills the consciousness. To close a book at a moment of recognition and
muse on its significance may dispel any realistic illusion, but it fosters the
deeper engagement that depends on one's own thoughts unfolding in the
same imaginative space as those of the hero or the author. The point of
reading about other human lives, the exploits of heroes and the destinies of
exemplary figures, is to bring the lessons they teach to bear on our own
lives. When our notions of good and evil, motive and desire, love and faith
are tested in the imagination, the results become part of the store of experience and wisdom that constitutes character. Ethical and spiritual life—our
relations with others, with ourselves, with the world—may be said to constitute a special aptitude of language, not limited to literature, of course,
but a virtue of all discourse—and in need of continual exercise if we are to
preserve our humanity. We can never properly be finished talking about
these concerns: this is why psychotherapy works (and goes on forever);
here are the wellsprings of gossip and diary-keeping; such is the justification for teaching the humanities to generation after generation.

In a society where no institution, not even the family, takes responsibility for moral training of citizens, literature may provide the detailed cases
in practical ethics through which the moral sense is strengthened and ma-
tured. The feelings are educated—this was Tolstoy's defense of art—
when we are moved by the lives of others, passionately realized in our own
imagination. Certain plots purge the spirit—they are cathartic—while in
reading others it is more appropriate to say with Gide that we are "pastur-
ing the soul." As we grow familiar with characters and their dispositions,
recognize their motives, take account of the social complications and ob-

stacles, we too come to have an investment in the developing pattern of event and significance that uses up the possibilities and slowly coheres as fate.

All narrative mediums share the same subject matter—human life. Therefore they provide raw material for ethics, psychology, and philosophy. The way human beings behave in art is enough like the way they behave in life to allow us to incorporate the former among practical cases for understanding and judging our own behavior. Literature has an advantage here over other mediums, for it not only can represent events in a wider context of history and culture, motive and consequence, but also lends itself immediately to interpretation and analysis. The work of the moral sense, human sympathies, the soul's enlargement, all go forth by means of language. You cannot take a moving-picture of an ethical judgment (Eisenstein proved this), though you can show someone making one. Literature can present both the judge and the judgment.

Of course we also experience the world in nonverbal ways, and a purely verbal medium has its disadvantages, indicated well enough by the desire novelists have so often felt to render nonverbal experience. The gulf between verbal and nonverbal worlds is the central theme of the two great novels I have already referred to, *Moby-Dick* and *War and Peace*. As the gulf widens, we find ourselves standing on the far shore from our bodily nature. Modern society, so thoroughly verbal in its education, economics, social intercourse, government, and private life, has produced two literatures: one a chant of popular fantasies, words at their furthest remove from things, like knots on a prayer string; the other a mandarin art turning in on itself in stream of consciousness, wordplay, lyricism, and other symptoms of self-reflexive formalism.

Certainly the ubiquity of popular fiction—and the conniving of publishers, reviewers, school teachers, and other authorities to legitimate it—is a disaster unparalleled in the history of cultures. But the other, more pretentious literature we have created—what we call "modernism"—has not provided any very hopeful alternative or antidote. It cannot be a healthy sign that the major novelists of our century have been such verbal athletes. The power of the novel to deal with the traditional subjects—ethical and spiritual realities—depends on the natural use of language to mediate between consciousness and life, to struggle with the limitations of mimesis. As modernism focuses more and more exclusively on mere verbal effects, voyeur of its own processes, prose fiction abandons its essential purpose and becomes little more than a higher branch of mathematics. Between such thin-blooded formalist novels and the formulaic commodities mass-produced for popular consumption, there is not much to choose.

Meanwhile generations of technically expert readers are raised and schooled without benefit of the cultural experience traditionally conveyed by literature. It is only right that each epoch find moral truth and spiritual salvation in its own books—but what a commentary on our society! Not only do we produce such grim lessons and sugar-coated placebos, from Kafka to Vonnegut, but we also neglect those classics of our heritage that were still available to the imagination hardly a generation ago. *Huckleberry Finn* and *The House of the Seven Gables* used to be read in high school classes; *Gulliver's Travels* and *Great Expectations* were standard texts in Freshman English. Now it is the latest fad literature, with an occasional "classic" like *The Stranger*.

Let me also remind the reader of the methods by which the kernel is extracted from such books. The natural impulse of students, to gossip about the characters they meet in novels, has been stifled by high school teachers with warnings "not to read too much into the text." College professors reduce moral and psychological problems to an analysis, performed on the blackboard, of patterns in the carpet such as never meet the untutored eye. These matters may be interesting to the specialist but not to the ordinary reader, who learns precisely the wrong thing in English class, that high art is a bore and has nothing to do with life.

The job of the literary critic should be to act as a moral philosopher, not a structural exegete. The first thing criticism ought to do is confront this present situation, so much of its own making, rather than pursue any further evolutions in meta-thought. As for the rest of us, it is our duty to abjure the media and begin once again to think for ourselves, to live—and not merely imagine—our own lives.

Notes

1. REALISM AND VERISIMILITUDE

1. Introduction to *The Monk* (New York, 1952), p. 14.
2. Paul Goodman, "Literary Method and Author-Attitude," in *Art and Social Nature* (New York, 1946), pp. 91–92.

2. HAWTHORNE'S FAITH IN WORDS

1. *The American Notebooks*, ed. Claude M. Simpson (Columbus: Ohio State University Press, 1973), pp. 228, 184, 15, and 123. For the tales as well I have used the Centenary Edition of the Works of Nathaniel Hawthorne; page references are not given, since the reader will have no difficulty locating passages in such brief works.
2. *American Notebooks*, pp. 254, 228, and 178.
3. *American Notebooks*, p. 180.
4. *The Blithedale Romance* and *Fanshawe*, eds. William Charvat, et al., vol. 3 of the Centenary Edition (Columbus: Ohio State University Press, 1965), p. 11.
5. *American Notebooks*, p. 240.
6. *American Notebooks*, p. 181.
7. *American Notebooks*, p. 153.
8. *American Notebooks*, p. 182.
9. *American Notebooks*, p. 16.
10. *Collected Works of Ralph Waldo Emerson: Nature, Addresses, and Lectures*, eds. Robert E. Spiller and Alfred R. Ferguson (Cambridge, Mass.: Harvard University Press, 1971), p. 39.
11. *American Notebooks*, p. 251.
12. *Nature*, pp. 18, 21, 22.
13. *Nature*, p. 20.
14. *Nature*, p. 19.
15. *Nature*, p. 20.

173

3. "UNSPEAKABLE HORROR" IN POE

1. I have used as my text for Poe's tales Thomas Ollive Mabbott's two-volume edition of the *Tales and Sketches*, in the *Collected Works of Edgar Allan Poe* (Cambridge, Mass.: Harvard University Press, 1978-   ). For quotations from the shorter works I have not provided page references, since the reader will easily find the passages cited.

2. *The Complete Works of Edgar Allan Poe*, ed. James A. Harrison, 16 vols. (New York, 1902), XVI, 88–90.

3. *Complete Works*, XVI, 292.

4. *Complete Works*, XVI, 306–307.

4. PROPAGANDA BY THE DEED IN JAMES

1. *The Art of the Novel*, ed. R. P. Blackmur (New York, 1934), p. 76.

2. *The Art of the Novel*, p. 59.

3. *The Art of the Novel*, pp. 77–78.

4. Parenthetical page references are to the following editions: *The Princess Casamassima* (New York: Harper Colophon, 1964); *Sentimental Education*, trans. Robert Baldick (Baltimore: Penguin, 1964); *The Devils* [*The Possessed*], trans. David Magarshack (Baltimore: Penguin, 1953); *Virgin Soil*, trans. Rochelle S. Townsend (New York: Dutton, 1963); *Under Western Eyes* (Garden City, N.J.: Anchor, 1963).

5. See "Ivan Turgenef's New Novel," *The Nation*, XXIV (1877), 252–253; "Ivan Turgenieff," *Atlantic Monthly*, LIII (1884), 52; and Virginia Harlow, *Thomas Sergeant Perry: A Biography* (Durham, N.C., 1950), p. 293.

6. Harlow, p. 296.

7. James, "Turgenev," *The Future of the Novel*, ed. Leon Edel (New York, 1956), p. 231.

8. "The Influence of Turgenev on Henry James," *The Slavonic and East German Review*, XX (1941), 28-54. Unfortunately, Lerner's article cannot be trusted for accuracy; on p. 50, for example, he confuses Mariana and Madame Sipiagina, a mistake that his desire to identify the latter with Christina in *The Princess Casamassima* leads him into.

9. In this and the next two quotations I use the translation of A. W. Dilke (London, 1878), pp. 92, 137, and 166. For comparison, see the Townsend translation, pp. 84, 125, and 152.

10. *Translations from the Philosophical Writings of Gottlob Frege*, ed. and trans. Peter Geach and Max Black (Oxford, 1960), p. 70. That Frege chooses a political example in this passage seems revealing.

11. *Frege*, p. 58.

12. *Frege*, p. 63.

13. "The Art of Fiction," *The Future of the Novel*, p. 14.

14. *The Rise of the Novel* (Berkeley, Calif., 1957), p. 30.

15. Ed. F. O. Matthiessen and Kenneth B. Murdock (New York, 1955). An exception to

James's practice may be found on page 69, where a bit of London dialogue is preserved. It is also true, by the way, that he made a data-collecting trip to a prison for use in *The Princess Casamassima.*

16. John Henry Mackay, *The Anarchists,* trans. George Schumm (Boston, 1891), pp. 163-164.

17. "The Art of Fiction," pp. 5-6, 9-10.

18. *"The Princess Casamassima," The Liberal Imagination* (New York, 1953), p. 79.

19. *The Background of the Princess Casamassima* (Gainesville, Fla., 1960). See also John Quail's excellent history of British anarchism during this period, *The Slowly Burning Fuse* (London: Paladin, 1978).

20. This is from Richard Henry Savage's potboiler of 1894, *The Anarchist* (2 vols.; Leipzig), I, 63, which is of some interest here not merely because of its subject, but also because it is obviously indebted to James for its "international theme." The young heiress is a healthy Milly Theale, who (one might think in macabre parody of *The Wings of the Dove*) finally becomes engaged to the American hero—her own kind—at the end of the novel, *literally* over the dead body of the anarchist Oborski, who has been commissioned by the central committee to get his hands on her person and her money.

21. Trilling, p. 67. The phrase is from a letter written by James to A. C. Benson in 1896.

22. Savage, II, 27.

23. Peter Kropotkin, *Memoirs of a Revolutionist* (Boston and New York, 1899), p. 442. James himself was in Lyons, gathering materials for a travel series he was doing for an American magazine, when the bomb was thrown; see *A Little Tour of France* (Boston, 1884), pp. 237-239.

24. Kropotkin, p. 493.

25. Mackay, pp. 231-233.

26. Savage, II, 51.

27. As reported in the *Boston Herald,* 8 April 1885.

28. *The Great Republic* (New York, 1884); *The Fall of the Great Republic* (Boston, 1885).

29. Orginally entitled "The Two Countries"; see *The Notebooks of Henry James,* p. 66.

30. *The Letters of Henry James,* ed. Percy Lubbock (New York, 1920), I, 80, 114.

31. "Ivan Turgenef's New Novel," p. 252.

32. Quoted in Harlow, *Thomas Sargeant Perry,* p. 320.

33. "Ivan Turgenef's New Novel," p. 252.

34. Frédéric Moreau avoids both vow and avowal; hence *Sentimental Education* has no "action," is an absolutely non-dramatic novel.

35. In *Contemporary Socialism* (London, 1884), p. 295.

36. "The revolutionist is a doomed man" (Max Nomad, *Apostles of Revolution* [Boston, 1939], p. 228); "The revolutionary is a lost man" (Franco Venturi, *Roots of Revolution,* trans. Francis Haskell [New York, 1964; Italian edition, 1952], p. 365).

37. Quoted in F. O. Matthiessen, *The James Family* (New York, 1947), p. 256.

38. *The James Family,* pp. 666-667.

39. *The Political Philosophy of Bakunin*, ed. G. P. Maximoff (London, 1964 [c. 1953]), p. 403.

40. *The Russian Storm-Cloud* (London, 1886), p. 28.

41. The phrase is found in Henry B. Brewster's *The Theories of Anarchy and of Law* (London, 1887). Brewster and James may have first met in 1887 or 1888, and at least by 1889, when Brewster sent James a copy of *The Theories* for Christmas. James reported that he found it "rather exquisite and remarkable." See Martin Halpern, "The Life and Writings of Henry B. Brewster," Diss. Harvard 1959, p. 97, and Leon Edel, "Who *Was* Gilbert Osmond?," *Modern Fiction Studies*, VI (1960), 164.

42. *What I Believe* [1884], *The Works of Leo Tolstoy*, trans. Aylmer Maude (London, 1933), IX, 388, 390.

43. *The James Family*, p. 669.

44. See Halpern, p. 38.

45. Brewster, pp. 14-20.

46. Brewster, p. 28.

47. Brewster, p. 33.

48. In *War and Peace* or *God and the State*. For example, this passage from the latter: "The general idea is always an abstraction and, for that very reason, in some sort a negation of real life. . . . [H]uman thought and, in consequence of this, science can grasp and name only the general significance of real facts, their relations, their laws—in short, that which is permanent in their continual transformations—but never their material, individual side, palpitating, so to speak, with reality and life, and therefore fugitive and intangible. Science comprehends the thought of the reality, not reality itself; the thought of life, not life. . . . In this respect it is infinitely inferior to art, which, in its turn, is peculiarly concerned also with general types and general situations, but which incarnates them by an artifice of its own in forms which, if they are not living in the sense of real life, none the less excite in our imagination the memory and sentiment of life; art in a certain sense individualizes the types and situations which it conceives; by means of the individualities without flesh and bone, and consequently permanent and immortal, which it has the power to create, it recalls to our minds the living, real individualities which appear and disappear under our eyes. Art, then, is as it were the return of abstraction of life; science, on the contrary, is the perpetual immolation of life fugitive, temporary, but real, on the altar of eternal abstractions."—*God and the State*, trans. anon. (Bombay, n. d. [originally published in 1882]), pp. 64–65, 67.

49. Compare the following passage from *Virgin Soil*:

   "You had better take care, Boris Andraevitch is sometimes such a Jacobin—"
   "Jacko, jacko, jacko," the parrot screamed.
   Valentina Mihailovna waves her handkerchief at him.
   "Don't interrupt an intelligent conversation!"   (42)

50. Brewster, p. 144.

51. *Henry James: Letters to A. C. Benson and Auguste Monod*, ed. E. F. Benson (London, 1930), p. 35.

52. *The Notebooks*, pp. 44-45.

53. *The Question of Our Speech* [and] *The Lesson of Balzac: Two Lectures* (Boston and New York, 1905), pp. 10, 14-15.

5. "MENTALIZED SEX" IN D. H. LAWRENCE

1. *Letters*, ed. Harry T. Moore (London, 1962), p. 972. The first typist *did* interfere; Nelly Morrison refused to go on after five chapters, and Lawrence had to farm it out to his friends.
2. *Letters*, p. 1035. "A Propos of *Lady Chatterley's Lover*," in *Sex, Literature, and Censorship*, ed. Harry T. Moore (New York, 1959), p. 84.
3. "A Propos . . . ," p. 84.
4. Ibid., p. 85.
5. Ibid., p. 86.
6. Edmund Wilson, "Signs of Life: *Lady Chatterley's Lover*" [1929], in *Shores of Light* (New York, 1961), p. 407.
7. *Letters*, p. 1111.
8. "A Propos . . . ," p. 99.
9. Ibid., p. 85.
10. *Lady Chatterley's Lover* [Grove Press edition] (New York, 1959), p. 290.
11. Ibid., pp. 311-312.
12. Ibid., pp. 312-313.
13. *The Trial of Lady Chatterley*, ed. C. H. Rolph (Baltimore, 1961), p. 224.
14. *Letters*, p. 725.
15. Ibid., p. 1111.
16. "A Propos . . . ," p. 84.
17. Ibid., p. 84.
18. Ibid., p. 85.
19. Ibid., pp. 88-89.
20. "Mr. Noon," in *Phoenix II*, eds. Warren Roberts and Harry T. Stone (New York, 1968), pp. 125–127.
21. Ibid., pp. 127–128.
22. Ibid., p. 169.
23. *Lady Chatterley's Lover*, p. 229.
24. "Pornography and Obscenity," in *Sex, Literature, and Censorship*, pp. 71-73.
25. Ibid., pp. 71, 77.
26. "Surgery for the Novel—or a Bomb" [1923], in *Phoenix*, ed. Edward D. McDonald (London, 1936), p. 517.
27. Marcel Proust, *Swann's Way*, trans. C. K. Scott Moncrieff (New York, 1928) pp. 226-227.
28. "Pornography and Obscenity," pp. 71-74.
29. Ibid., p. 74.

30. E. J. Dingwall, *Male Infibulation* (London, 1925), p. 51. The uses of infibulation, from classical times, were chiefly to prevent fornication by actors, singers, and athletes, whose continence was thought beneficial to their arts. I might point out here that various methods of discouraging masturbation by females were also entertained in the nineteenth century—notably the excision of the clitoris—but Lawrence is not interested in that side of the story, and the terms of his discussion tend to be masculine, not to say sexist.

31. John Hunter, *A Treatise on the Venereal Disease* (London, 1786) p. 200.

32. Ibid., 3d edn., ed. Everard Home (London, 1810), p. 214.

33. Michael Ryan, *Prostitution in London* (London, 1839), p. 273.

34. Ibid., p. 267.

35. "Pornography and Obscenity," p. 73.

36. Quoted in Alec Craig, *Suppressed Books* (Cleveland, 1963), p. 226.

37. *Trial*, p. 13.

38. Alexander M. Gow, *Good Morals and Gentle Manners* (New York, 1873), pp. 51-53.

39. Quoted in Ronald Pearsall, *The Worm in the Bud* (Toronto, 1969), p. 515.

40. Chandler Robbins, *Disorders of Literary Men* (Boston, 1825), pp. 18-19.

41. William Acton, *The Functions and Disorders of the Reproductive Organs*, 5th edn. (London, 1871), p. 159.

42. Ryan, p. 259.

43. *Letters*, p. 373-374.

44. "Pornography and Obscenity," p. 79.

45. *Kangaroo* (New York, 1960), p. 64.

46. Ibid., p. 95.

47. Ibid., p. 335.

48. *The Plumed Serpent* (New York, 1951), p. 277.

49. *Psychoanalysis and the Unconscious* and *Fantasia of the Unconscious* (New York, 1960), p. 194.

50. *Kangaroo*, pp. 196–197.

51. Ibid., p. 95.

52. Acton, p. 230.

53. *Studies in Classic American Literature* (New York, 1961), p. 132.

54. "Pornography and Obscenity," p. 71.

55. Ibid., p. 79.

56. *Letters*, p. 320.

57. Ibid., p. 993.

58. Ibid., pp. 989–990.

59. *Kangaroo*, p. 271.

60. Ibid., p. 334.

61. Ibid., p. 285.

62. Ibid., p. 289.

6. PORNOGRAPHY, MASTURBATION AND THE NOVEL

1. Dingwall mentions S. G. Vogel, *Unterricht fur Eltern . . .* (Stendal, 1786), and J. C. Jaeger, *Grundriss der Wund-Arzneylkunst in dem altern Zeiten der Romer* (Frankfurt am Main, 1789).

2. Milton's book, by the way, is what Marcus partly takes Dingwall's to be, that is, the place to begin if one is interested in the history of devices like the "urethral ring," spiked or toothed, and the "electric alarum," which were used to prevent (not, as it turns out, masturbation, but a related complaint) nocturnal emission.

3. The range of interest in this problem is worth recalling. Different approaches include, for example, both mesmerism and phrenology—Michael Ryan, *Prostitution in London* (London, 1839), devotes a long section to Gall's theory of amativeness and the cerebellum, while Carpenter's later *Principles of Mental Physiology* (London, 1874), the first work to use the term "unconscious cerebration," takes account of the investigations of Braid. Other significant contributions were Darwin's *Expression of the Emotions* (1872), Lewes's *Problems of Life and Mind* (1874-1879), Daniel Hack Tuke's *Illustrations of the Influences of the Mind on the Body* (1872).

4. It ought to be said that both metaphors were in use during Victoria's reign; compare *My Secret Life*: "The three voices blended whatever baudy, stimulating words fell from us. 'Oh! fuck—cunt—spunk—oh—I am coming—I'm spending—spunk—ballocks—aha—ahre.'" Also compare the eighteenth-century "I'm going," as in Cleland.

5. *Pornography and Obscenity* (1930). Lawrence continues: "The sentimentalism and the niggling analysis, often self-analysis, of most of our modern literature, is a sign of self-abuse. It is the manifestation of masturbation, the sort of conscious activity stimulated by masturbation, whether male or female. The outstanding feature of such consciousness is that there is no real object, there is only subject." Compare Marcus (1966): ". . . since in pornography there is no 'other person,' only oneself, the emotions—even the lust—that one feels toward an actual living object, in contradistinction to the abstract and self-referential lust of fantasy—which might be expected to accompany a representation of sexual activities between two persons have no real place there and no way of being expressed." Compare Ryan (1839): "Every one will admit that, he who is addicted to the unmanly habit of masturbation or onanism, is isolated from society, concentrates all his affections on himself, exerts none of the mutual sympathies of the different members of society, which contribute most powerfully to the good of all."

7. ADAM AND EVERYMAN: PAUL GOODMAN IN HIS STORIES

1. All quotations are from my edition of *The Collected Stories of Paul Goodman*, 4 vols. (Santa Barbara, Calif.: Black Sparrow Press, 1978–80).